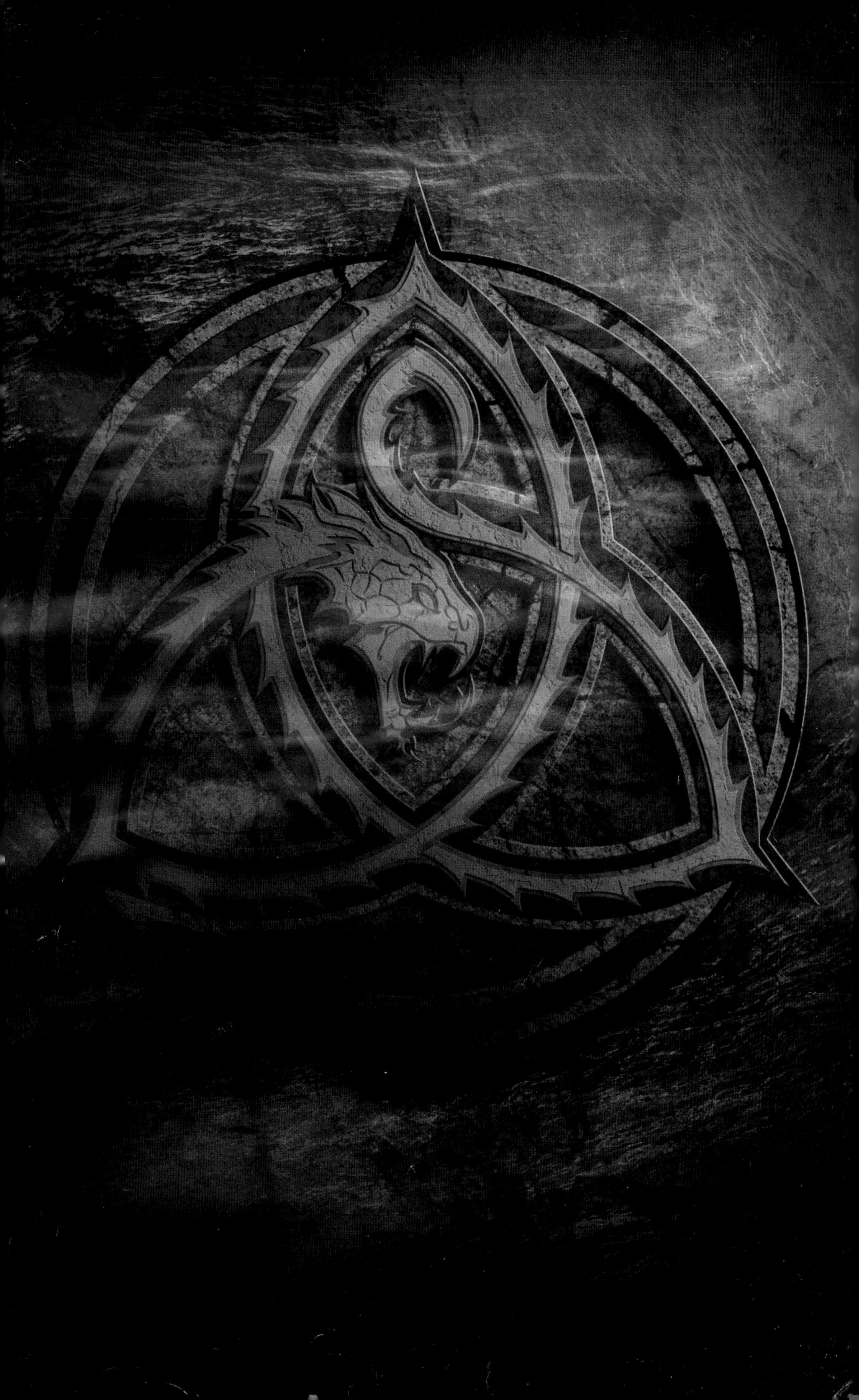

FEAR ITSELF
ITSELF
SPIDER-MAN

WRITER
CHRIS YOST
ARTIST
MIKE McKONE
COLORS
JEROMY COX
LETTERS
VC'S JOE CARAMAGNA
COVER ART
MARKO DJURDJEVIC
ASSISTANT EDITOR
ELLIE PYLE
EDITOR
STEPHEN WACKER

FEAR ITSELF: FF
WRITER: **CULLEN BUNN**
PENCILER: **TOM GRUMMETT**
INKERS: **CORY HAMSCHER**
WITH RICK MAGYAR
COLORIST: **RAIN BEREDO**
LETTERER: **VC'S CLAYTON COWLES**
COVER ARTIST: **GABRIELE DELL'OTTO**
ASSOCIATE EDITOR: **LAUREN SANKOVITCH**
EDITOR: **TOM BREVOORT**

FEAR ITSELF: THE WORTHY
WRITERS: **CHRISTOS GAGE, JEFF PARKER,
JEN VAN METER, FRANK TIERI, GREG PAK,
TOM DEFALCO, TOM PEYER
& ROBERTO AGUIRRE-SACASA**
ARTISTS: **ELIA BONETTI, DECLAN SHALVEY,
CLAYTON HENRY, ERIC CANETE, LEE WEEKS,
MARIO ALBERTI, SERGIO CARIELLO
& JAVIER PULIDO**
COLORISTS: **MATTHEW WILSON, FRANK MARTIN JR.,
CHRIS CHUCKRY, MARIO ALBERTI,
CHRIS SOTOMAYOR & MUNTSA VICENTE**
LETTERER: **VC'S JOE SABINO**
COVER ART: **JELENA DJURDJEVIC**
HAMMER-WIELDER ART:
MARKO DJURDJEVIC & STUART IMMONEN
EDITORS: **RACHEL PINNELAS & TOM BRENNAN**
VP DIGITAL CONTENT & PROGRAMMING:
JOHN CERILLI
ASSOCIATE PRODUCER: **HARRY GO**
DIGITAL PRODUCTION MANAGER: **TIM SMITH 3**

PREVIOUSLY:

A time of uncertainty and fear grips the world.

Sin, the daughter of the Red Skull, has unleashed an ancient evil into the world: the forgotten Asgardian god known only as the Serpent! He has summoned forth seven mystical hammers from the cosmos, and those that grasp these hammers become uncontrollable engines of destruction. With his hammer-wielding minions, the Serpent devastates the Earth in his march towards revenge on Odin and Asgard.

COLLECTION EDITOR: JENNIFER GRÜNWALD • ASSISTANT EDITORS: ALEX STARBUCK & NELSON RIBEIRO
EDITOR, SPECIAL PROJECTS: MARK D. BEAZLEY • SENIOR EDITOR, SPECIAL PROJECTS: JEFF YOUNGQUIST
SENIOR VICE PRESIDENT OF SALES: DAVID GABRIEL • SVP OF BRAND PLANNING & COMMUNICATIONS: MICHAEL PASCIULLO

EDITOR IN CHIEF: AXEL ALONSO • CHIEF CREATIVE OFFICER: JOE QUESADA • PUBLISHER: DAN BUCKLEY • EXECUTIVE PRODUCER: ALAN FINE

FEAR ITSELF: SPIDER-MAN. Contains material originally published in magazine form as FEAR ITSELF SPIDER-MAN #1-3, FEAR ITSELF: FF #1 and FEAR ITSELF: THE WORTHY #1. First printing 2012. ISBN# 978-0-7851-5804-2. Published by MARVEL WORLDWIDE, INC., a subsidiary of MARVEL ENTERTAINMENT, LLC. OFFICE OF PUBLICATION: 135 West 50th Street, New York, NY 10020. $19.99 per copy in the U.S. and $21.99 in Canada (GST #R127032852); Canadian Agreement #40668537. **Printed in the U.S.A.** ALAN FINE, EVP - Office of the President, Marvel Worldwide, Inc. and EVP & CMO Marvel Characters B.V.; DAN BUCKLEY, Publisher & President - Print, Animation & Digital Divisions; JOE QUESADA, Chief Creative Officer; DAVID BOGART, SVP of Business Affairs & Talent Management; TOM BREVOORT, SVP of Publishing; C.B. CEBULSKI, SVP of Creator & Content Development; DAVID GABRIEL, SVP of Publishing Sales & Circulation; MICHAEL PASCIULLO, SVP of Brand Planning & Communications; JIM O'KEEFE, VP of Operations & Logistics; DAN CARR, Executive Director of Publishing Technology; SUSAN CRESPI, Editorial Operations Manager; ALEX MORALES, Publishing Operations Manager; STAN LEE, Chairman Emeritus. For information regarding advertising in Marvel Comics or on Marvel.com, please contact John Dokes, SVP Integrated Sales and Marketing, at jdokes@marvel.com. For Marvel subscription inquiries, please call 800-217-9158. **Manufactured between 2/6/2012 and 3/5/2012 by R.R. DONNELLEY, INC., SALEM, VA, USA.**

10 9 8 7 6 5 4 3 2 1

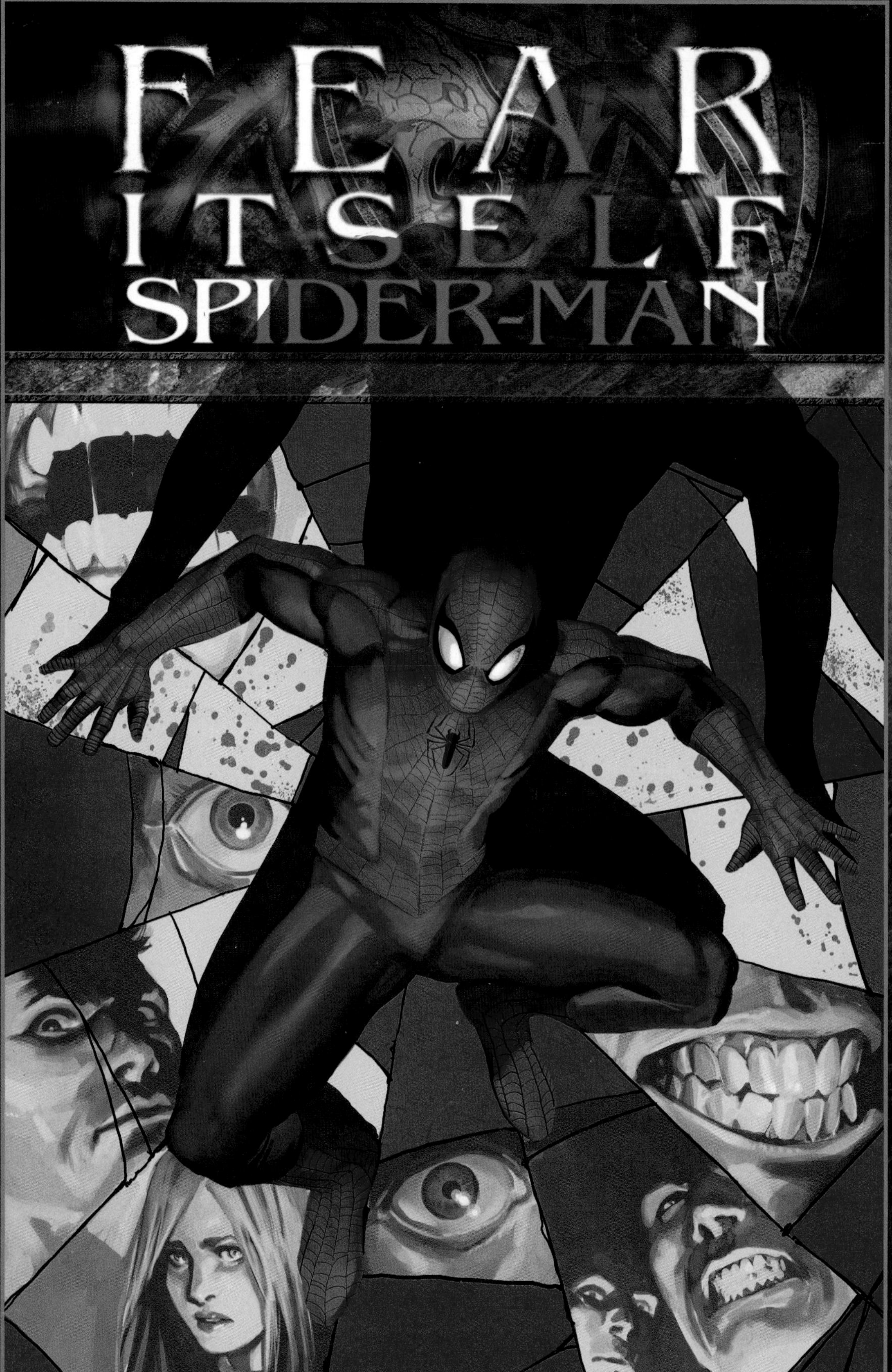
FEAR
ITSELF
SPIDER-MAN

DAY ONE

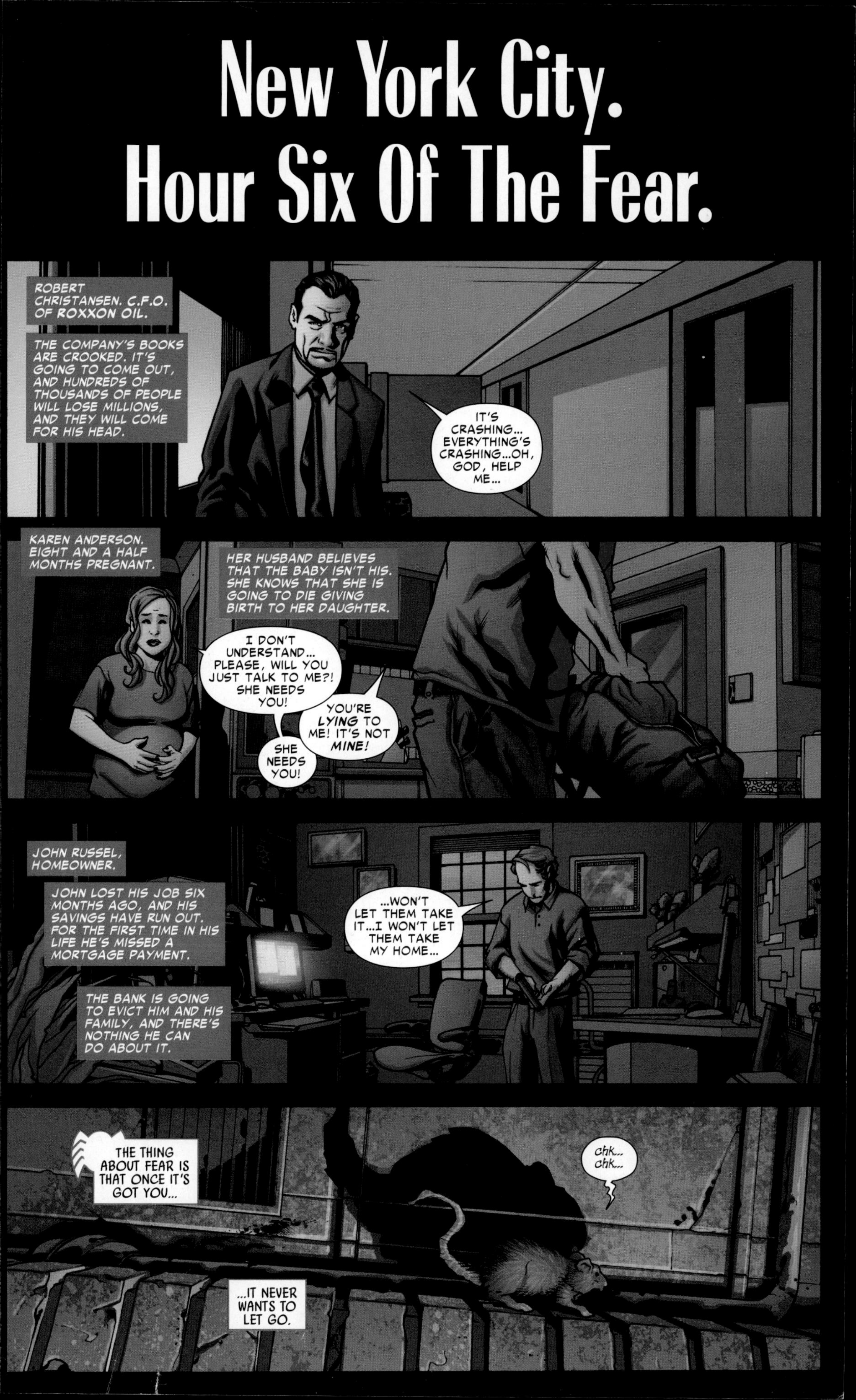
New York City.
Hour Six Of The Fear.
ROBERT CHRISTANSEN. C.F.O. OF ROXXON OIL.
THE COMPANY'S BOOKS ARE CROOKED. IT'S GOING TO COME OUT, AND HUNDREDS OF THOUSANDS OF PEOPLE WILL LOSE MILLIONS, AND THEY WILL COME FOR HIS HEAD.
IT'S CRASHING... EVERYTHING'S CRASHING...OH, GOD, HELP ME...
KAREN ANDERSON. EIGHT AND A HALF MONTHS PREGNANT.
HER HUSBAND BELIEVES THAT THE BABY ISN'T HIS. SHE KNOWS THAT SHE IS GOING TO DIE GIVING BIRTH TO HER DAUGHTER.
I DON'T UNDERSTAND... PLEASE, WILL YOU JUST TALK TO ME?! SHE NEEDS YOU!
YOU'RE LYING TO ME! IT'S NOT MINE!
SHE NEEDS YOU!
JOHN RUSSEL, HOMEOWNER.
JOHN LOST HIS JOB SIX MONTHS AGO, AND HIS SAVINGS HAVE RUN OUT. FOR THE FIRST TIME IN HIS LIFE HE'S MISSED A MORTGAGE PAYMENT.
...WON'T LET THEM TAKE IT...I WON'T LET THEM TAKE MY HOME...
THE BANK IS GOING TO EVICT HIM AND HIS FAMILY, AND THERE'S NOTHING HE CAN DO ABOUT IT.
THE THING ABOUT FEAR IS THAT ONCE IT'S GOT YOU...
Chk... Chk...
...IT NEVER WANTS TO LET GO.

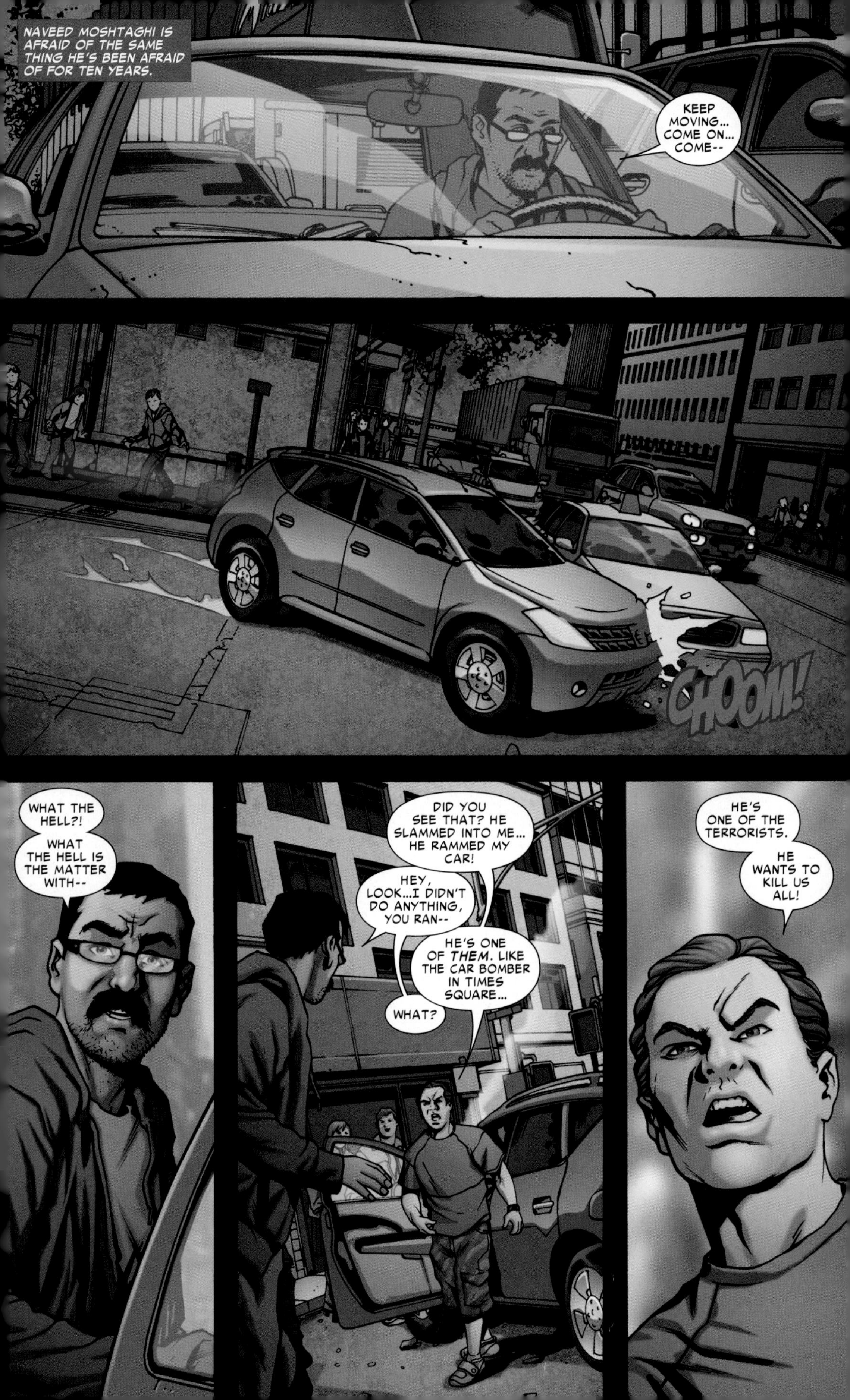
NAVEED MOSHTAGHI IS AFRAID OF THE SAME THING HE'S BEEN AFRAID OF FOR TEN YEARS.
KEEP MOVING... COME ON... COME--
CHOOM!
WHAT THE HELL?!
WHAT THE HELL IS THE MATTER WITH--
DID YOU SEE THAT? HE SLAMMED INTO ME... HE RAMMED MY CAR!
HEY, LOOK...I DIDN'T DO ANYTHING, YOU RAN--
HE'S ONE OF *THEM*. LIKE THE CAR BOMBER IN TIMES SQUARE...
WHAT?
HE'S ONE OF THE TERRORISTS.
HE WANTS TO KILL US ALL!

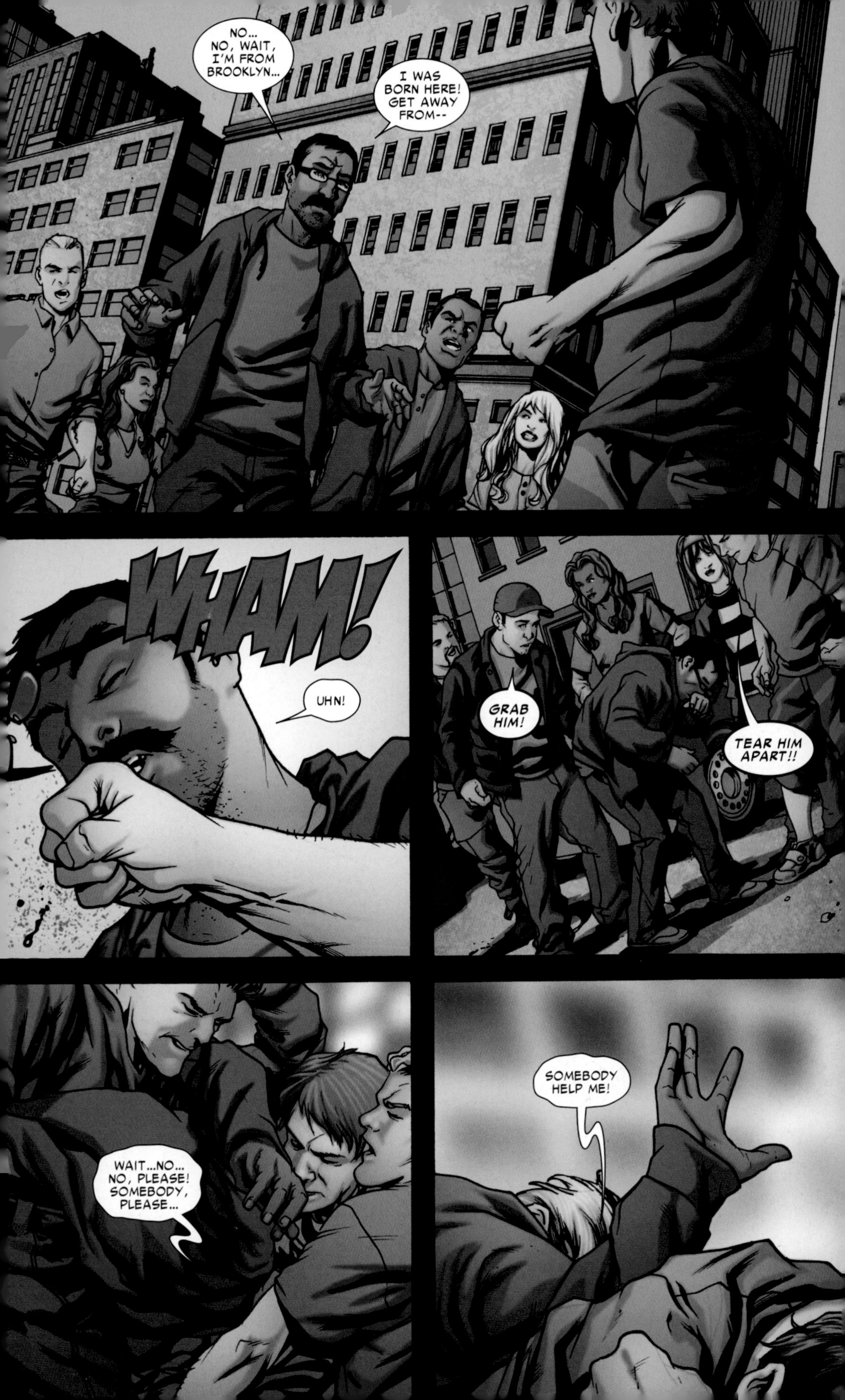
NO... NO, WAIT, I'M FROM BROOKLYN...
I WAS BORN HERE! GET AWAY FROM--
WHAM!
UHN!
GRAB HIM!
TEAR HIM APART!!
WAIT...NO... NO, PLEASE! SOMEBODY, PLEASE...
SOMEBODY HELP ME!

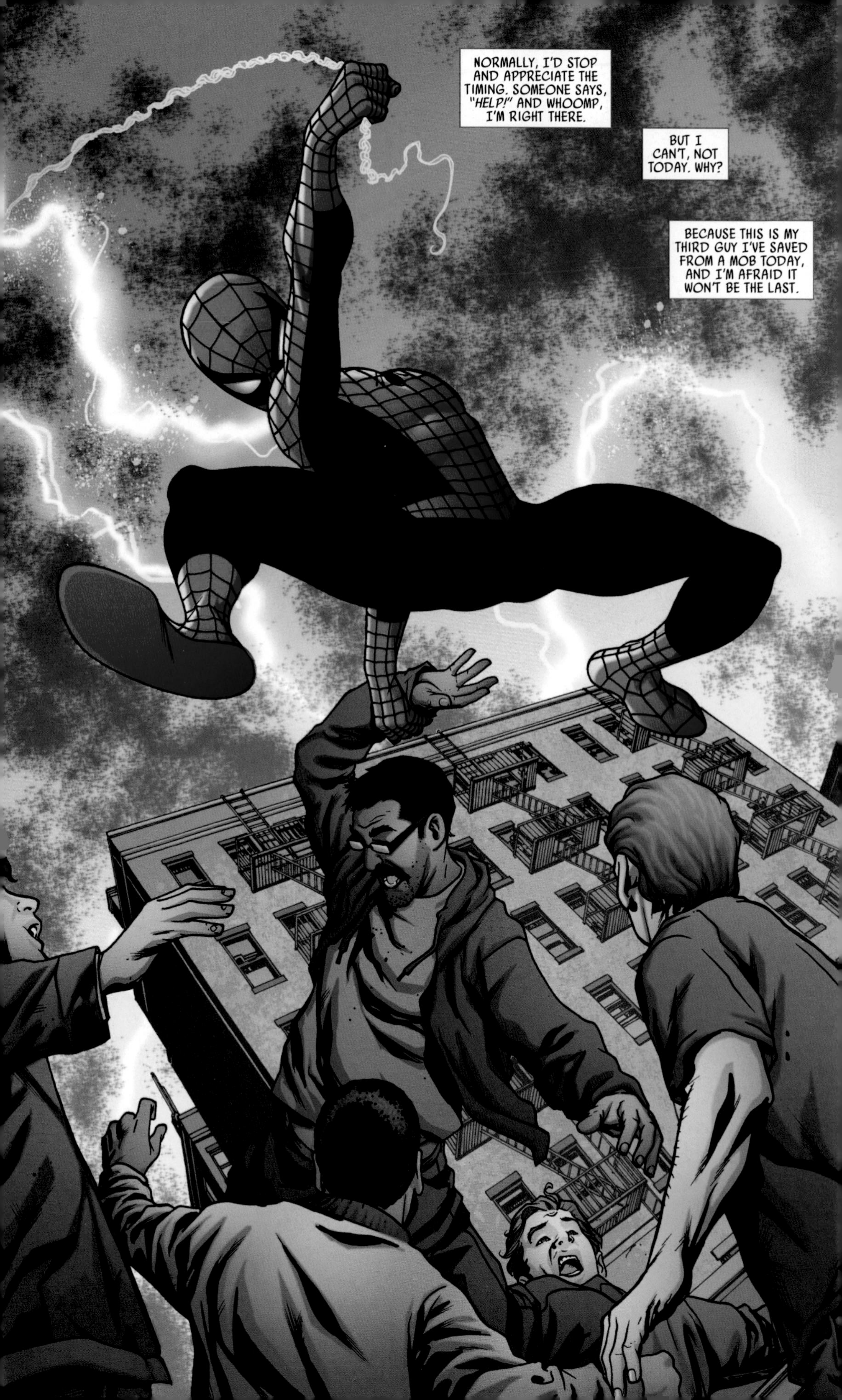
NORMALLY, I'D STOP AND APPRECIATE THE TIMING. SOMEONE SAYS, "HELP!" AND WHOOMP, I'M RIGHT THERE.
BUT I CAN'T, NOT TODAY. WHY?
BECAUSE THIS IS MY THIRD GUY I'VE SAVED FROM A MOB TODAY, AND I'M AFRAID IT WON'T BE THE LAST.

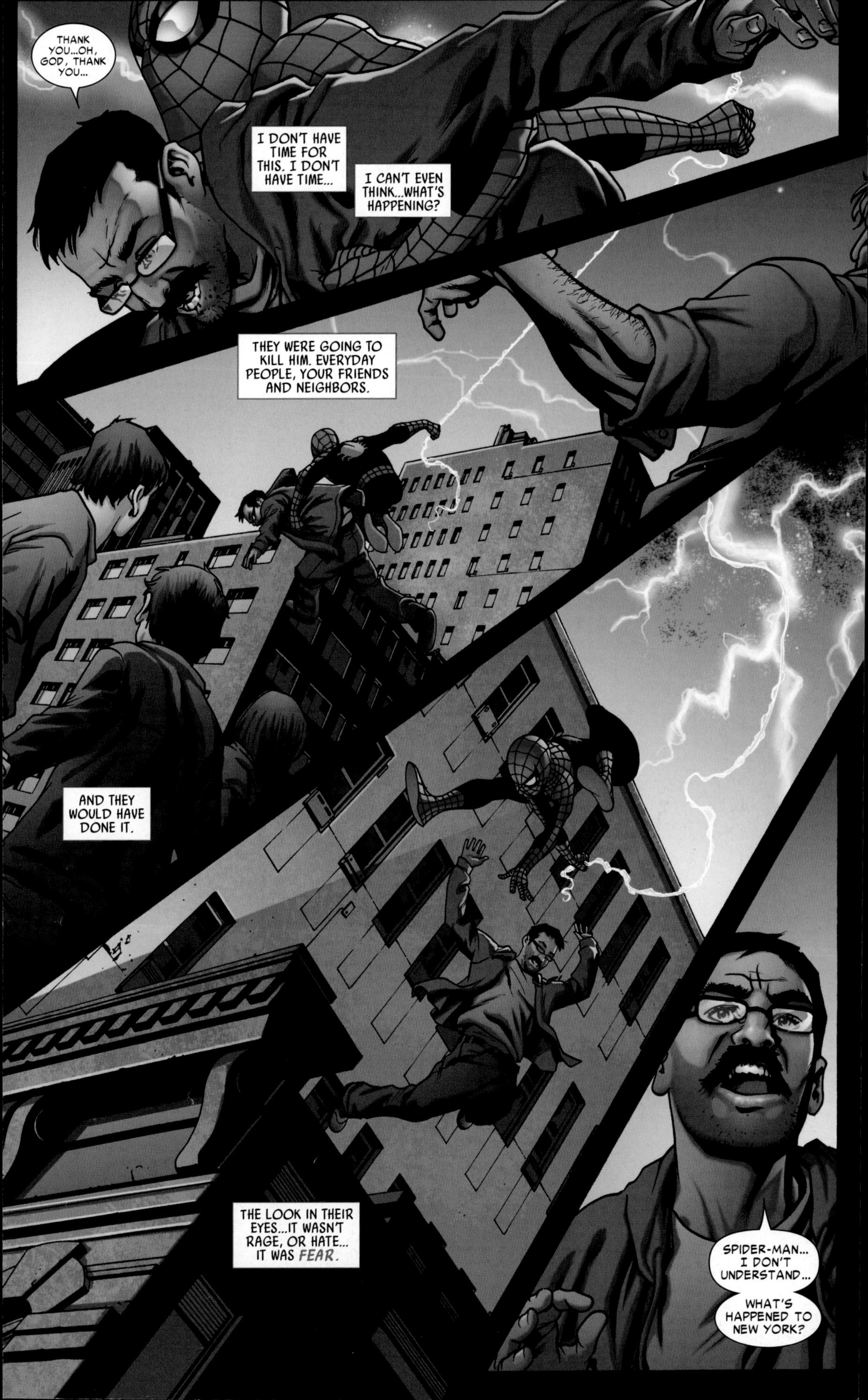
THANK YOU...OH, GOD, THANK YOU...
I DON'T HAVE TIME FOR THIS. I DON'T HAVE TIME...
I CAN'T EVEN THINK...WHAT'S HAPPENING?
THEY WERE GOING TO KILL HIM. EVERYDAY PEOPLE, YOUR FRIENDS AND NEIGHBORS.
AND THEY WOULD HAVE DONE IT.
THE LOOK IN THEIR EYES...IT WASN'T RAGE, OR HATE... IT WAS FEAR.
SPIDER-MAN... I DON'T UNDERSTAND...
WHAT'S HAPPENED TO NEW YORK?

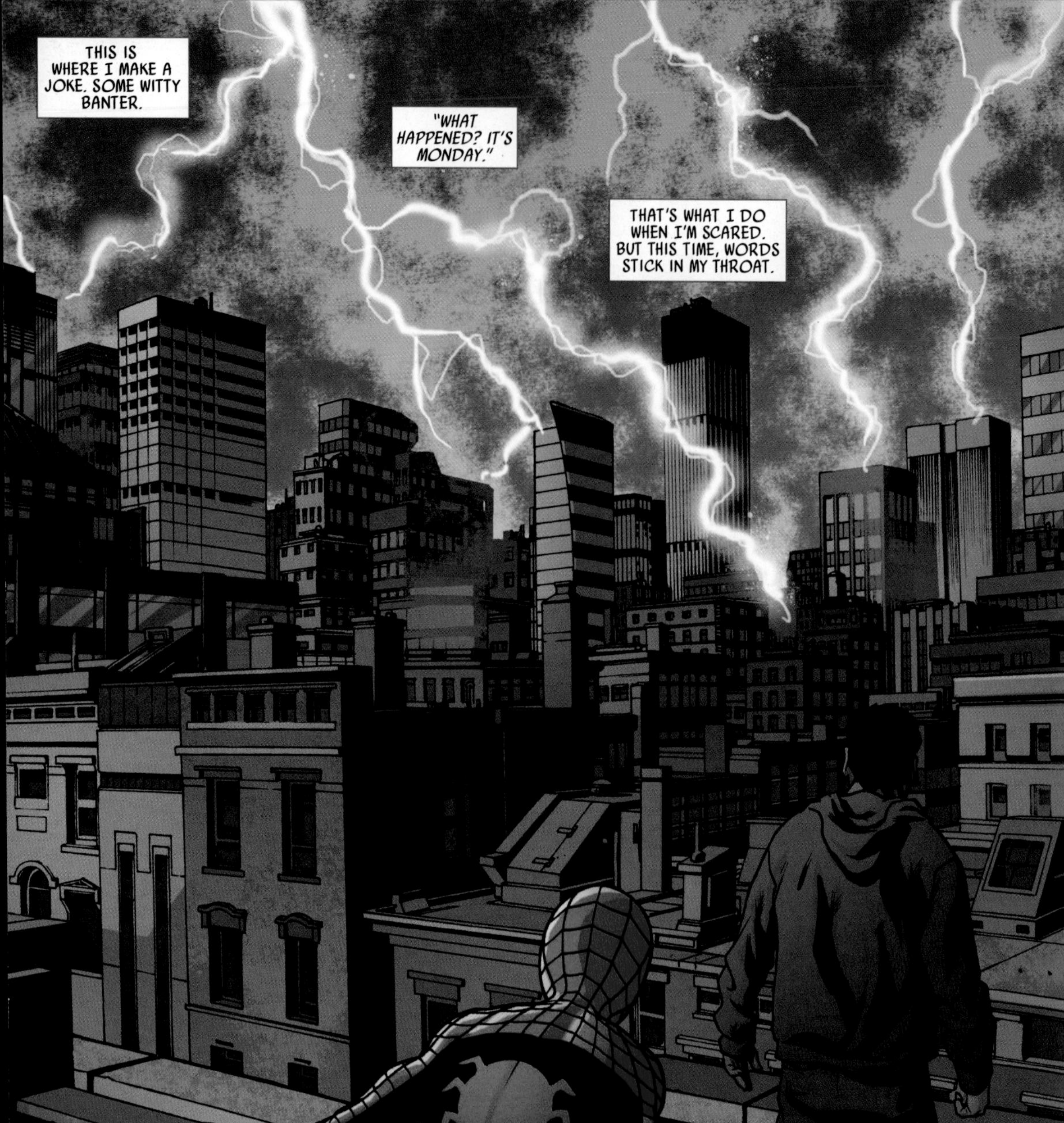
THIS IS WHERE I MAKE A JOKE. SOME WITTY BANTER.
"WHAT HAPPENED? IT'S MONDAY."
THAT'S WHAT I DO WHEN I'M SCARED. BUT THIS TIME, WORDS STICK IN MY THROAT.

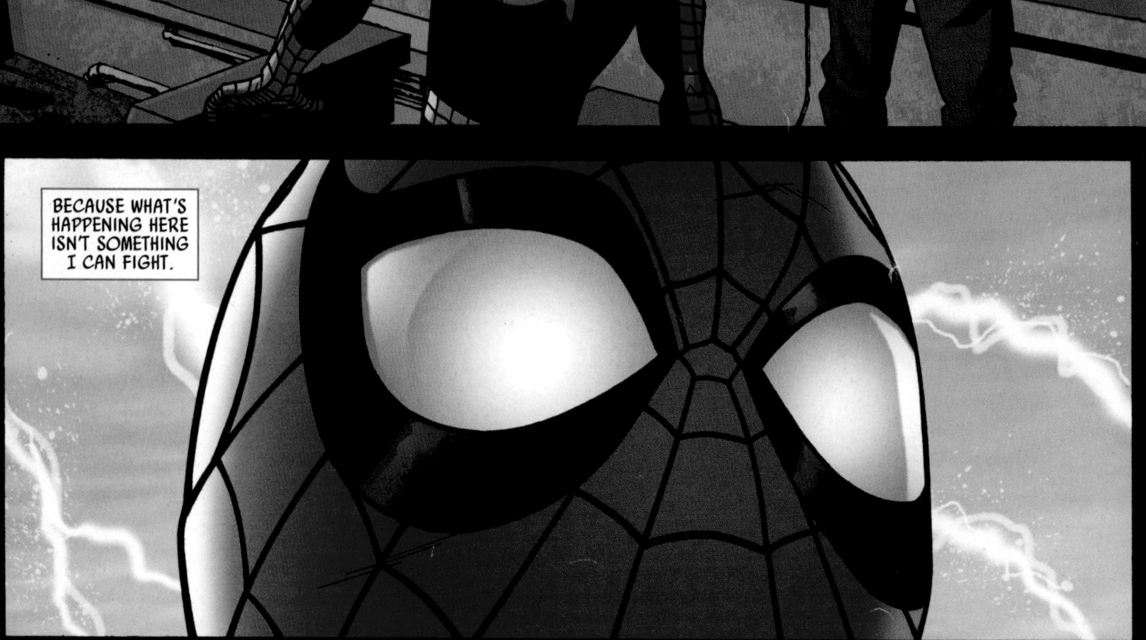
BECAUSE WHAT'S HAPPENING HERE ISN'T SOMETHING I CAN FIGHT.

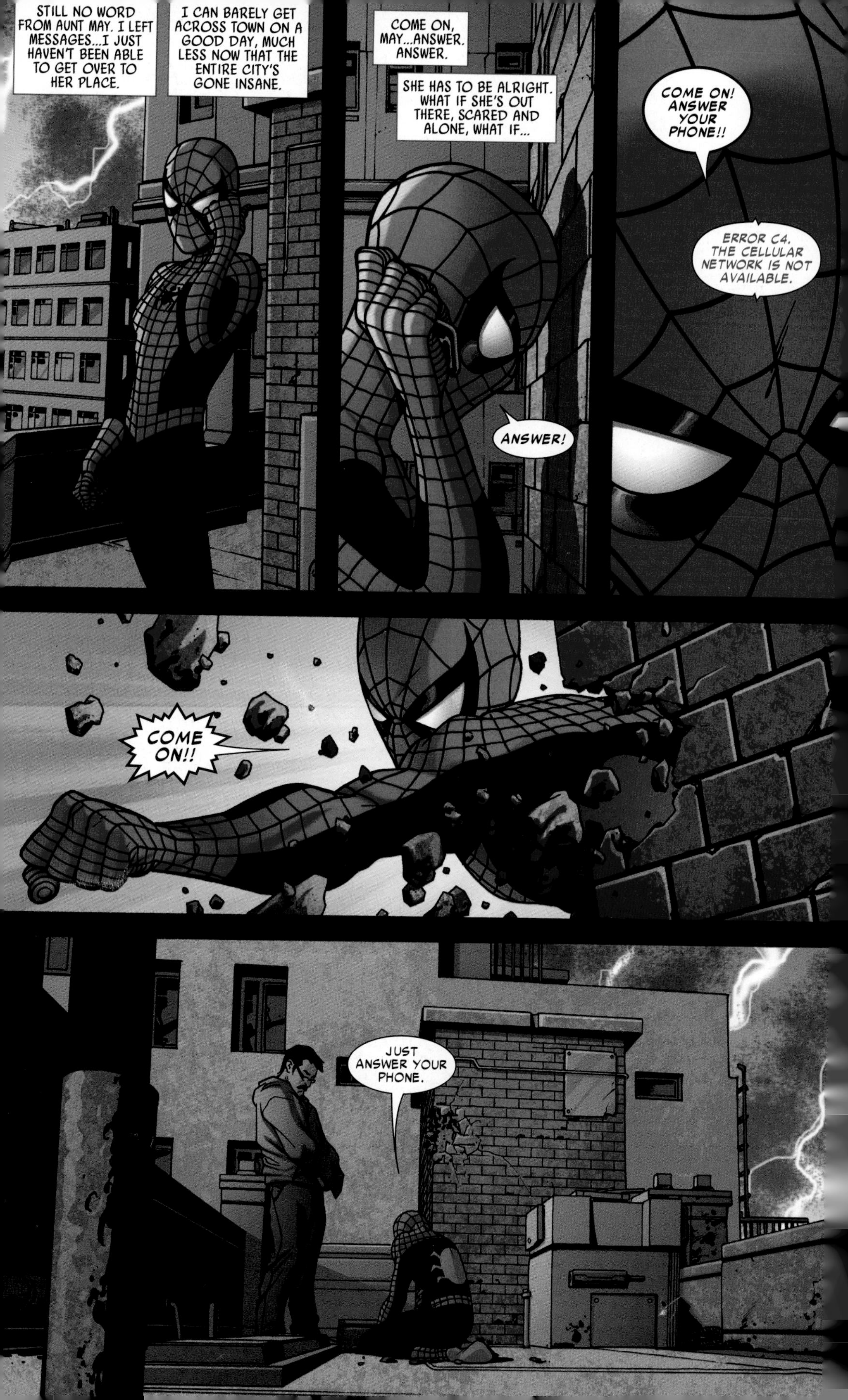
STILL NO WORD FROM AUNT MAY. I LEFT MESSAGES...I JUST HAVEN'T BEEN ABLE TO GET OVER TO HER PLACE.
I CAN BARELY GET ACROSS TOWN ON A GOOD DAY, MUCH LESS NOW THAT THE ENTIRE CITY'S GONE INSANE.
COME ON, MAY...ANSWER. ANSWER.
SHE HAS TO BE ALRIGHT. WHAT IF SHE'S OUT THERE, SCARED AND ALONE, WHAT IF...
ANSWER!
COME ON! ANSWER YOUR PHONE!!
ERROR C4. THE CELLULAR NETWORK IS NOT AVAILABLE.
COME ON!!
JUST ANSWER YOUR PHONE.

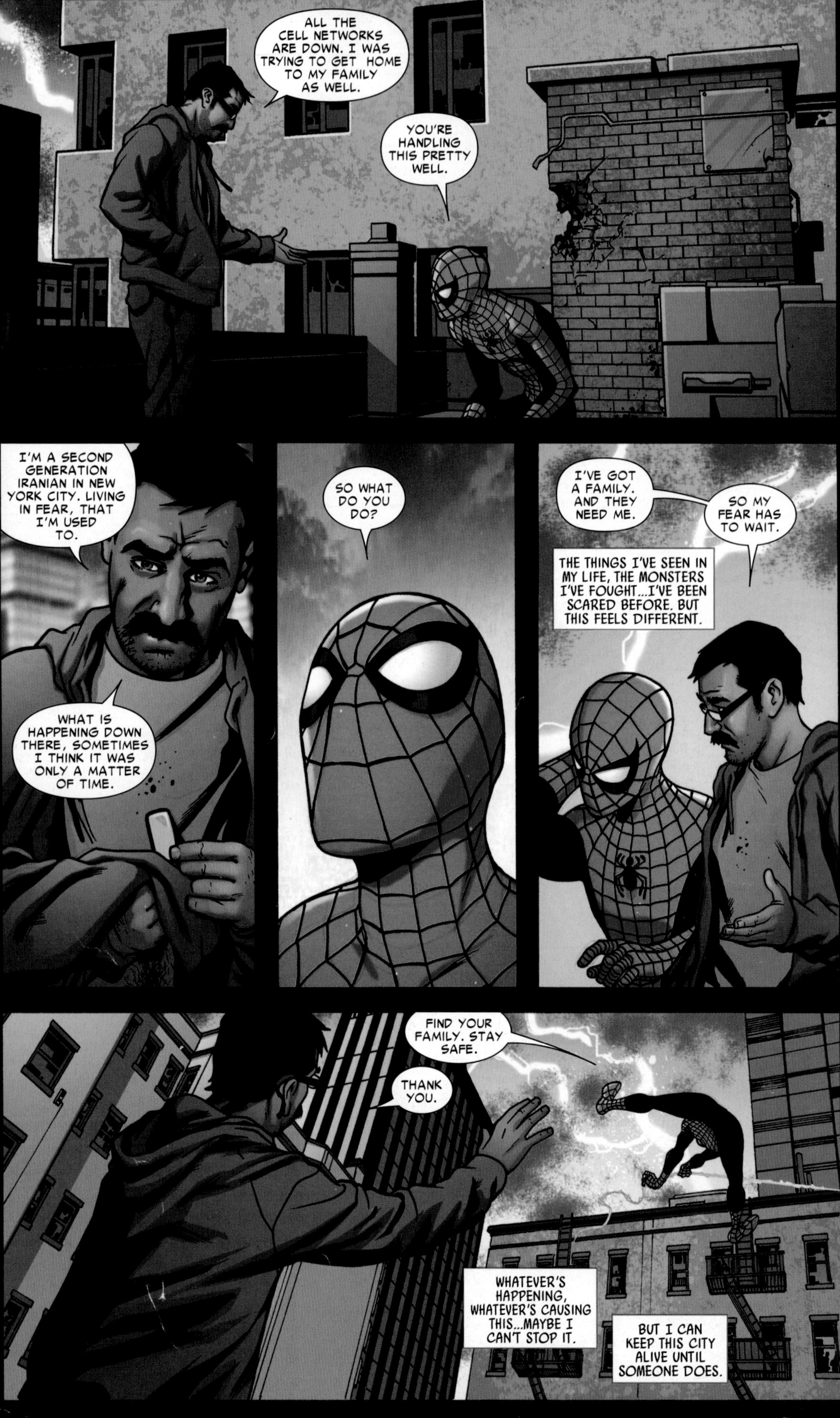
ALL THE CELL NETWORKS ARE DOWN. I WAS TRYING TO GET HOME TO MY FAMILY AS WELL.
YOU'RE HANDLING THIS PRETTY WELL.
I'M A SECOND GENERATION IRANIAN IN NEW YORK CITY. LIVING IN FEAR, THAT I'M USED TO.
WHAT IS HAPPENING DOWN THERE, SOMETIMES I THINK IT WAS ONLY A MATTER OF TIME.
SO WHAT DO YOU DO?
I'VE GOT A FAMILY. AND THEY NEED ME.
SO MY FEAR HAS TO WAIT.
THE THINGS I'VE SEEN IN MY LIFE, THE MONSTERS I'VE FOUGHT...I'VE BEEN SCARED BEFORE. BUT THIS FEELS DIFFERENT.
FIND YOUR FAMILY. STAY SAFE.
THANK YOU.
WHATEVER'S HAPPENING, WHATEVER'S CAUSING THIS...MAYBE I CAN'T STOP IT.
BUT I CAN KEEP THIS CITY ALIVE UNTIL SOMEONE DOES.

Hour Eleven of The Fear.

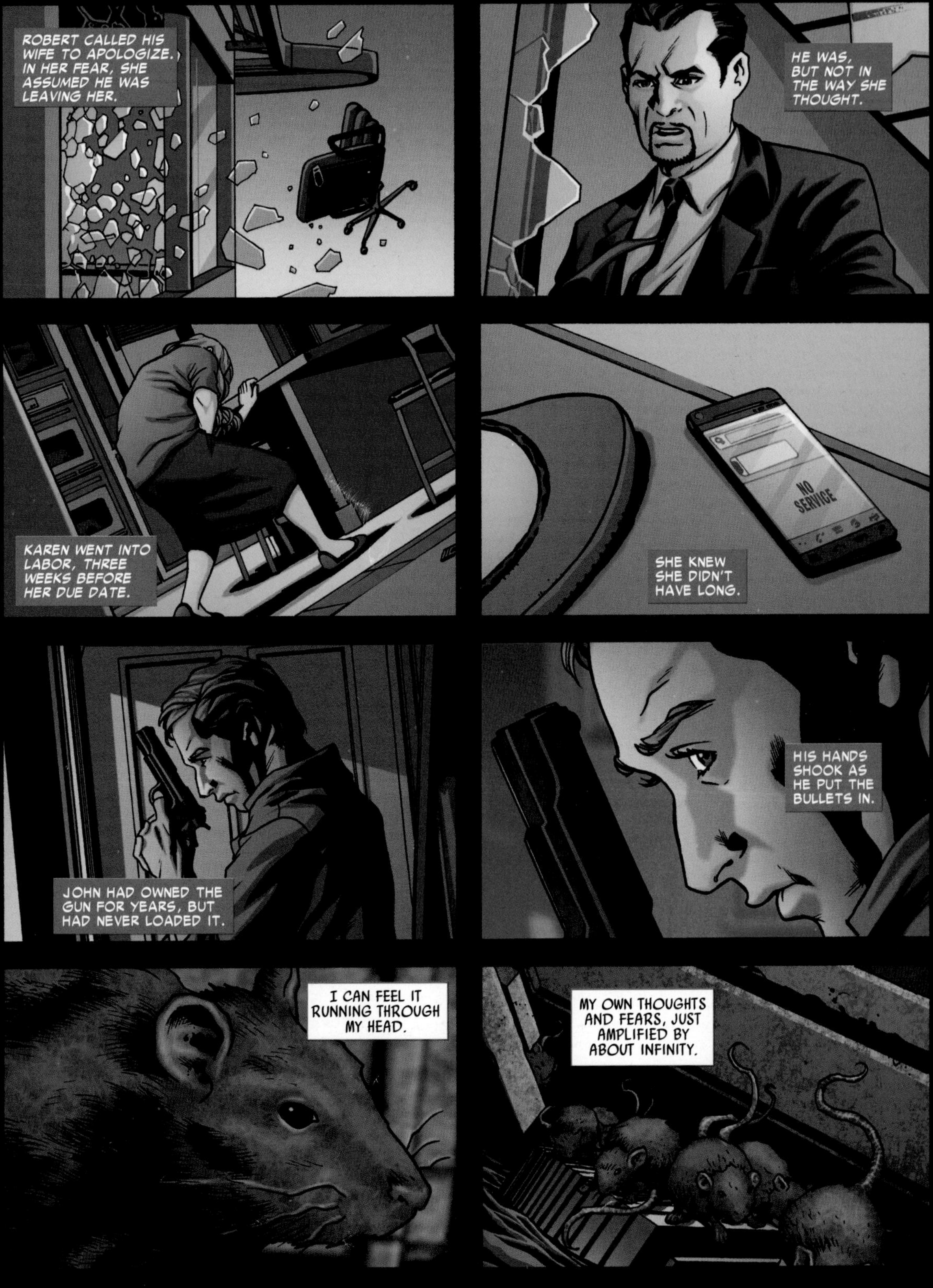
ROBERT CALLED HIS WIFE TO APOLOGIZE. IN HER FEAR, SHE ASSUMED HE WAS LEAVING HER.
HE WAS, BUT NOT IN THE WAY SHE THOUGHT.
KAREN WENT INTO LABOR, THREE WEEKS BEFORE HER DUE DATE.
NO SERVICE
SHE KNEW SHE DIDN'T HAVE LONG.
JOHN HAD OWNED THE GUN FOR YEARS, BUT HAD NEVER LOADED IT.
HIS HANDS SHOOK AS HE PUT THE BULLETS IN.
I CAN FEEL IT RUNNING THROUGH MY HEAD.
MY OWN THOUGHTS AND FEARS, JUST AMPLIFIED BY ABOUT INFINITY.

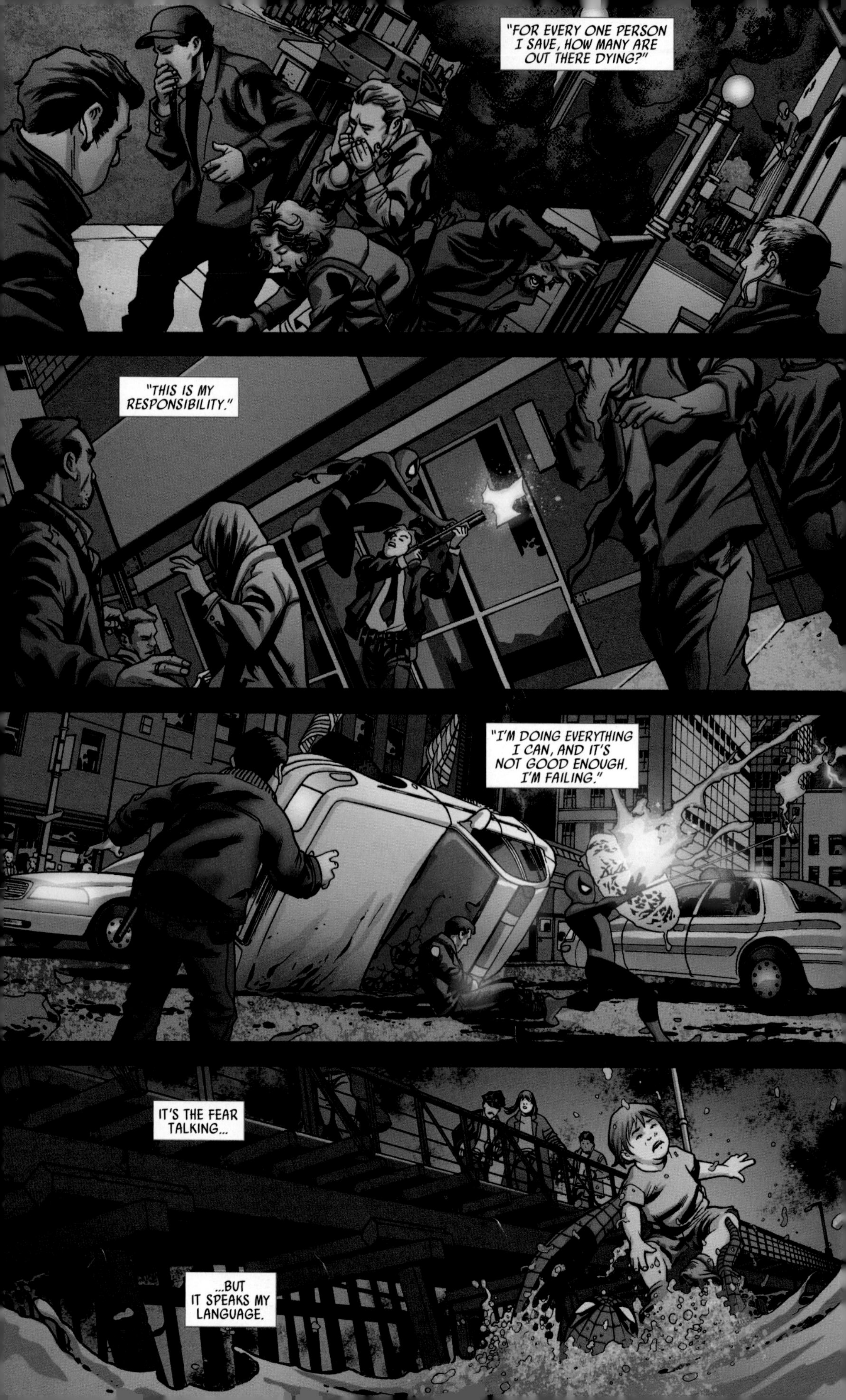
"FOR EVERY ONE PERSON I SAVE, HOW MANY ARE OUT THERE DYING?"
"THIS IS MY RESPONSIBILITY."
"I'M DOING EVERYTHING I CAN, AND IT'S NOT GOOD ENOUGH. I'M FAILING."
IT'S THE FEAR TALKING...
...BUT IT SPEAKS MY LANGUAGE.

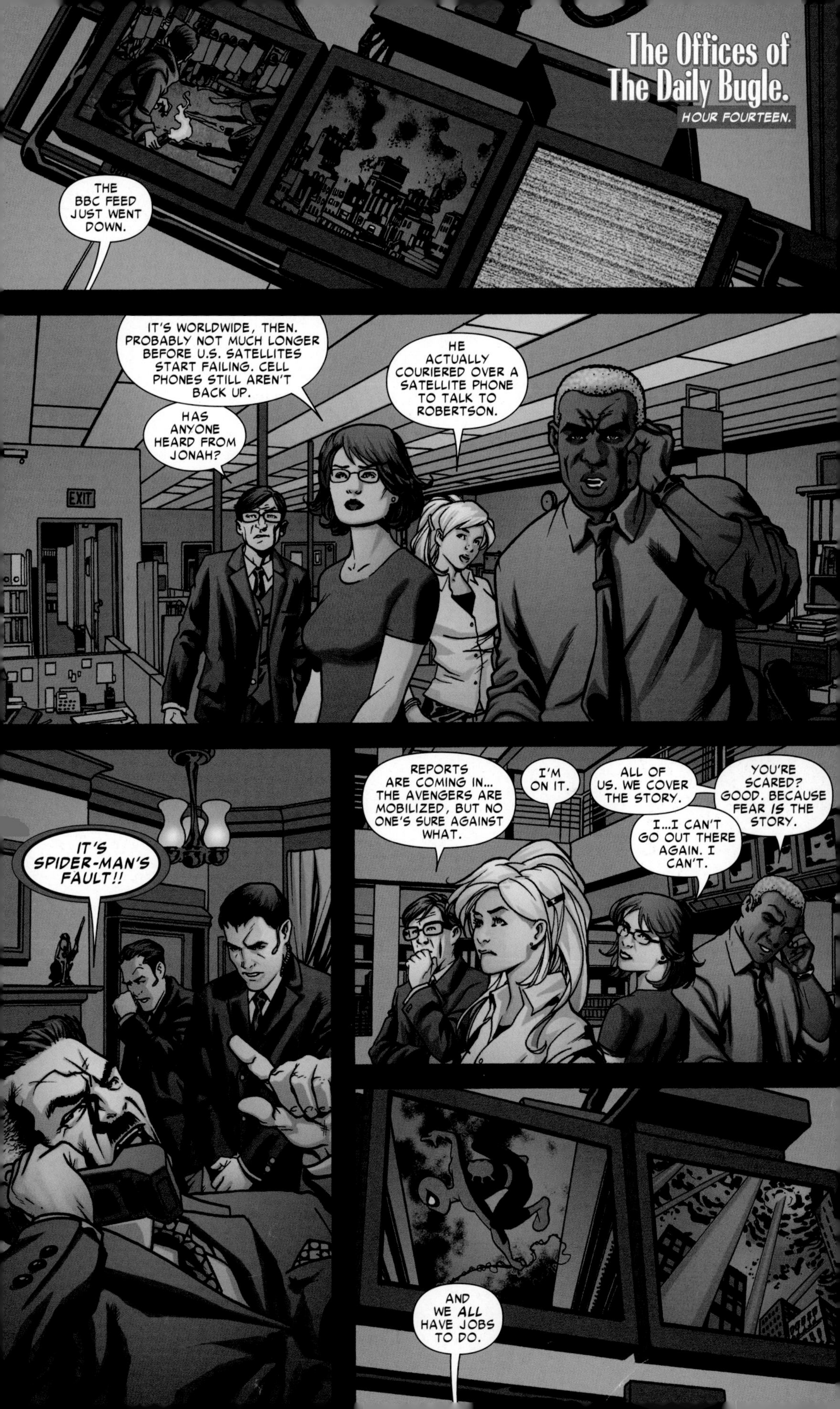
The Offices of The Daily Bugle.
HOUR FOURTEEN.
THE BBC FEED JUST WENT DOWN.
IT'S WORLDWIDE, THEN. PROBABLY NOT MUCH LONGER BEFORE U.S. SATELLITES START FAILING. CELL PHONES STILL AREN'T BACK UP.
HAS ANYONE HEARD FROM JONAH?
HE ACTUALLY COURIERED OVER A SATELLITE PHONE TO TALK TO ROBERTSON.
EXIT
IT'S SPIDER-MAN'S FAULT!!
REPORTS ARE COMING IN... THE AVENGERS ARE MOBILIZED, BUT NO ONE'S SURE AGAINST WHAT.
I'M ON IT.
ALL OF US. WE COVER THE STORY.
I...I CAN'T GO OUT THERE AGAIN. I CAN'T.
YOU'RE SCARED? GOOD. BECAUSE FEAR IS THE STORY.
AND WE ALL HAVE JOBS TO DO.

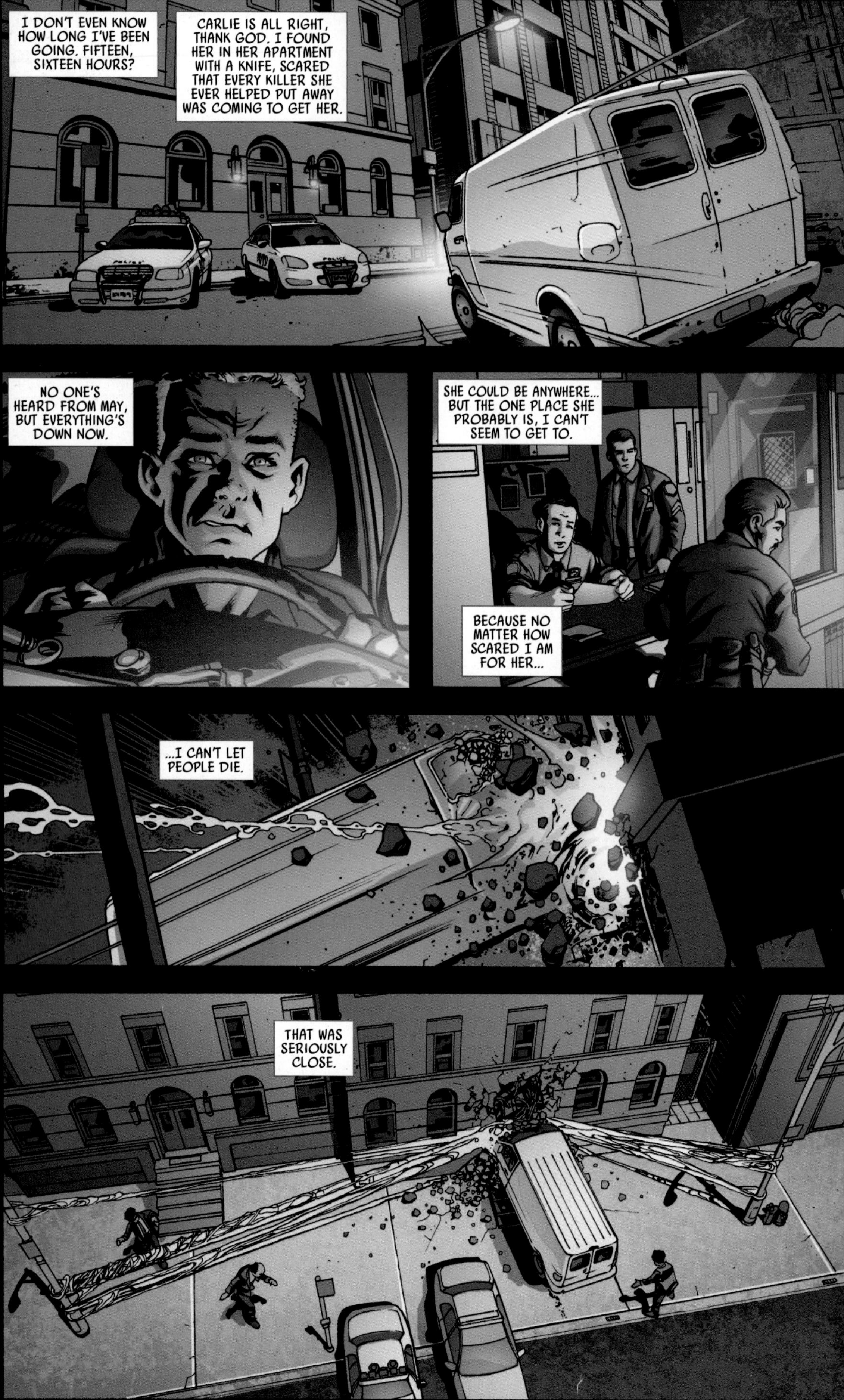
I DON'T EVEN KNOW HOW LONG I'VE BEEN GOING. FIFTEEN, SIXTEEN HOURS?
CARLIE IS ALL RIGHT, THANK GOD. I FOUND HER IN HER APARTMENT WITH A KNIFE, SCARED THAT EVERY KILLER SHE EVER HELPED PUT AWAY WAS COMING TO GET HER.
NO ONE'S HEARD FROM MAY, BUT EVERYTHING'S DOWN NOW.
SHE COULD BE ANYWHERE... BUT THE ONE PLACE SHE PROBABLY IS, I CAN'T SEEM TO GET TO.
BECAUSE NO MATTER HOW SCARED I AM FOR HER...
...I CAN'T LET PEOPLE DIE.
THAT WAS SERIOUSLY CLOSE.

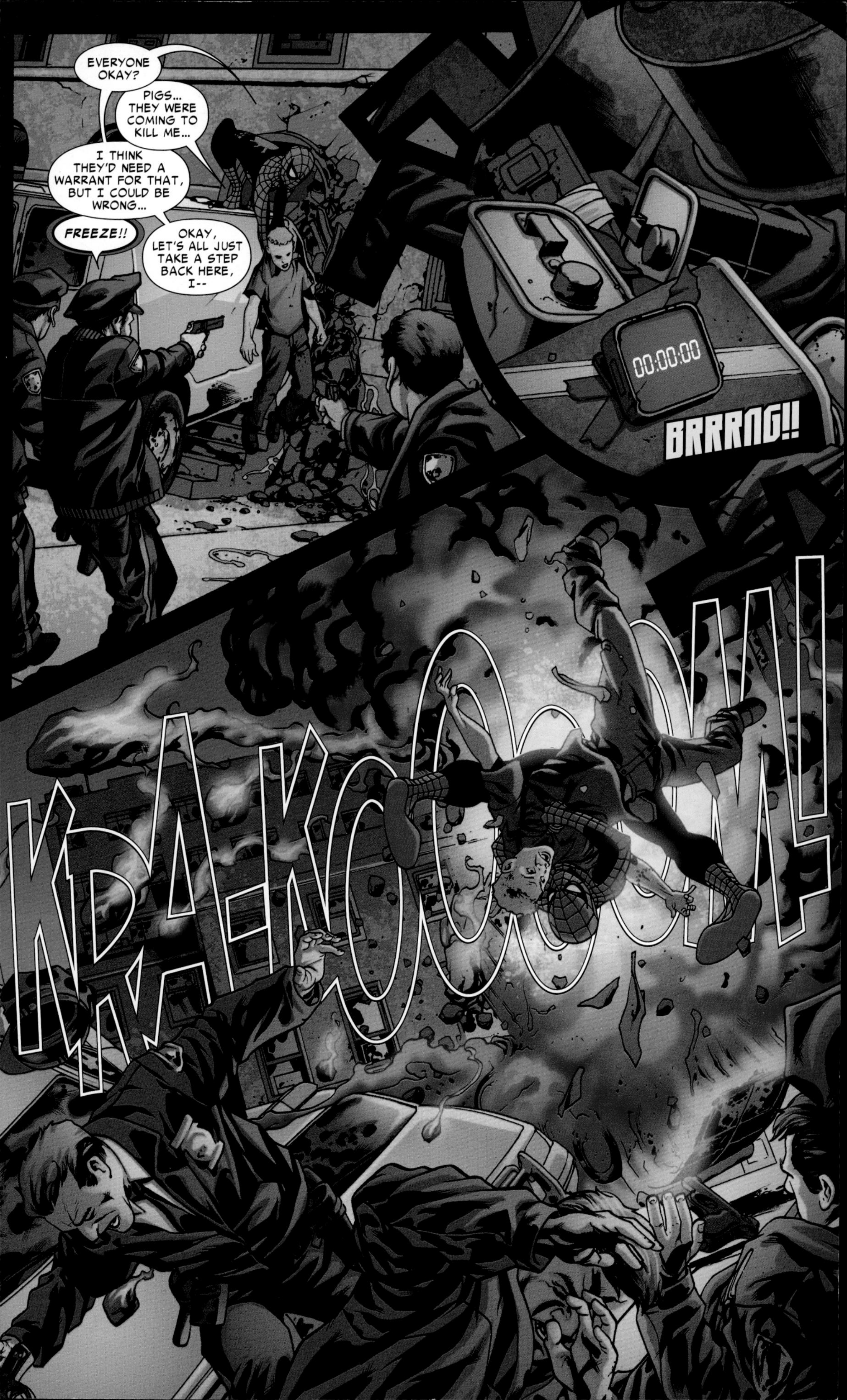
EVERYONE OKAY?
PIGS... THEY WERE COMING TO KILL ME...
I THINK THEY'D NEED A WARRANT FOR THAT, BUT I COULD BE WRONG...
FREEZE!!
OKAY, LET'S ALL JUST TAKE A STEP BACK HERE, I--
00:00:00
BRRRNG!!
KRA-KOOOOOM!

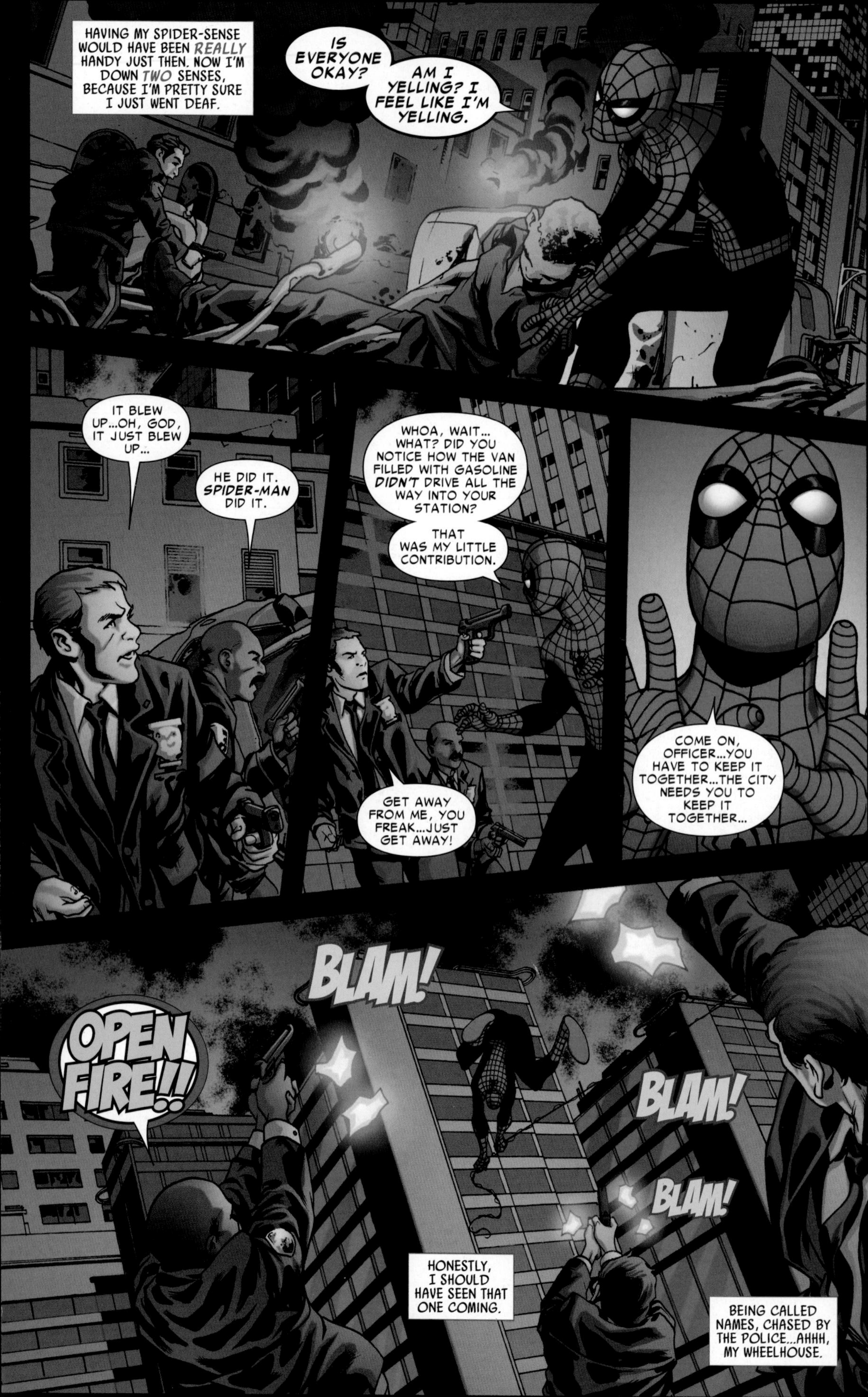

HAVING MY SPIDER-SENSE WOULD HAVE BEEN REALLY HANDY JUST THEN. NOW I'M DOWN TWO SENSES, BECAUSE I'M PRETTY SURE I JUST WENT DEAF.
IS EVERYONE OKAY?
AM I YELLING? I FEEL LIKE I'M YELLING.
IT BLEW UP...OH, GOD, IT JUST BLEW UP...
HE DID IT. SPIDER-MAN DID IT.
WHOA, WAIT... WHAT? DID YOU NOTICE HOW THE VAN FILLED WITH GASOLINE DIDN'T DRIVE ALL THE WAY INTO YOUR STATION?
THAT WAS MY LITTLE CONTRIBUTION.
GET AWAY FROM ME, YOU FREAK...JUST GET AWAY!
COME ON, OFFICER...YOU HAVE TO KEEP IT TOGETHER...THE CITY NEEDS YOU TO KEEP IT TOGETHER...
BLAM!
OPEN FIRE!!
BLAM!
BLAM!
HONESTLY, I SHOULD HAVE SEEN THAT ONE COMING.
BEING CALLED NAMES, CHASED BY THE POLICE...AHHH, MY WHEELHOUSE.

Hour Twenty of The Fear.

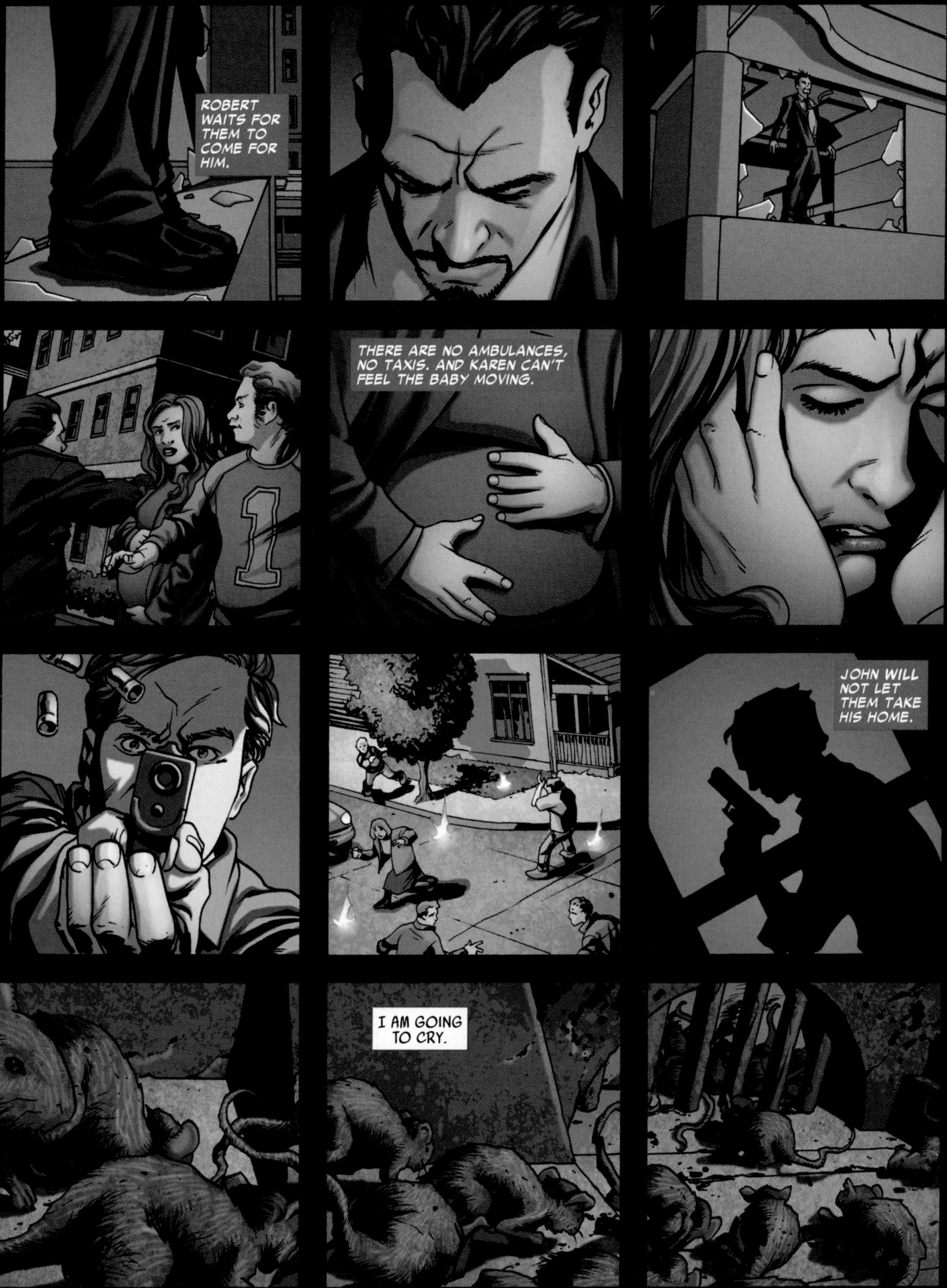
ROBERT WAITS FOR THEM TO COME FOR HIM.
THERE ARE NO AMBULANCES, NO TAXIS. AND KAREN CAN'T FEEL THE BABY MOVING.
JOHN WILL NOT LET THEM TAKE HIS HOME.
I AM GOING TO CRY.

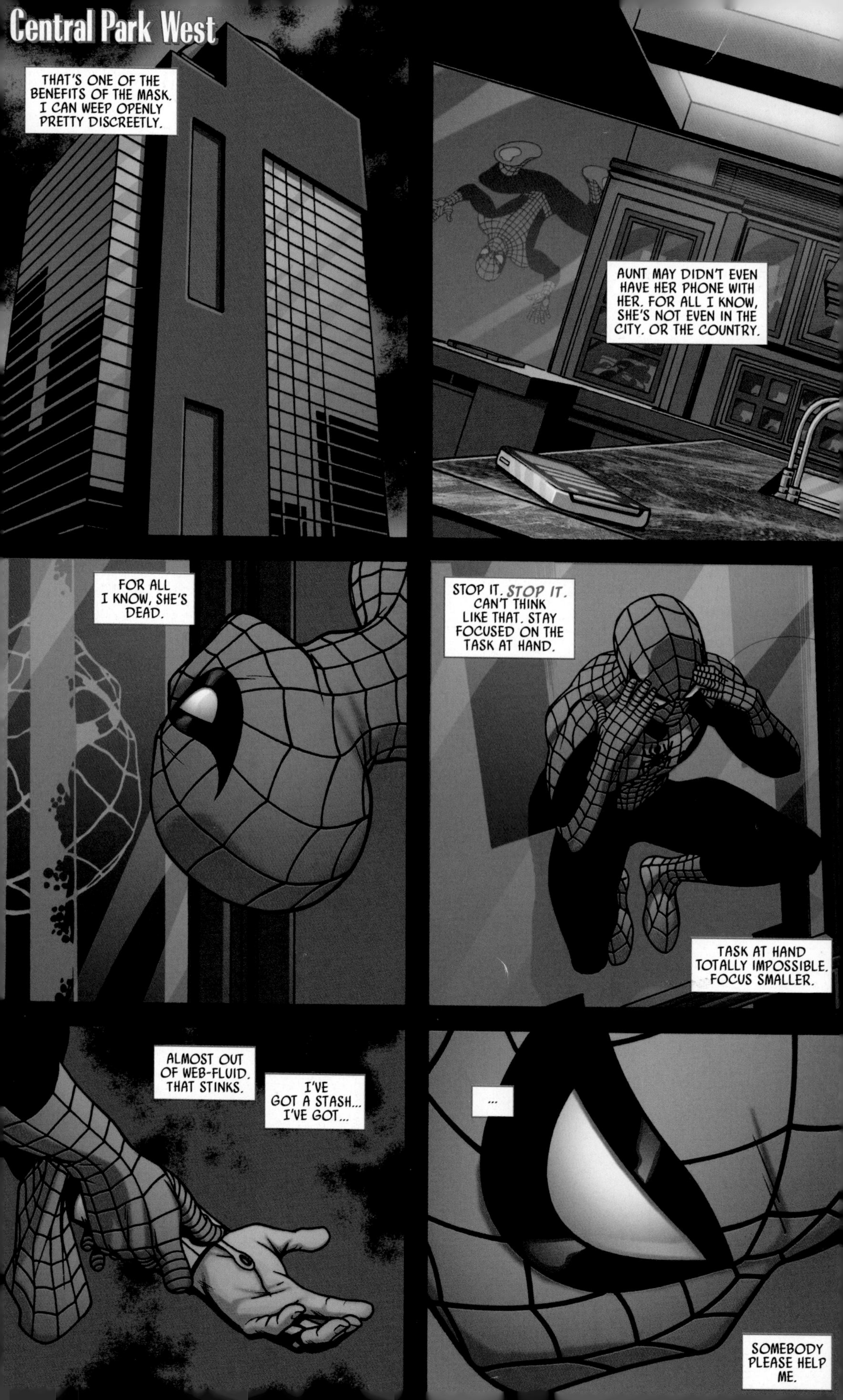

Central Park West
THAT'S ONE OF THE BENEFITS OF THE MASK. I CAN WEEP OPENLY PRETTY DISCREETLY.
AUNT MAY DIDN'T EVEN HAVE HER PHONE WITH HER. FOR ALL I KNOW, SHE'S NOT EVEN IN THE CITY. OR THE COUNTRY.
FOR ALL I KNOW, SHE'S DEAD.
STOP IT. STOP IT. CAN'T THINK LIKE THAT. STAY FOCUSED ON THE TASK AT HAND.
TASK AT HAND TOTALLY IMPOSSIBLE. FOCUS SMALLER.
ALMOST OUT OF WEB-FLUID. THAT STINKS.
I'VE GOT A STASH... I'VE GOT...
...
SOMEBODY PLEASE HELP ME.

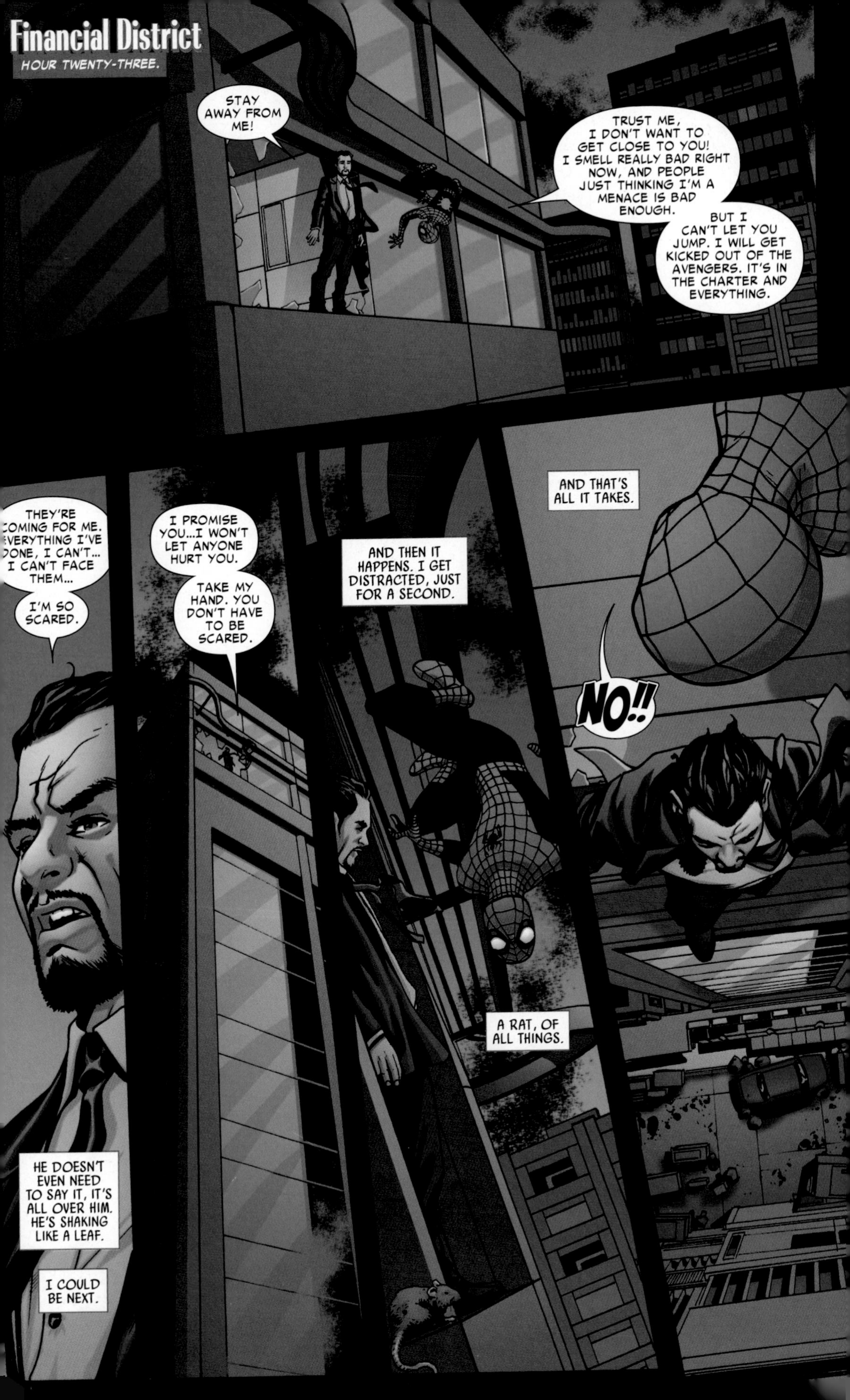
Financial District
HOUR TWENTY-THREE.
STAY AWAY FROM ME!
TRUST ME, I DON'T WANT TO GET CLOSE TO YOU! I SMELL REALLY BAD RIGHT NOW, AND PEOPLE JUST THINKING I'M A MENACE IS BAD ENOUGH.
BUT I CAN'T LET YOU JUMP. I WILL GET KICKED OUT OF THE AVENGERS. IT'S IN THE CHARTER AND EVERYTHING.
THEY'RE COMING FOR ME. VERYTHING I'VE ONE, I CAN'T... I CAN'T FACE THEM...
I'M SO SCARED.
HE DOESN'T EVEN NEED TO SAY IT, IT'S ALL OVER HIM. HE'S SHAKING LIKE A LEAF.
I COULD BE NEXT.
I PROMISE YOU...I WON'T LET ANYONE HURT YOU.
TAKE MY HAND. YOU DON'T HAVE TO BE SCARED.
AND THEN IT HAPPENS. I GET DISTRACTED, JUST FOR A SECOND.
A RAT, OF ALL THINGS.
AND THAT'S ALL IT TAKES.
NO!!

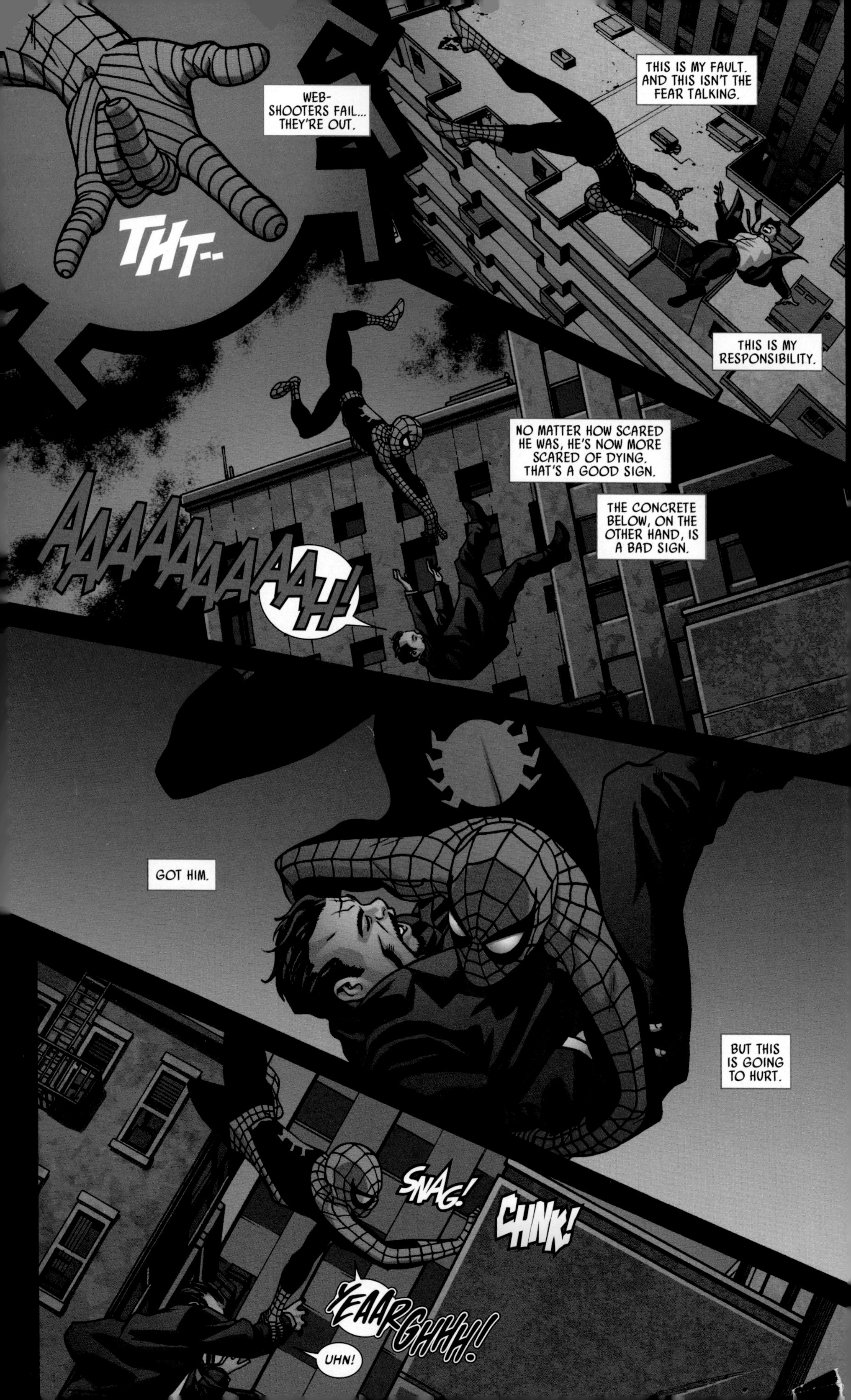
WEB-SHOOTERS FAIL... THEY'RE OUT.
THT--
THIS IS MY FAULT. AND THIS ISN'T THE FEAR TALKING.
THIS IS MY RESPONSIBILITY.
NO MATTER HOW SCARED HE WAS, HE'S NOW MORE SCARED OF DYING. THAT'S A GOOD SIGN.
THE CONCRETE BELOW, ON THE OTHER HAND, IS A BAD SIGN.
AAAAAAAAAAH!
GOT HIM.
BUT THIS IS GOING TO HURT.
SNAG!
CHNK!
YEAARGHHH!
UHN!

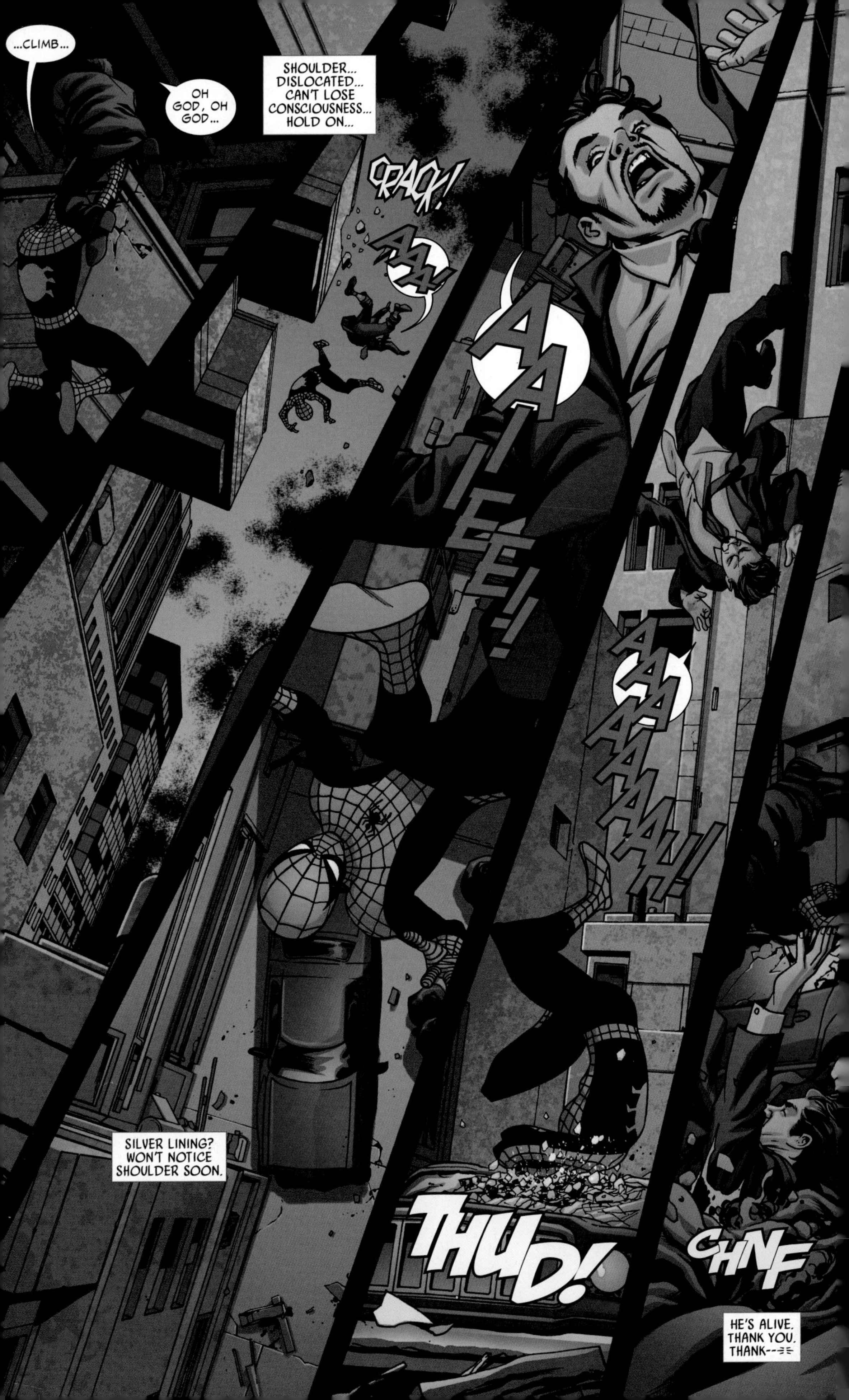
...CLIMB...
OH GOD, OH GOD...
SHOULDER... DISLOCATED... CAN'T LOSE CONSCIOUSNESS... HOLD ON...
CRACK!
AAAA
AAIIEEE!!
AAAAAAAAH!
SILVER LINING? WON'T NOTICE SHOULDER SOON.
THUD!
CHNF
HE'S ALIVE. THANK YOU. THANK--

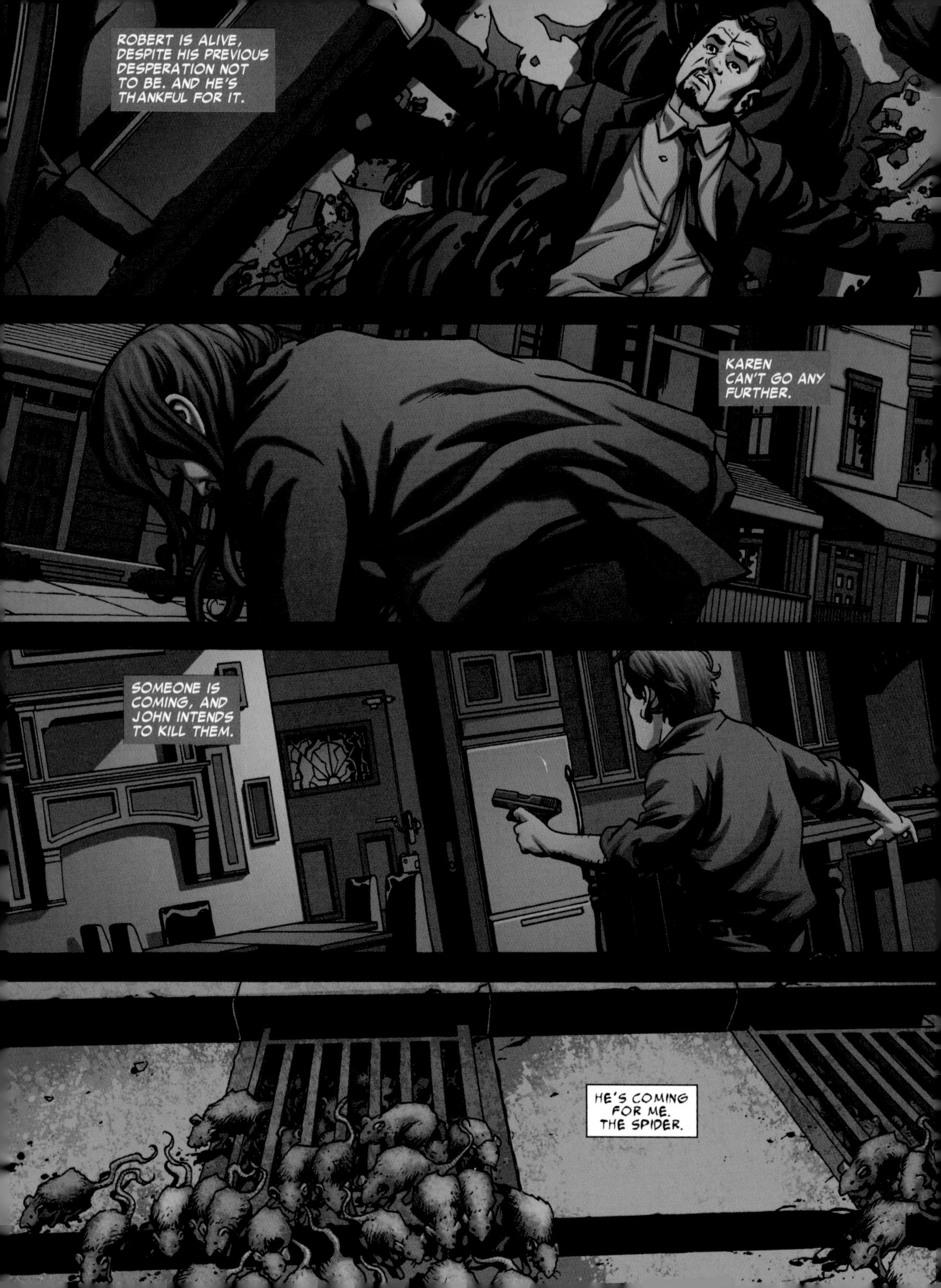
ROBERT IS ALIVE, DESPITE HIS PREVIOUS DESPERATION NOT TO BE. AND HE'S THANKFUL FOR IT.
KAREN CAN'T GO ANY FURTHER.
SOMEONE IS COMING, AND JOHN INTENDS TO KILL THEM.
HE'S COMING FOR ME. THE SPIDER.

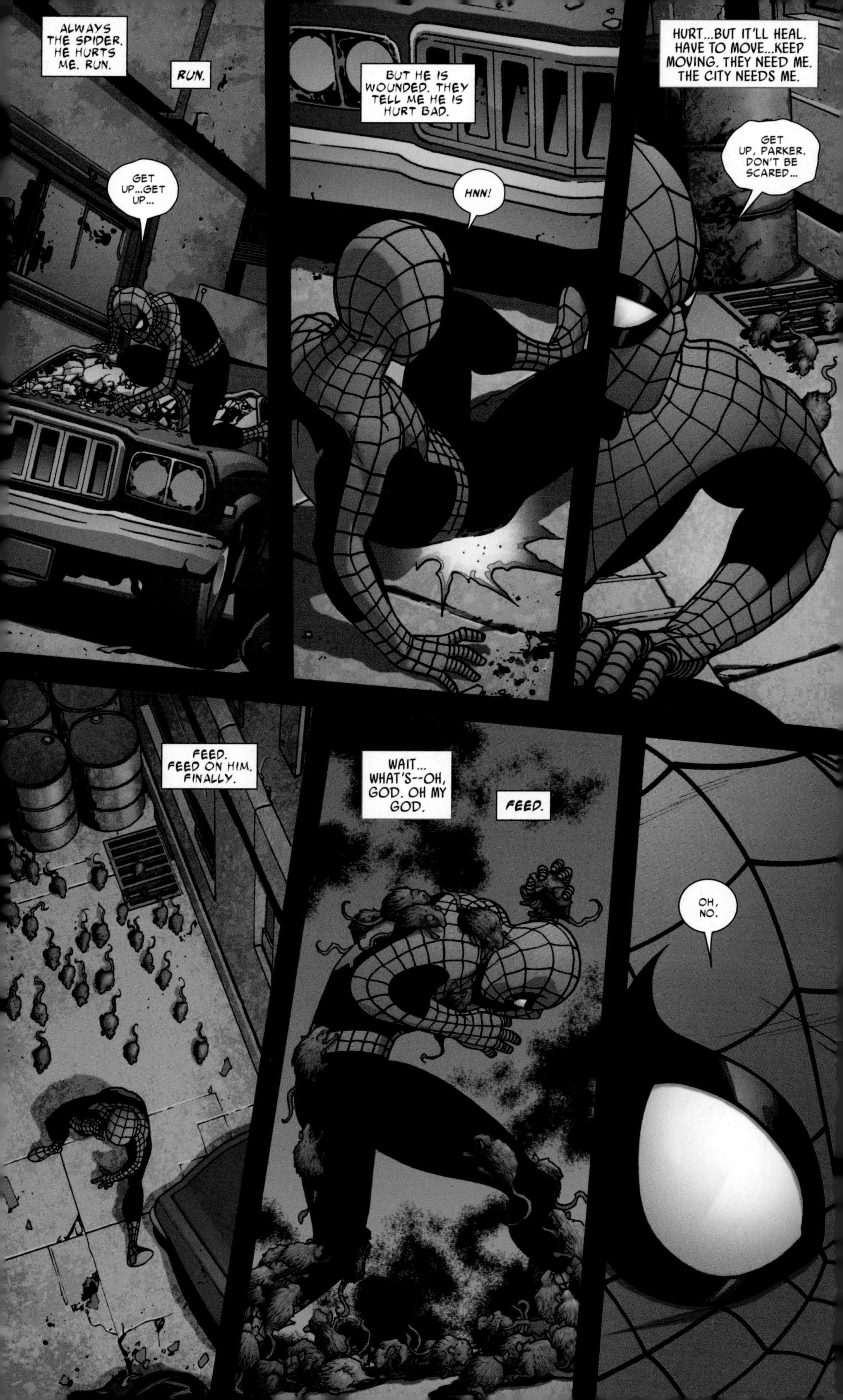
ALWAYS THE SPIDER. HE HURTS ME. RUN.
RUN.
GET UP...GET UP...
BUT HE IS WOUNDED. THEY TELL ME HE IS HURT BAD.
HNN!
HURT...BUT IT'LL HEAL. HAVE TO MOVE...KEEP MOVING. THEY NEED ME. THE CITY NEEDS ME.
GET UP, PARKER. DON'T BE SCARED...
FEED. FEED ON HIM. FINALLY.
WAIT... WHAT'S--OH, GOD. OH MY GOD.
FEED.
OH, NO.

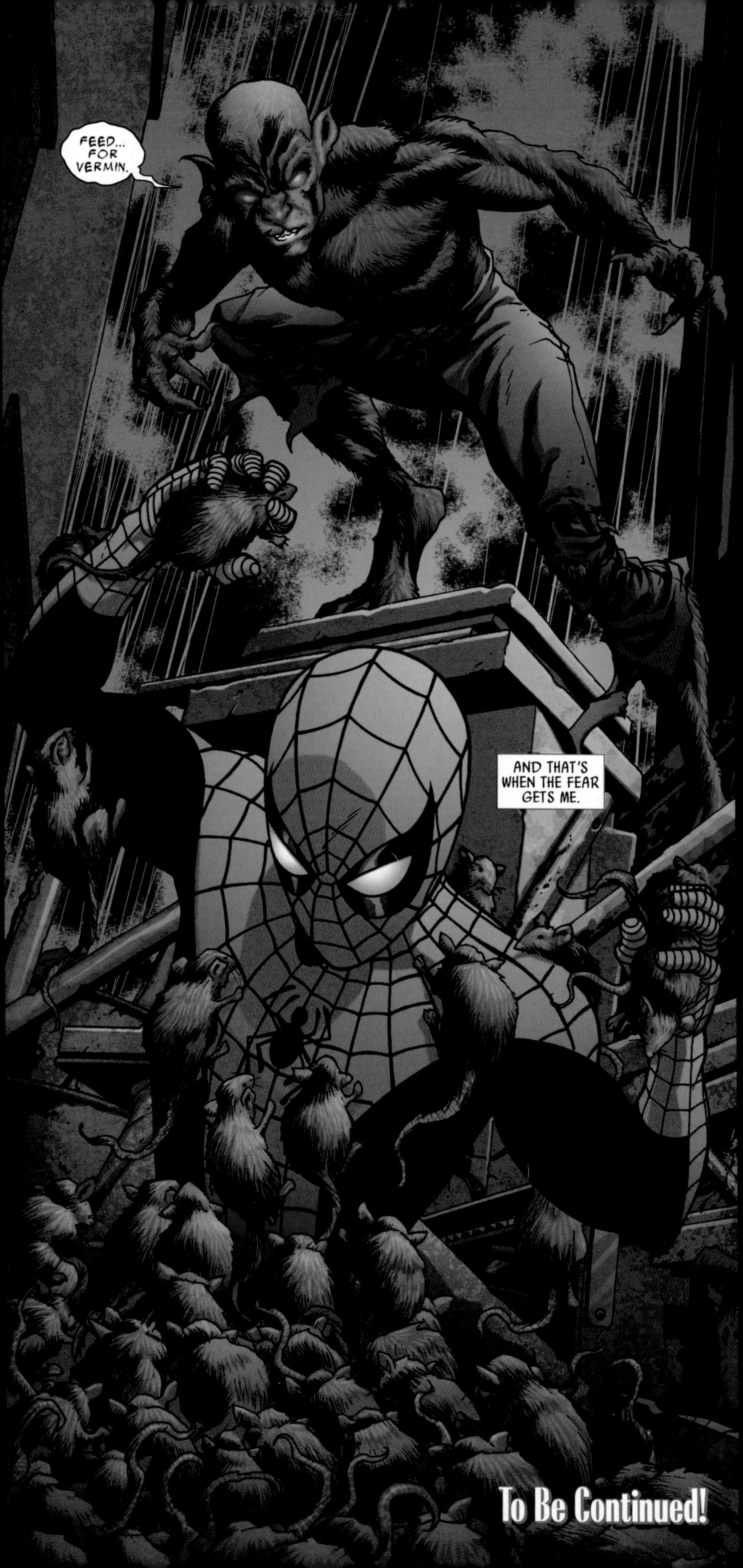
FEED... FOR VERMIN.
AND THAT'S WHEN THE FEAR GETS ME.
To Be Continued!

FEAR ITSELF
SPIDER-MAN

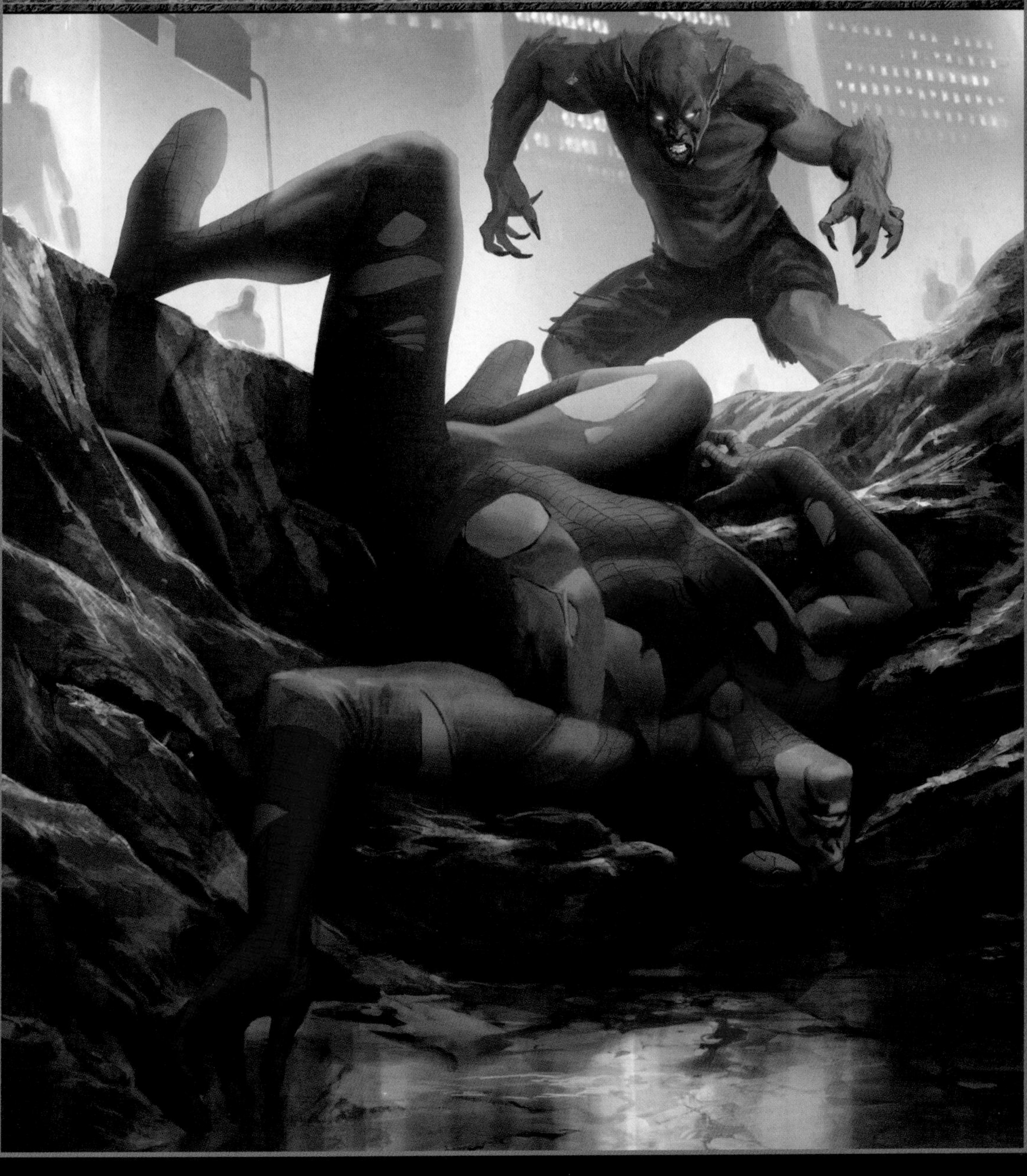

DAY TWO

Hour Twenty-Five Of The Fear.

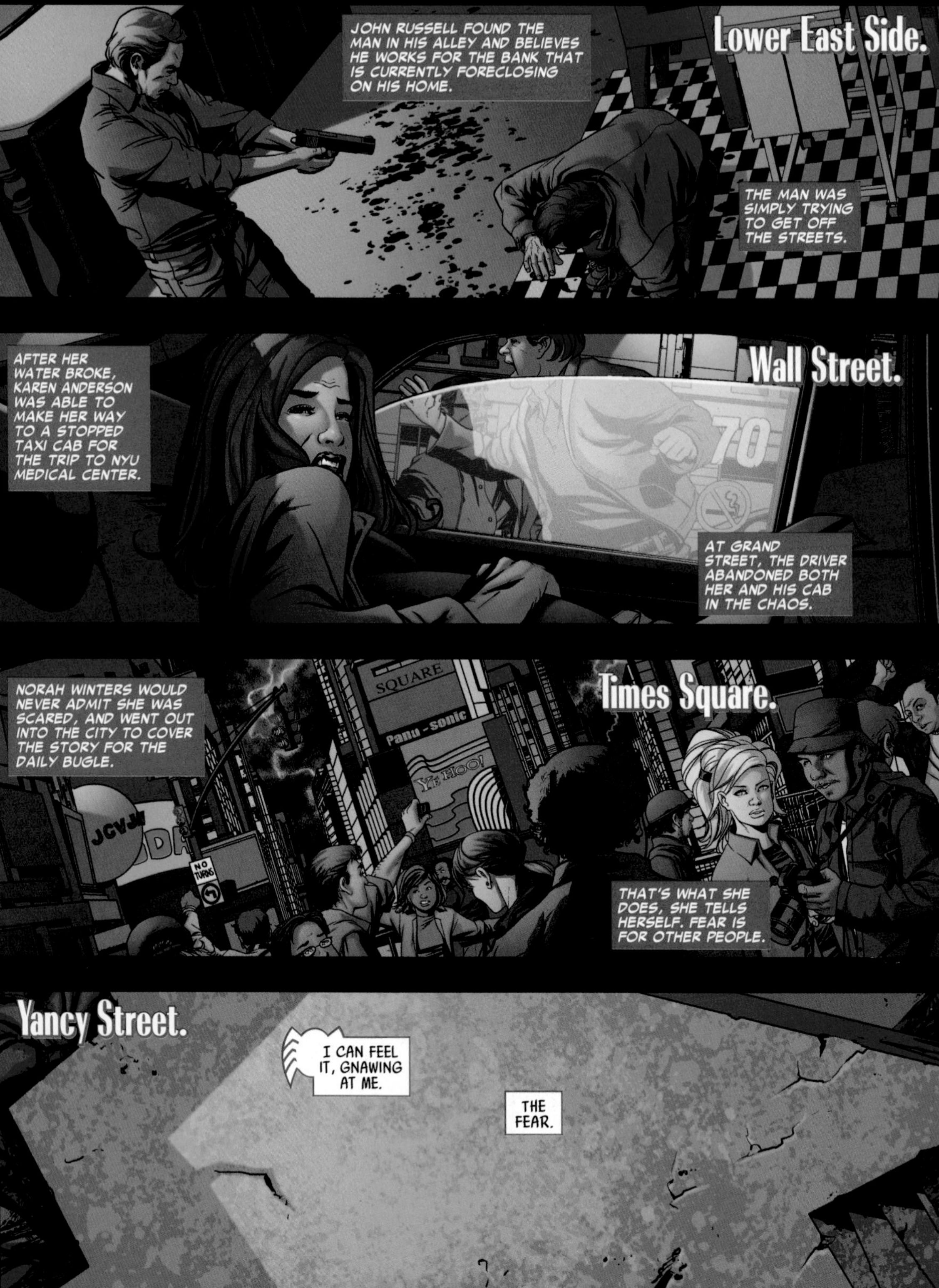
JOHN RUSSELL FOUND THE MAN IN HIS ALLEY AND BELIEVES HE WORKS FOR THE BANK THAT IS CURRENTLY FORECLOSING ON HIS HOME.
Lower East Side.
THE MAN WAS SIMPLY TRYING TO GET OFF THE STREETS.
AFTER HER WATER BROKE, KAREN ANDERSON WAS ABLE TO MAKE HER WAY TO A STOPPED TAXI CAB FOR THE TRIP TO NYU MEDICAL CENTER.
Wall Street.
70
AT GRAND STREET, THE DRIVER ABANDONED BOTH HER AND HIS CAB IN THE CHAOS.
NORAH WINTERS WOULD NEVER ADMIT SHE WAS SCARED, AND WENT OUT INTO THE CITY TO COVER THE STORY FOR THE DAILY BUGLE.
SQUARE
Panu-sonic
YE HOO!
NO TURNS
Times Square.
THAT'S WHAT SHE DOES, SHE TELLS HERSELF. FEAR IS FOR OTHER PEOPLE.
Yancy Street.
I CAN FEEL IT, GNAWING AT ME.
THE FEAR.

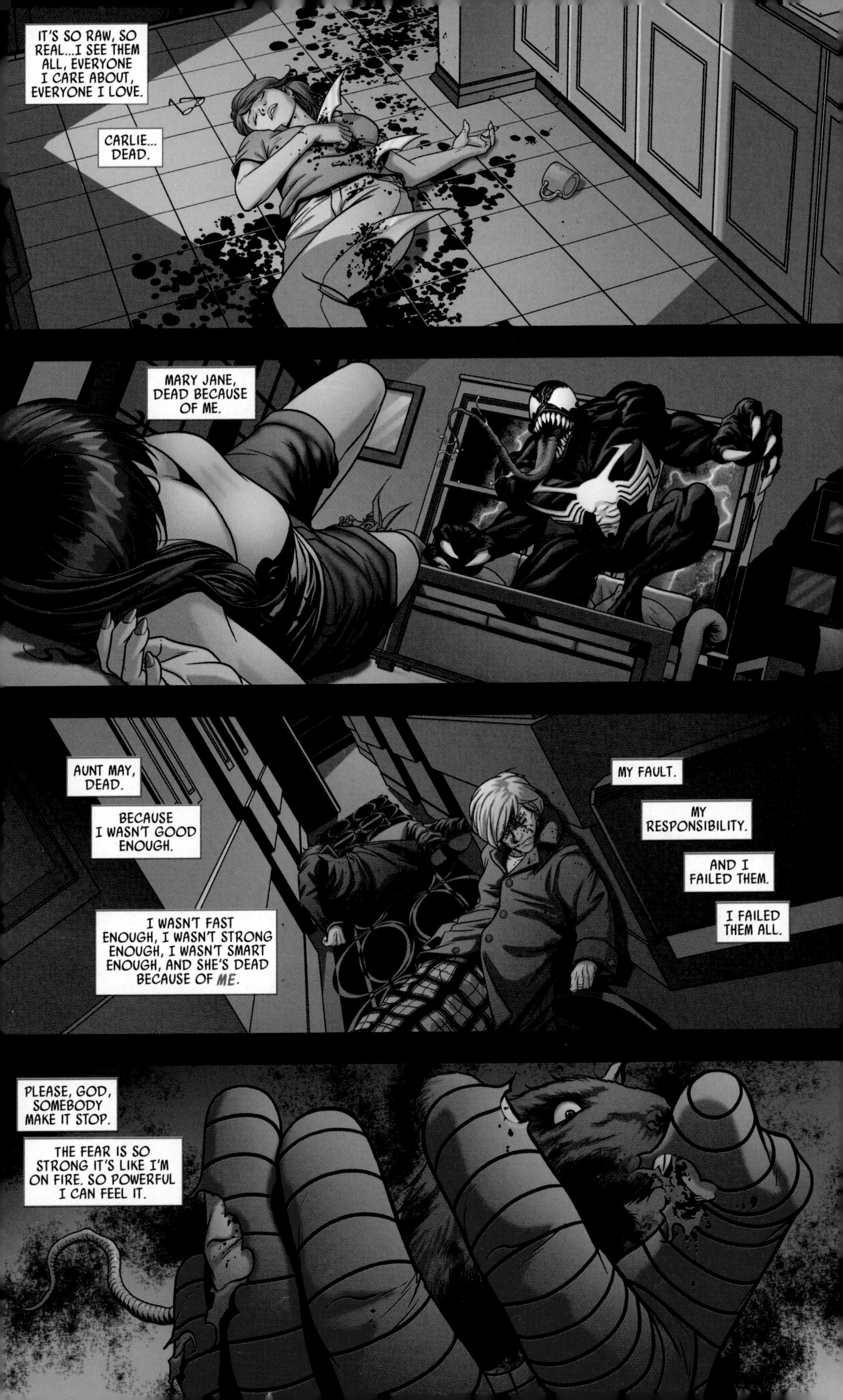
IT'S SO RAW, SO REAL...I SEE THEM ALL, EVERYONE I CARE ABOUT, EVERYONE I LOVE.
CARLIE... DEAD.
MARY JANE, DEAD BECAUSE OF ME.
AUNT MAY, DEAD.
BECAUSE I WASN'T GOOD ENOUGH.
I WASN'T FAST ENOUGH, I WASN'T STRONG ENOUGH, I WASN'T SMART ENOUGH, AND SHE'S DEAD BECAUSE OF ME.
MY FAULT.
MY RESPONSIBILITY.
AND I FAILED THEM.
I FAILED THEM ALL.
PLEASE, GOD, SOMEBODY MAKE IT STOP.
THE FEAR IS SO STRONG IT'S LIKE I'M ON FIRE. SO POWERFUL I CAN FEEL IT.

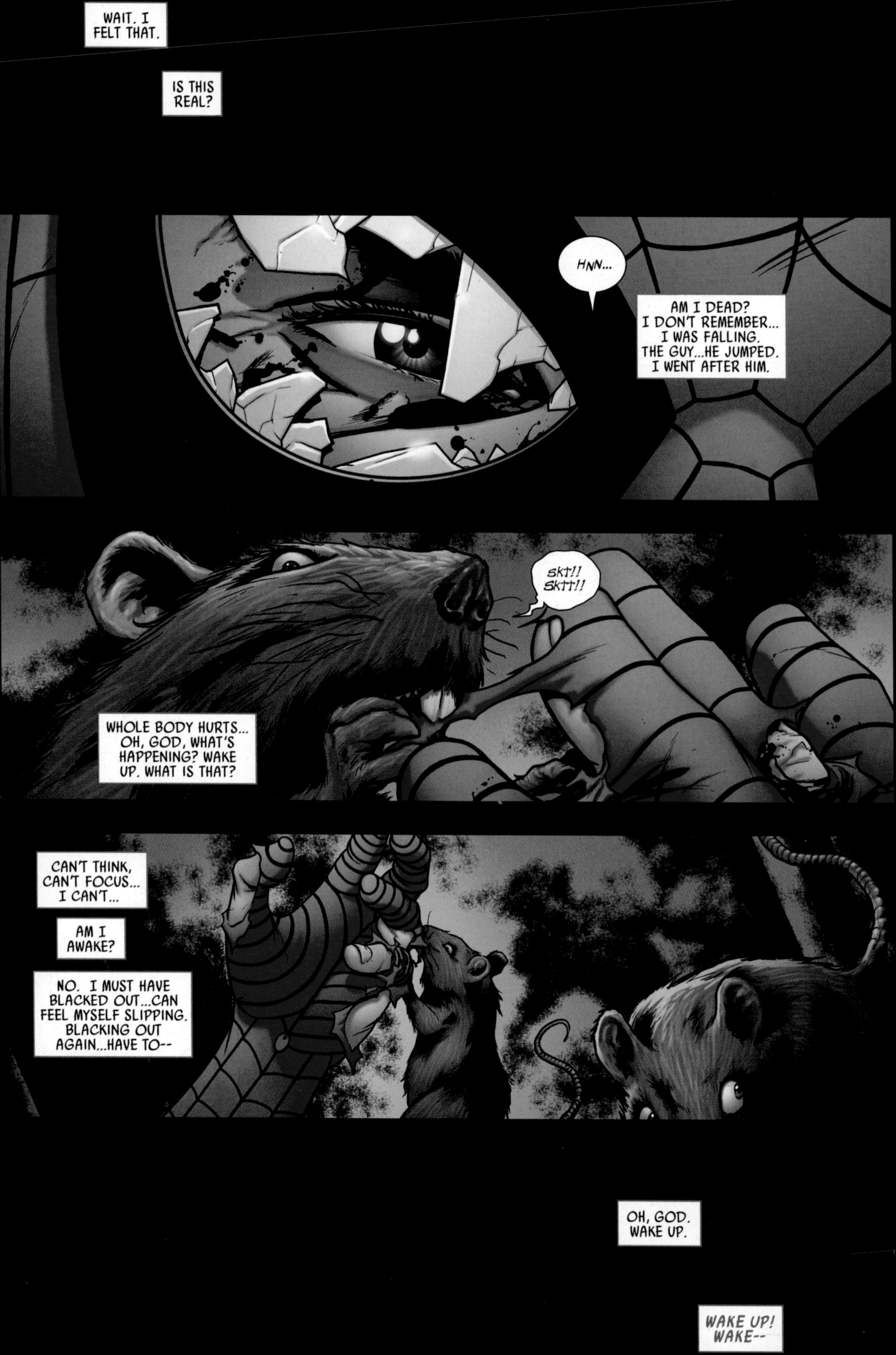
WAIT. I FELT THAT.
IS THIS REAL?
HNN...
AM I DEAD? I DON'T REMEMBER... I WAS FALLING. THE GUY...HE JUMPED. I WENT AFTER HIM.
SKT!! SKTT!!
WHOLE BODY HURTS... OH, GOD, WHAT'S HAPPENING? WAKE UP. WHAT IS THAT?
CAN'T THINK, CAN'T FOCUS... I CAN'T...
AM I AWAKE?
NO. I MUST HAVE BLACKED OUT...CAN FEEL MYSELF SLIPPING. BLACKING OUT AGAIN...HAVE TO--
OH, GOD. WAKE UP.
WAKE UP! WAKE--

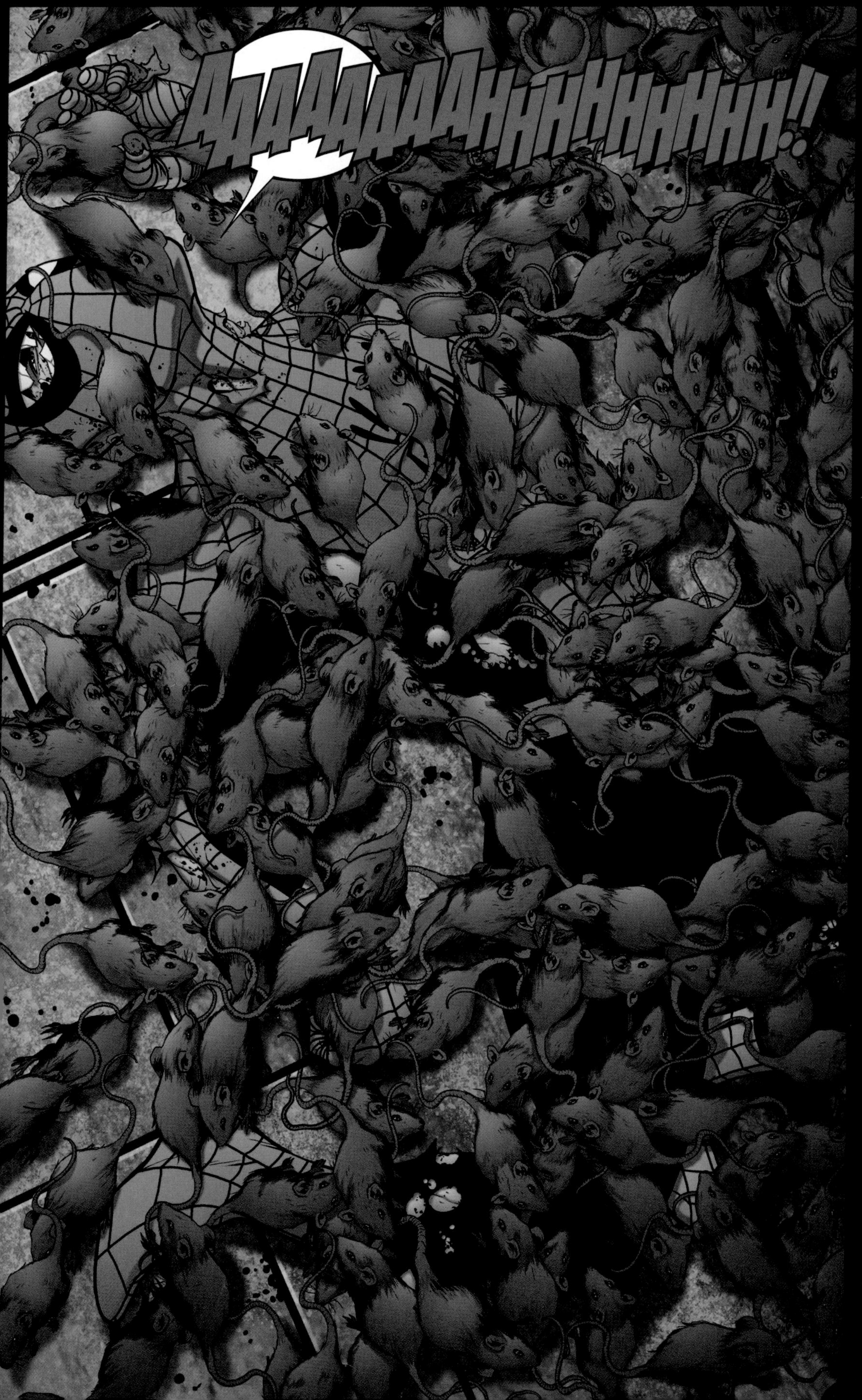
AAAAAAAAHHHHHHHHH!!

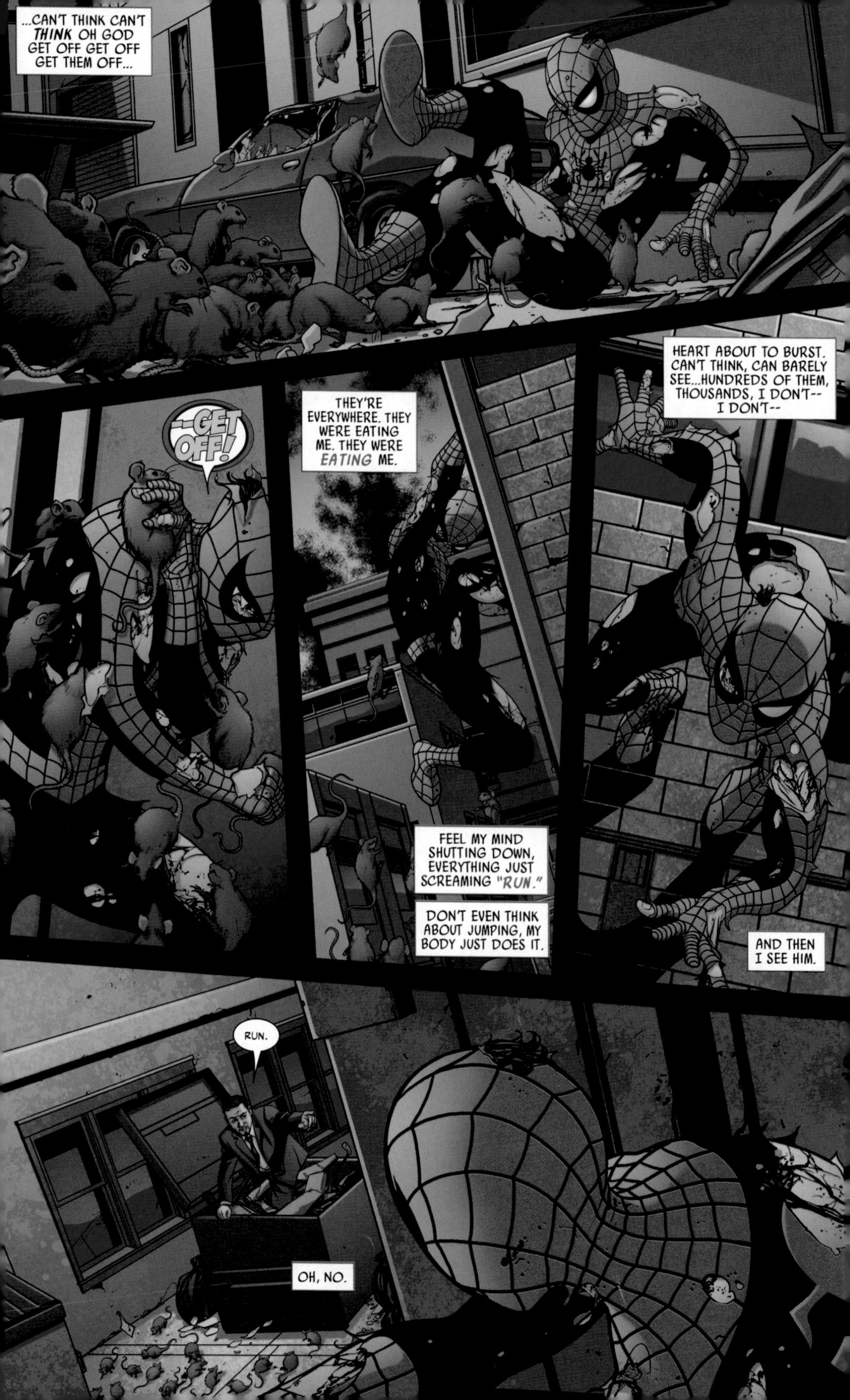
...CAN'T THINK CAN'T THINK OH GOD GET OFF GET OFF GET THEM OFF...
--GET OFF!
THEY'RE EVERYWHERE. THEY WERE EATING ME. THEY WERE EATING ME.
FEEL MY MIND SHUTTING DOWN, EVERYTHING JUST SCREAMING "RUN."
DON'T EVEN THINK ABOUT JUMPING, MY BODY JUST DOES IT.
HEART ABOUT TO BURST. CAN'T THINK, CAN BARELY SEE...HUNDREDS OF THEM, THOUSANDS, I DON'T-- I DON'T--
AND THEN I SEE HIM.
RUN.
OH, NO.

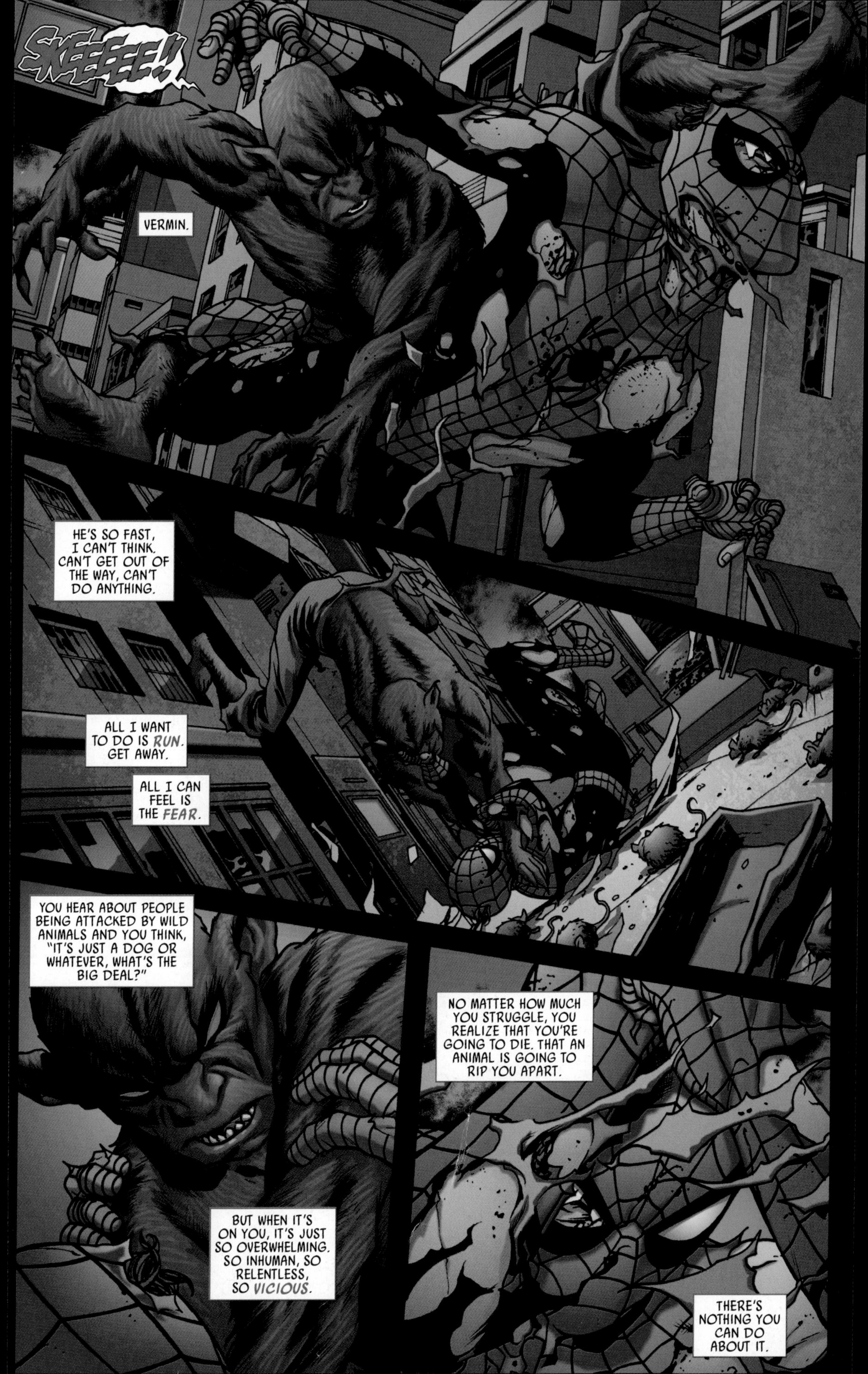
SKEEEEE!!
VERMIN.
HE'S SO FAST, I CAN'T THINK. CAN'T GET OUT OF THE WAY, CAN'T DO ANYTHING.
ALL I WANT TO DO IS RUN. GET AWAY.
ALL I CAN FEEL IS THE FEAR.
YOU HEAR ABOUT PEOPLE BEING ATTACKED BY WILD ANIMALS AND YOU THINK, "IT'S JUST A DOG OR WHATEVER, WHAT'S THE BIG DEAL?"
NO MATTER HOW MUCH YOU STRUGGLE, YOU REALIZE THAT YOU'RE GOING TO DIE. THAT AN ANIMAL IS GOING TO RIP YOU APART.
BUT WHEN IT'S ON YOU, IT'S JUST SO OVERWHELMING. SO INHUMAN, SO RELENTLESS, SO VICIOUS.
THERE'S NOTHING YOU CAN DO ABOUT IT.

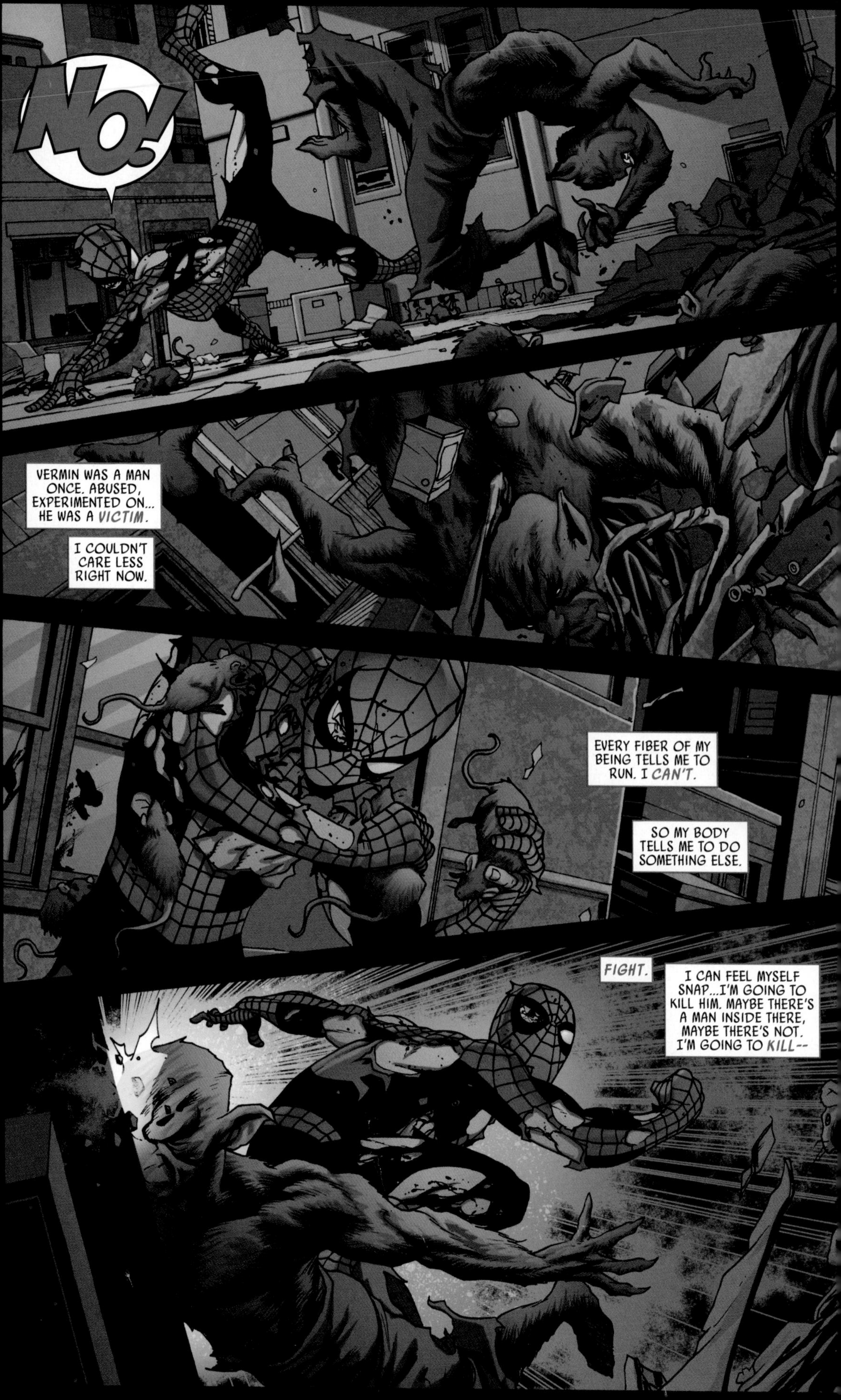
NO!
VERMIN WAS A MAN ONCE. ABUSED, EXPERIMENTED ON... HE WAS A VICTIM.
I COULDN'T CARE LESS RIGHT NOW.
EVERY FIBER OF MY BEING TELLS ME TO RUN. I CAN'T.
SO MY BODY TELLS ME TO DO SOMETHING ELSE.
FIGHT.
I CAN FEEL MYSELF SNAP...I'M GOING TO KILL HIM. MAYBE THERE'S A MAN INSIDE THERE, MAYBE THERE'S NOT. I'M GOING TO KILL--

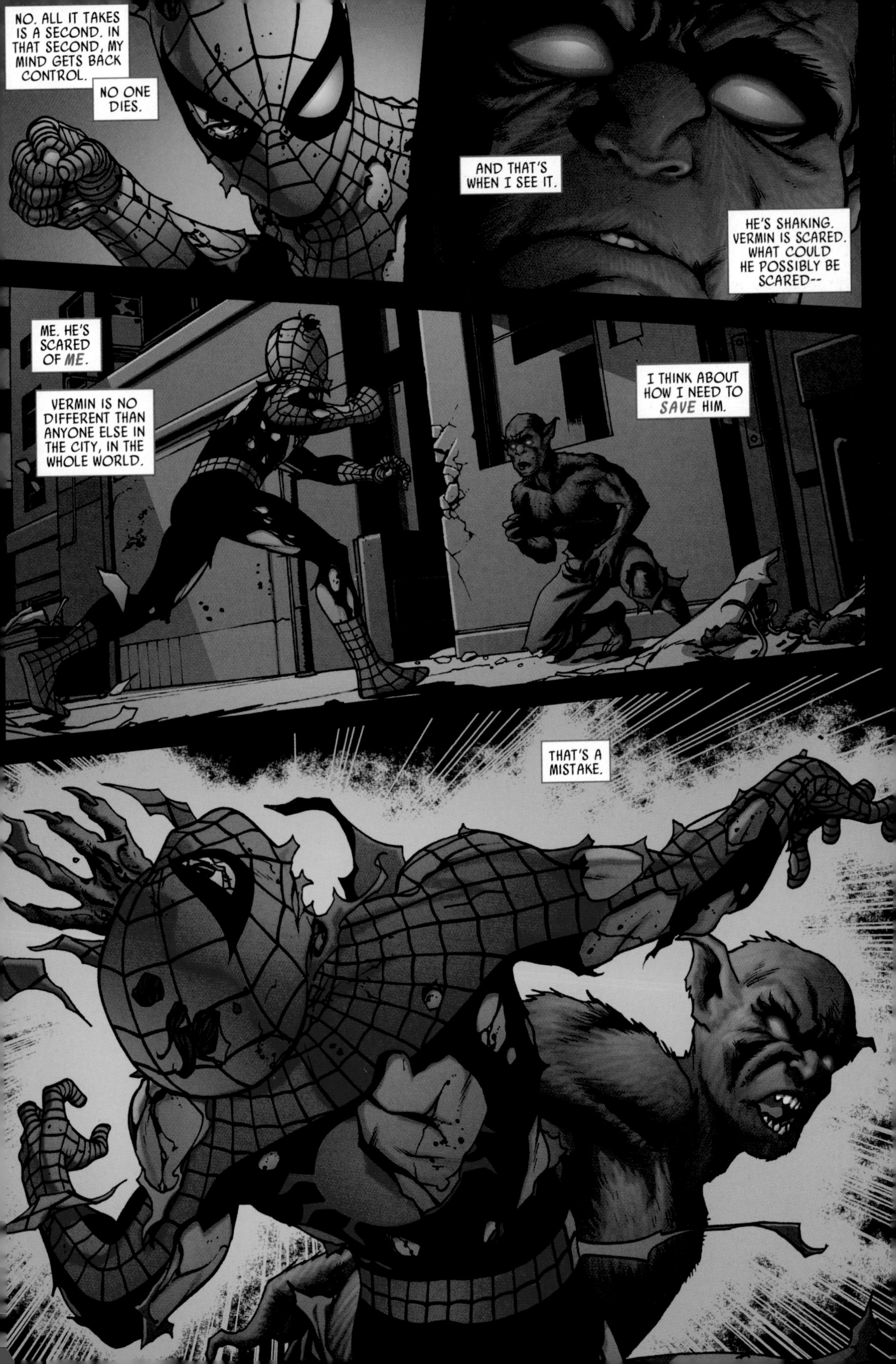
NO. ALL IT TAKES IS A SECOND. IN THAT SECOND, MY MIND GETS BACK CONTROL.
NO ONE DIES.
AND THAT'S WHEN I SEE IT.
HE'S SHAKING. VERMIN IS SCARED. WHAT COULD HE POSSIBLY BE SCARED--
ME. HE'S SCARED OF ME.
VERMIN IS NO DIFFERENT THAN ANYONE ELSE IN THE CITY, IN THE WHOLE WORLD.
I THINK ABOUT HOW I NEED TO SAVE HIM.
THAT'S A MISTAKE.

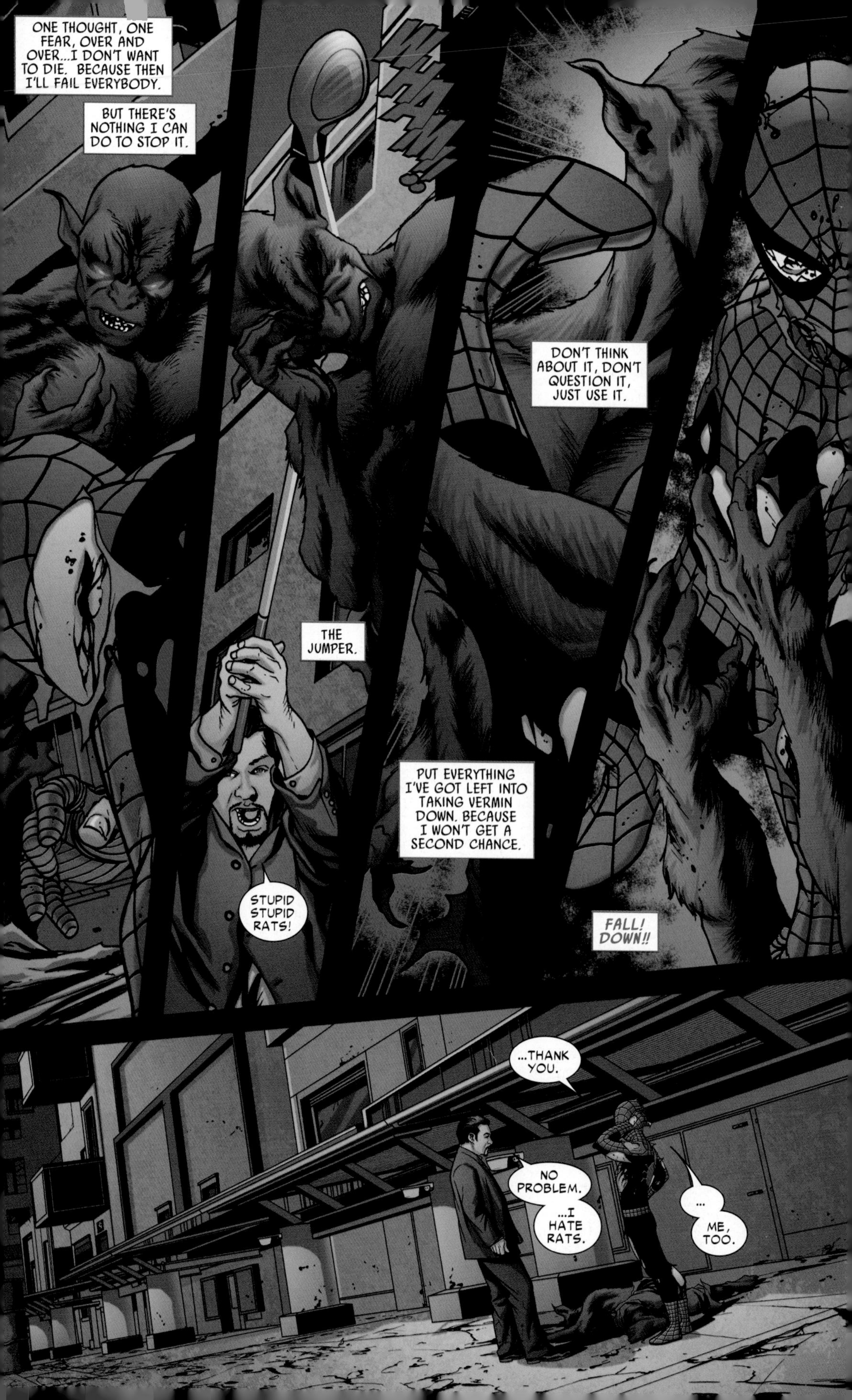
ONE THOUGHT, ONE FEAR, OVER AND OVER...I DON'T WANT TO DIE. BECAUSE THEN I'LL FAIL EVERYBODY.
BUT THERE'S NOTHING I CAN DO TO STOP IT.
WHAM!
THE JUMPER.
STUPID STUPID RATS!
DON'T THINK ABOUT IT, DON'T QUESTION IT, JUST USE IT.
PUT EVERYTHING I'VE GOT LEFT INTO TAKING VERMIN DOWN. BECAUSE I WON'T GET A SECOND CHANCE.
FALL! DOWN!!
...THANK YOU.
NO PROBLEM.
...I HATE RATS.
...
ME, TOO.

Hour Twenty-Eight Of The Fear.

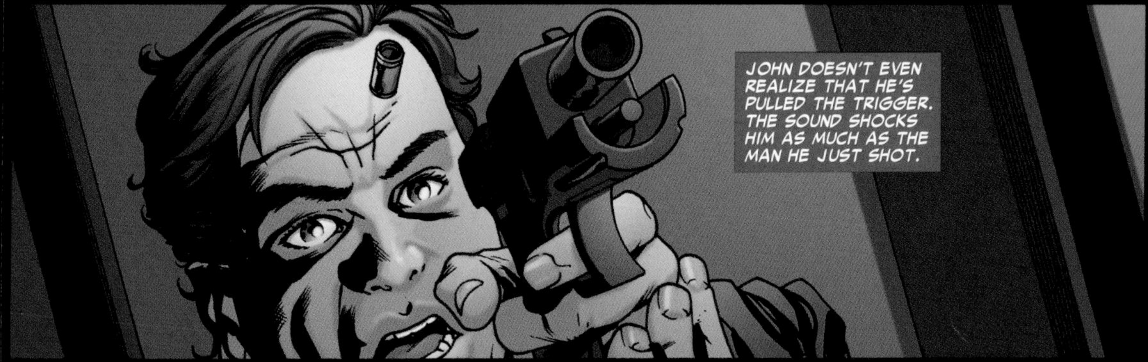
JOHN DOESN'T EVEN REALIZE THAT HE'S PULLED THE TRIGGER. THE SOUND SHOCKS HIM AS MUCH AS THE MAN HE JUST SHOT.

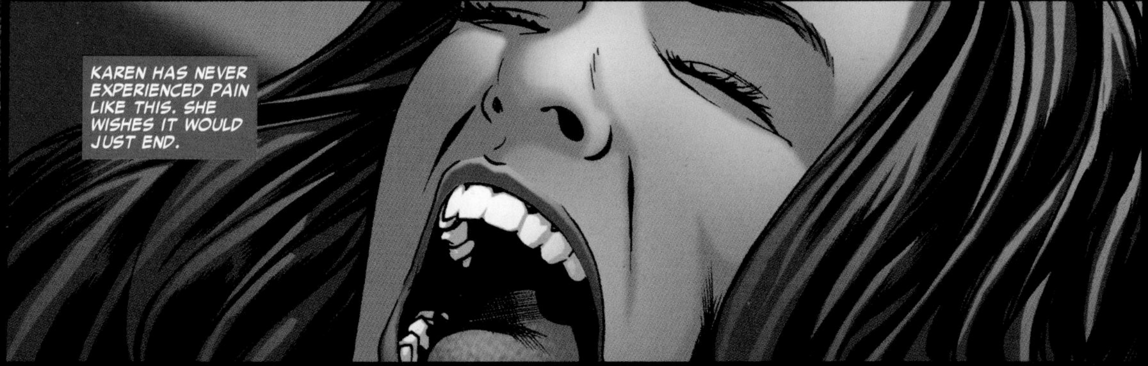
KAREN HAS NEVER EXPERIENCED PAIN LIKE THIS. SHE WISHES IT WOULD JUST END.

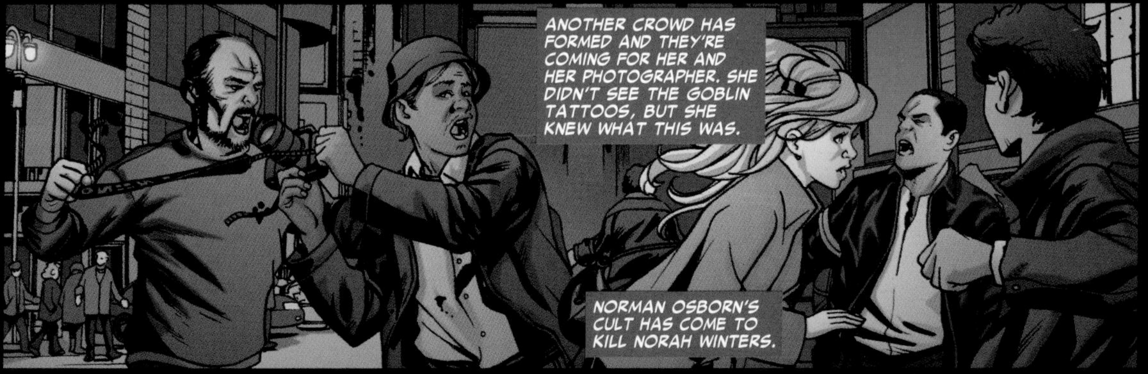
ANOTHER CROWD HAS FORMED AND THEY'RE COMING FOR HER AND HER PHOTOGRAPHER. SHE DIDN'T SEE THE GOBLIN TATTOOS, BUT SHE KNEW WHAT THIS WAS.
NORMAN OSBORN'S CULT HAS COME TO KILL NORAH WINTERS.

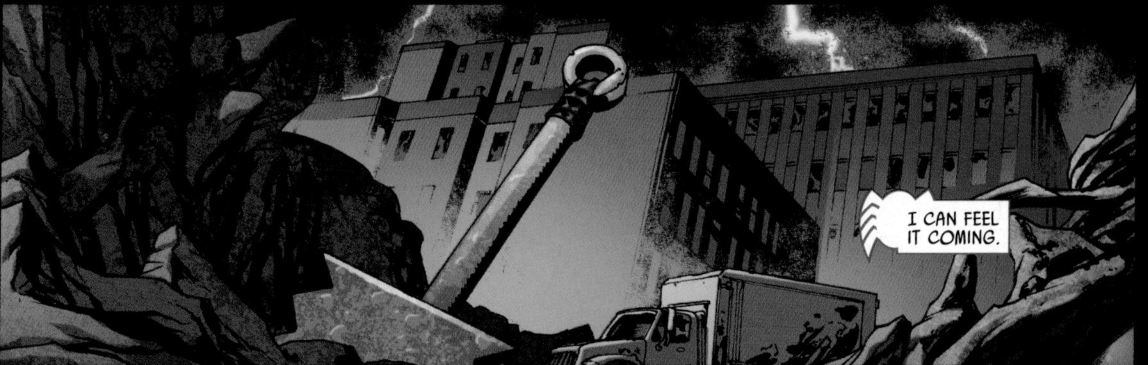
I CAN FEEL IT COMING.

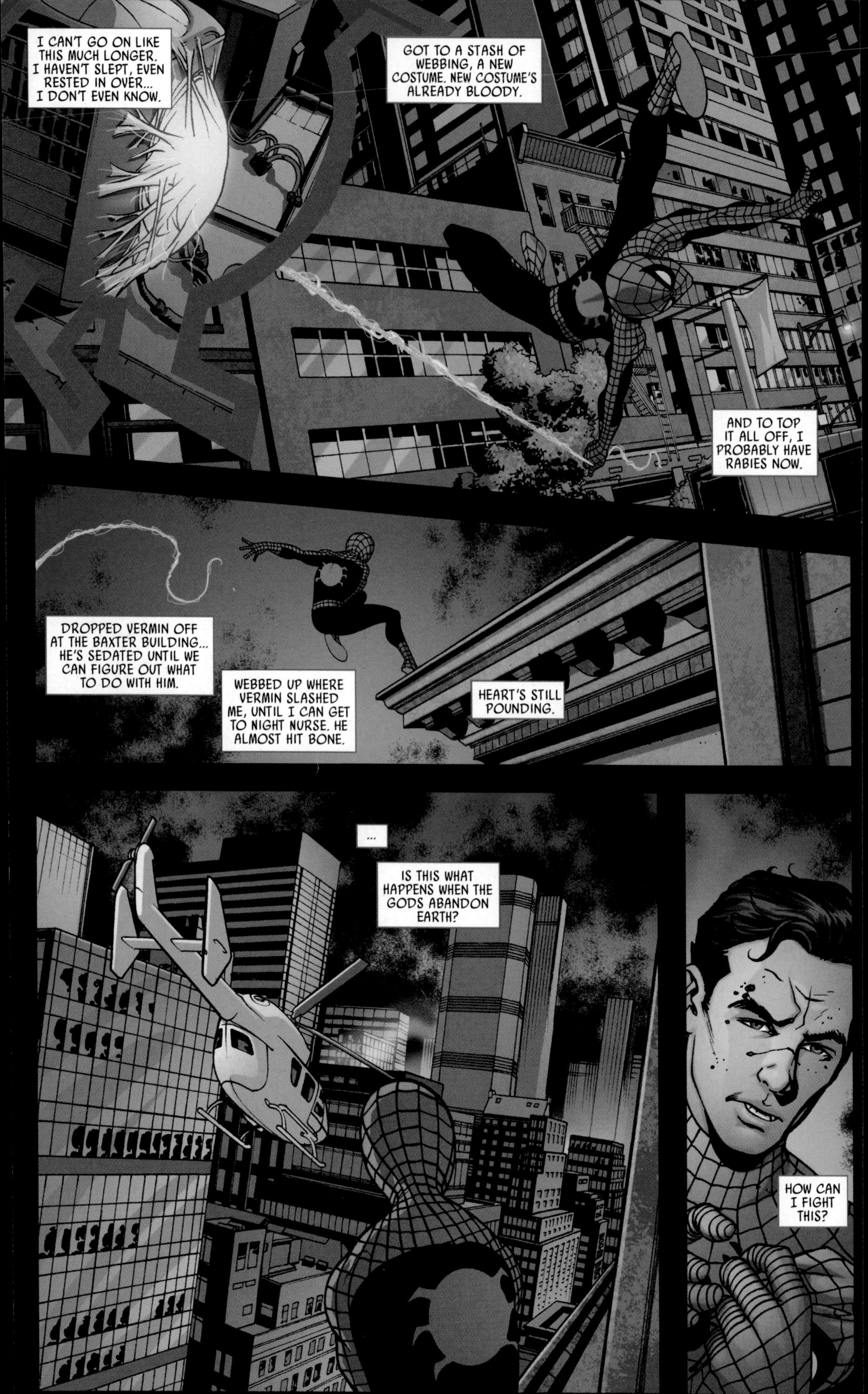
I CAN'T GO ON LIKE THIS MUCH LONGER. I HAVEN'T SLEPT, EVEN RESTED IN OVER... I DON'T EVEN KNOW.
GOT TO A STASH OF WEBBING, A NEW COSTUME. NEW COSTUME'S ALREADY BLOODY.
AND TO TOP IT ALL OFF, I PROBABLY HAVE RABIES NOW.
DROPPED VERMIN OFF AT THE BAXTER BUILDING... HE'S SEDATED UNTIL WE CAN FIGURE OUT WHAT TO DO WITH HIM.
WEBBED UP WHERE VERMIN SLASHED ME, UNTIL I CAN GET TO NIGHT NURSE. HE ALMOST HIT BONE.
HEART'S STILL POUNDING.
...
IS THIS WHAT HAPPENS WHEN THE GODS ABANDON EARTH?
HOW CAN I FIGHT THIS?

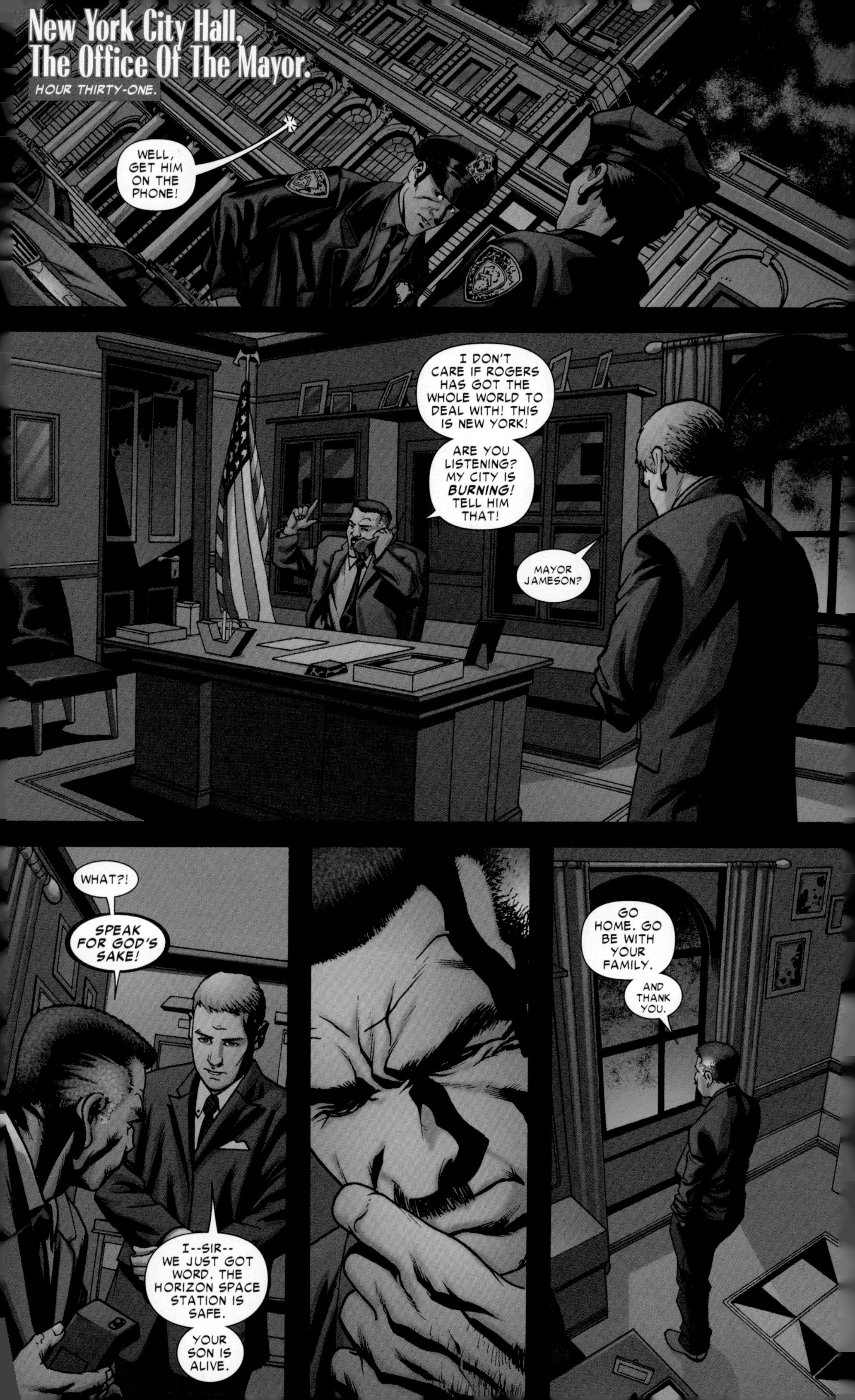
New York City Hall, The Office Of The Mayor.
HOUR THIRTY-ONE.
WELL, GET HIM ON THE PHONE!
I DON'T CARE IF ROGERS HAS GOT THE WHOLE WORLD TO DEAL WITH! THIS IS NEW YORK!
ARE YOU LISTENING? MY CITY IS BURNING! TELL HIM THAT!
MAYOR JAMESON?
WHAT?!
SPEAK FOR GOD'S SAKE!
I--SIR-- WE JUST GOT WORD. THE HORIZON SPACE STATION IS SAFE.
YOUR SON IS ALIVE.
GO HOME. GO BE WITH YOUR FAMILY.
AND THANK YOU.

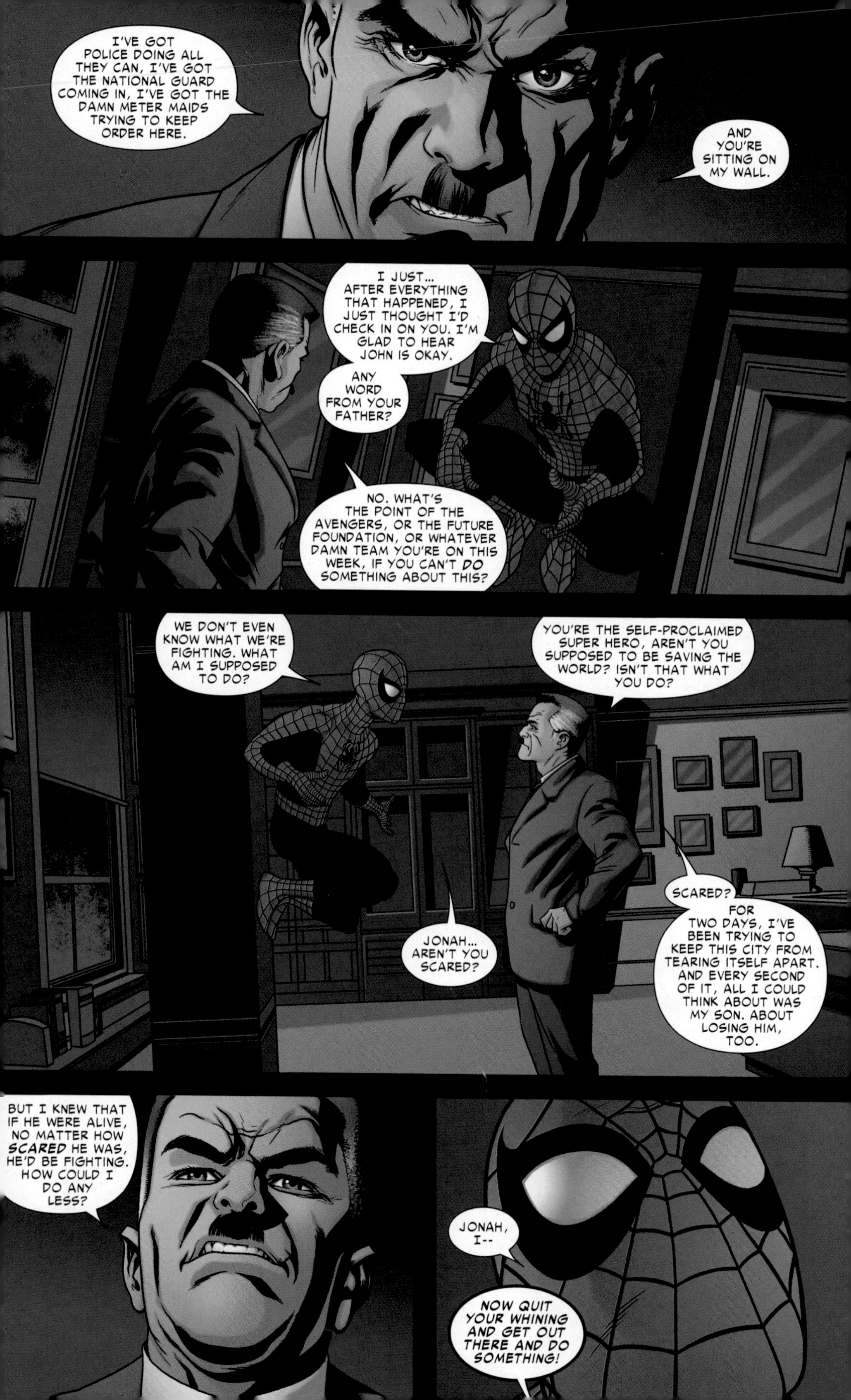
I'VE GOT POLICE DOING ALL THEY CAN, I'VE GOT THE NATIONAL GUARD COMING IN, I'VE GOT THE DAMN METER MAIDS TRYING TO KEEP ORDER HERE.
AND YOU'RE SITTING ON MY WALL.
I JUST... AFTER EVERYTHING THAT HAPPENED, I JUST THOUGHT I'D CHECK IN ON YOU. I'M GLAD TO HEAR JOHN IS OKAY.
ANY WORD FROM YOUR FATHER?
NO. WHAT'S THE POINT OF THE AVENGERS, OR THE FUTURE FOUNDATION, OR WHATEVER DAMN TEAM YOU'RE ON THIS WEEK, IF YOU CAN'T *DO* SOMETHING ABOUT THIS?
WE DON'T EVEN KNOW WHAT WE'RE FIGHTING. WHAT AM I SUPPOSED TO DO?
YOU'RE THE SELF-PROCLAIMED SUPER HERO, AREN'T YOU SUPPOSED TO BE SAVING THE WORLD? ISN'T THAT WHAT YOU DO?
JONAH... AREN'T YOU SCARED?
SCARED?
FOR TWO DAYS, I'VE BEEN TRYING TO KEEP THIS CITY FROM TEARING ITSELF APART. AND EVERY SECOND OF IT, ALL I COULD THINK ABOUT WAS MY SON. ABOUT LOSING HIM, TOO.
BUT I KNEW THAT IF HE WERE ALIVE, NO MATTER HOW *SCARED* HE WAS, HE'D BE FIGHTING. HOW COULD I DO ANY LESS?
JONAH, I--
NOW QUIT YOUR WHINING AND GET OUT THERE AND DO SOMETHING!

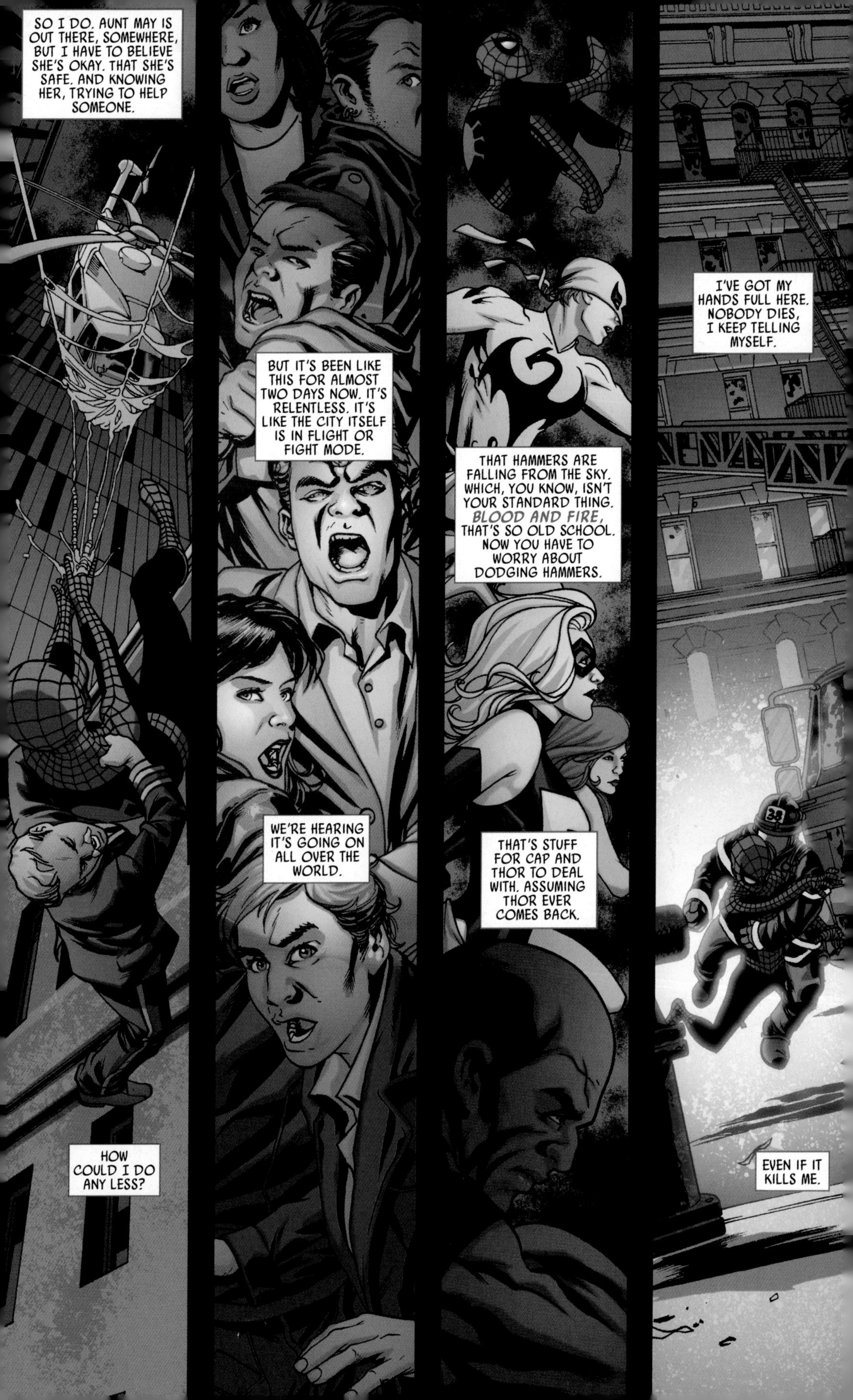
SO I DO. AUNT MAY IS OUT THERE, SOMEWHERE, BUT I HAVE TO BELIEVE SHE'S OKAY. THAT SHE'S SAFE. AND KNOWING HER, TRYING TO HELP SOMEONE.
HOW COULD I DO ANY LESS?
BUT IT'S BEEN LIKE THIS FOR ALMOST TWO DAYS NOW. IT'S RELENTLESS. IT'S LIKE THE CITY ITSELF IS IN FLIGHT OR FIGHT MODE.
WE'RE HEARING IT'S GOING ON ALL OVER THE WORLD.
THAT HAMMERS ARE FALLING FROM THE SKY. WHICH, YOU KNOW, ISN'T YOUR STANDARD THING. BLOOD AND FIRE, THAT'S SO OLD SCHOOL. NOW YOU HAVE TO WORRY ABOUT DODGING HAMMERS.
THAT'S STUFF FOR CAP AND THOR TO DEAL WITH. ASSUMING THOR EVER COMES BACK.
I'VE GOT MY HANDS FULL HERE. NOBODY DIES, I KEEP TELLING MYSELF.
EVEN IF IT KILLS ME.

Hour Thirty-Seven Of The Fear.

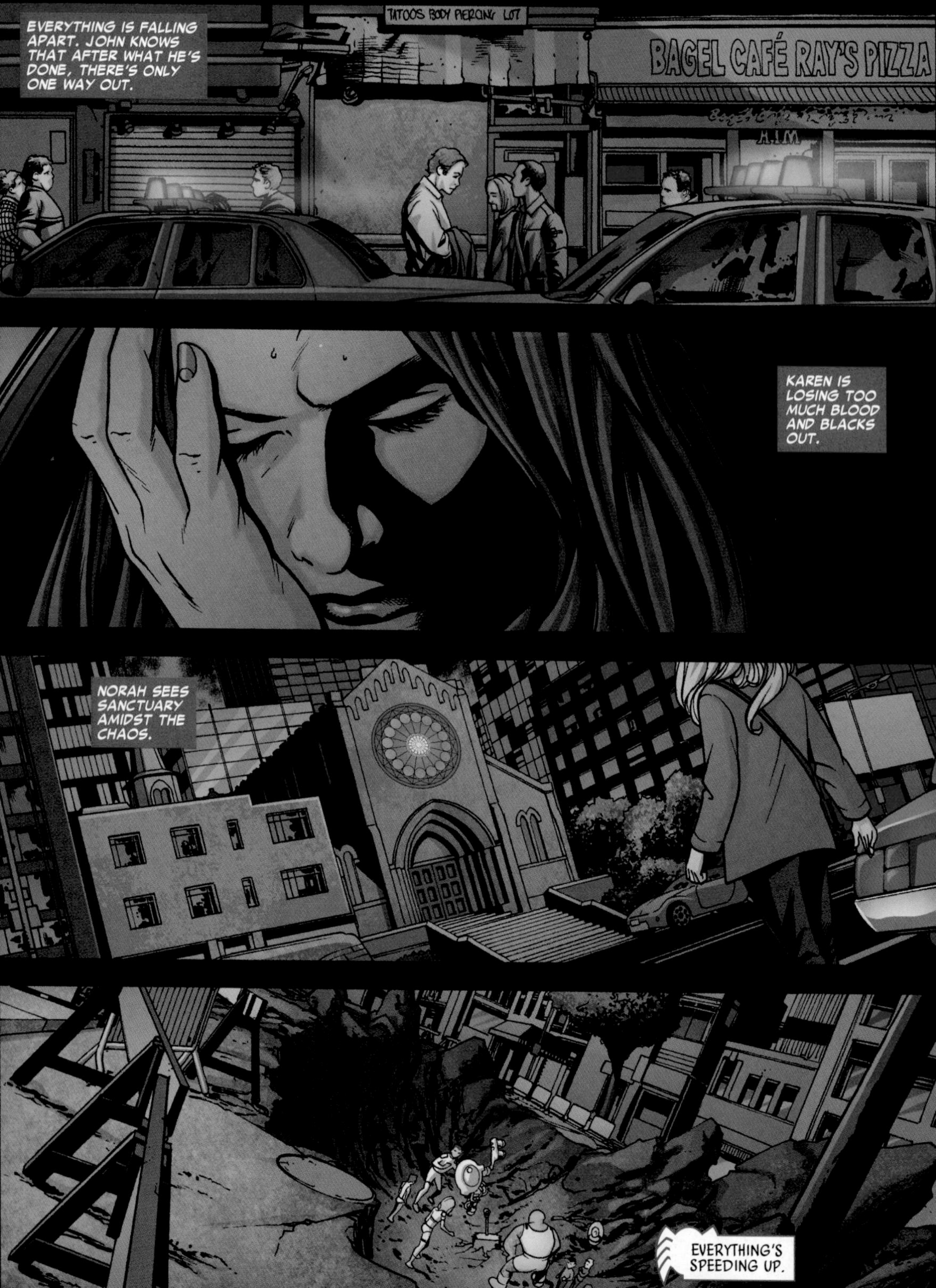
EVERYTHING IS FALLING APART. JOHN KNOWS THAT AFTER WHAT HE'S DONE, THERE'S ONLY ONE WAY OUT.
TATOOS BODY PIERCING LOT
BAGEL CAFÉ RAY'S PIZZA
KAREN IS LOSING TOO MUCH BLOOD AND BLACKS OUT.
NORAH SEES SANCTUARY AMIDST THE CHAOS.
EVERYTHING'S SPEEDING UP.

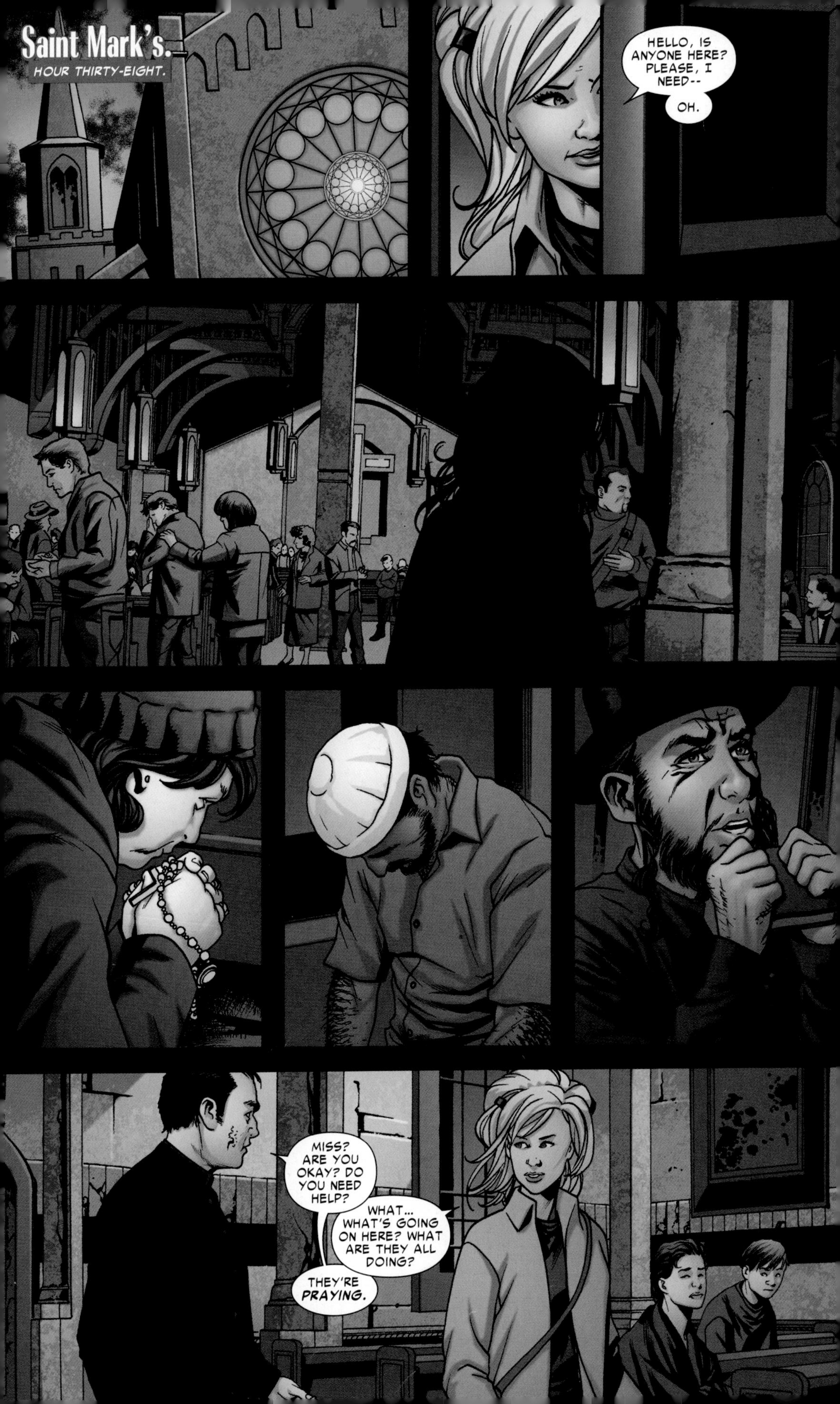
Saint Mark's.
HOUR THIRTY-EIGHT.
HELLO, IS ANYONE HERE? PLEASE, I NEED--
OH.
MISS? ARE YOU OKAY? DO YOU NEED HELP?
WHAT... WHAT'S GOING ON HERE? WHAT ARE THEY ALL DOING?
THEY'RE PRAYING.

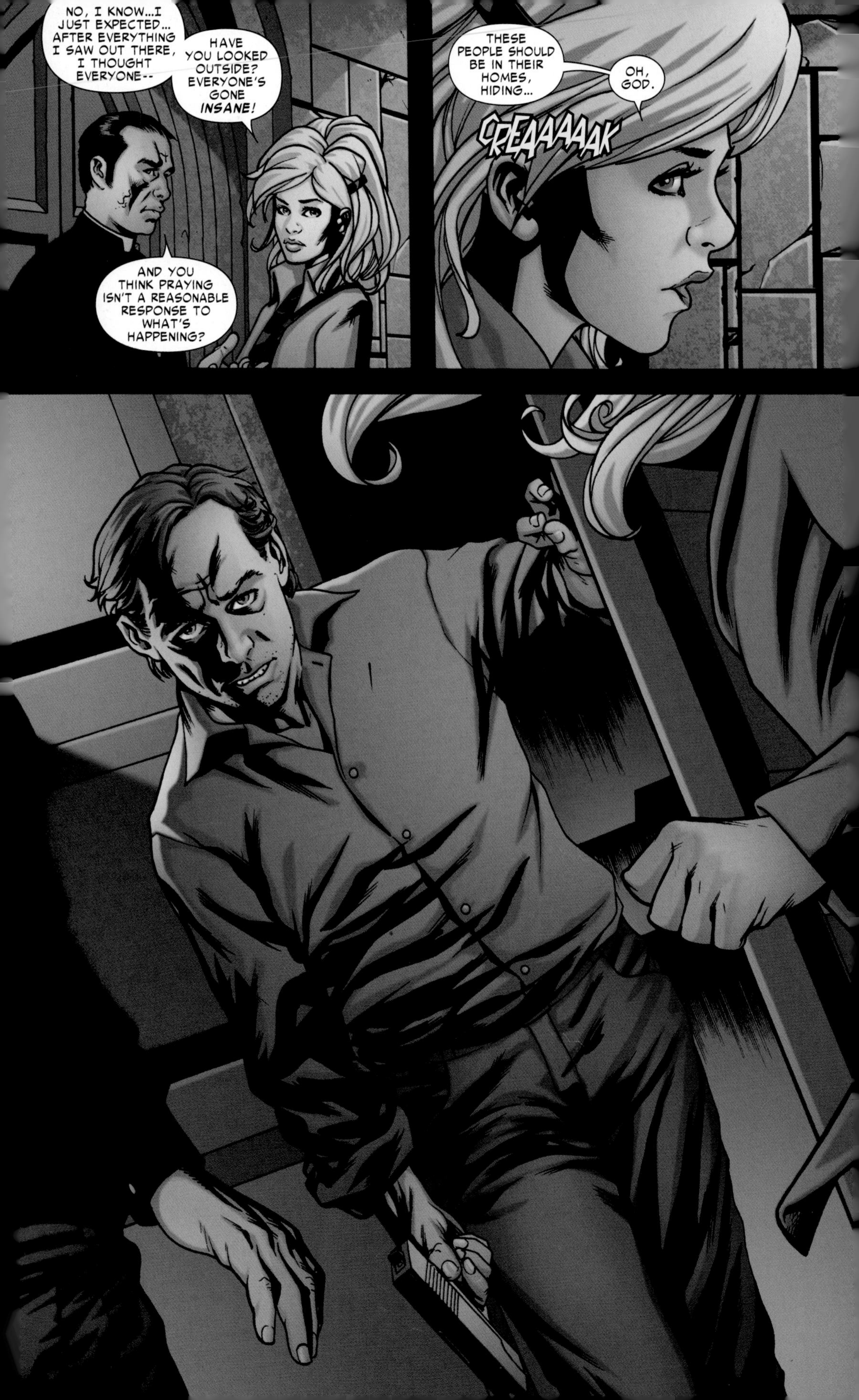
NO, I KNOW...I JUST EXPECTED... AFTER EVERYTHING I SAW OUT THERE, I THOUGHT EVERYONE--
HAVE YOU LOOKED OUTSIDE? EVERYONE'S GONE INSANE!
AND YOU THINK PRAYING ISN'T A REASONABLE RESPONSE TO WHAT'S HAPPENING?
THESE PEOPLE SHOULD BE IN THEIR HOMES, HIDING...
OH, GOD.
CREAAAAAK

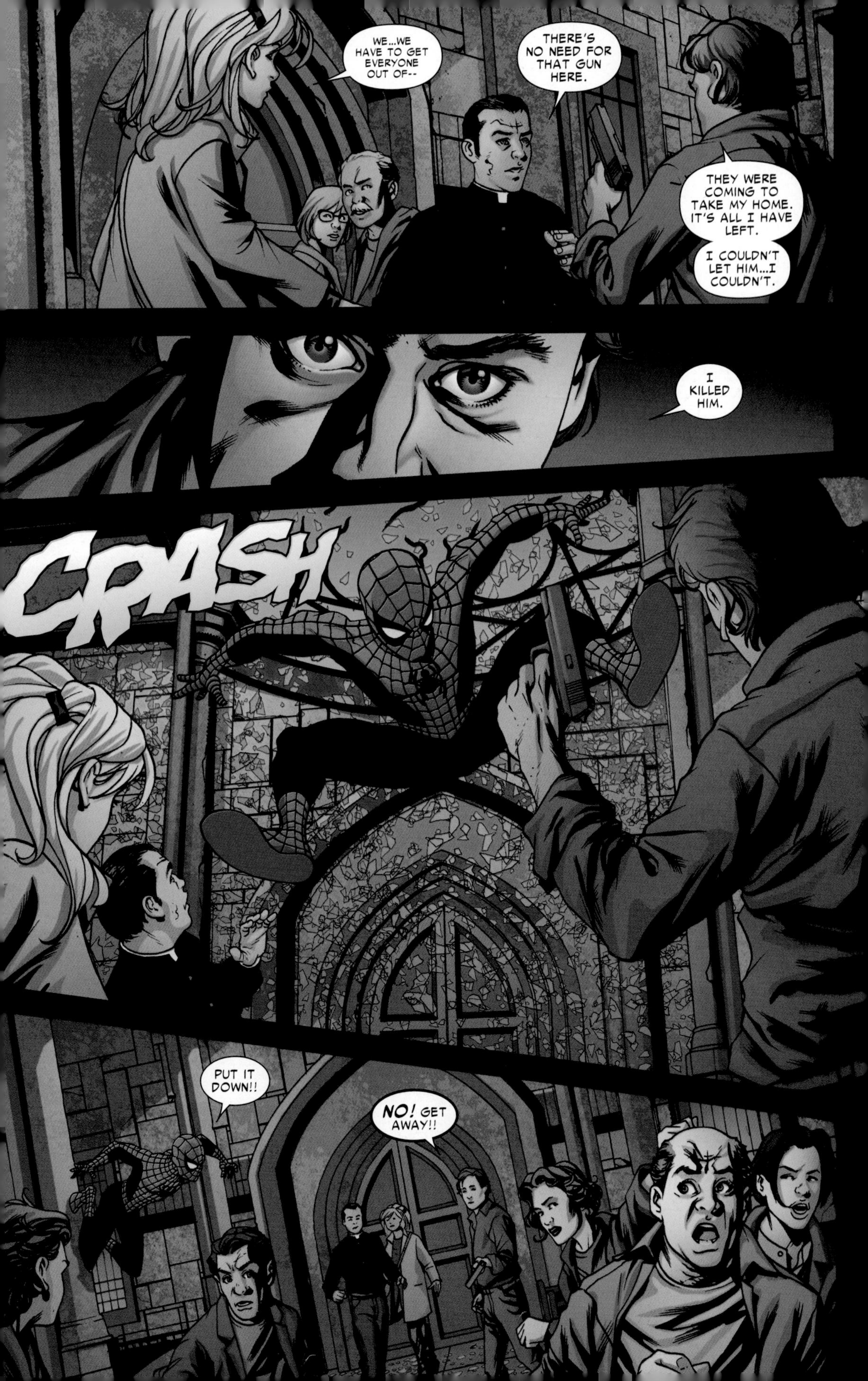
WE...WE HAVE TO GET EVERYONE OUT OF--
THERE'S NO NEED FOR THAT GUN HERE.
THEY WERE COMING TO TAKE MY HOME. IT'S ALL I HAVE LEFT.
I COULDN'T LET HIM...I COULDN'T.
I KILLED HIM.
CRASH
PUT IT DOWN!!
NO! GET AWAY!!

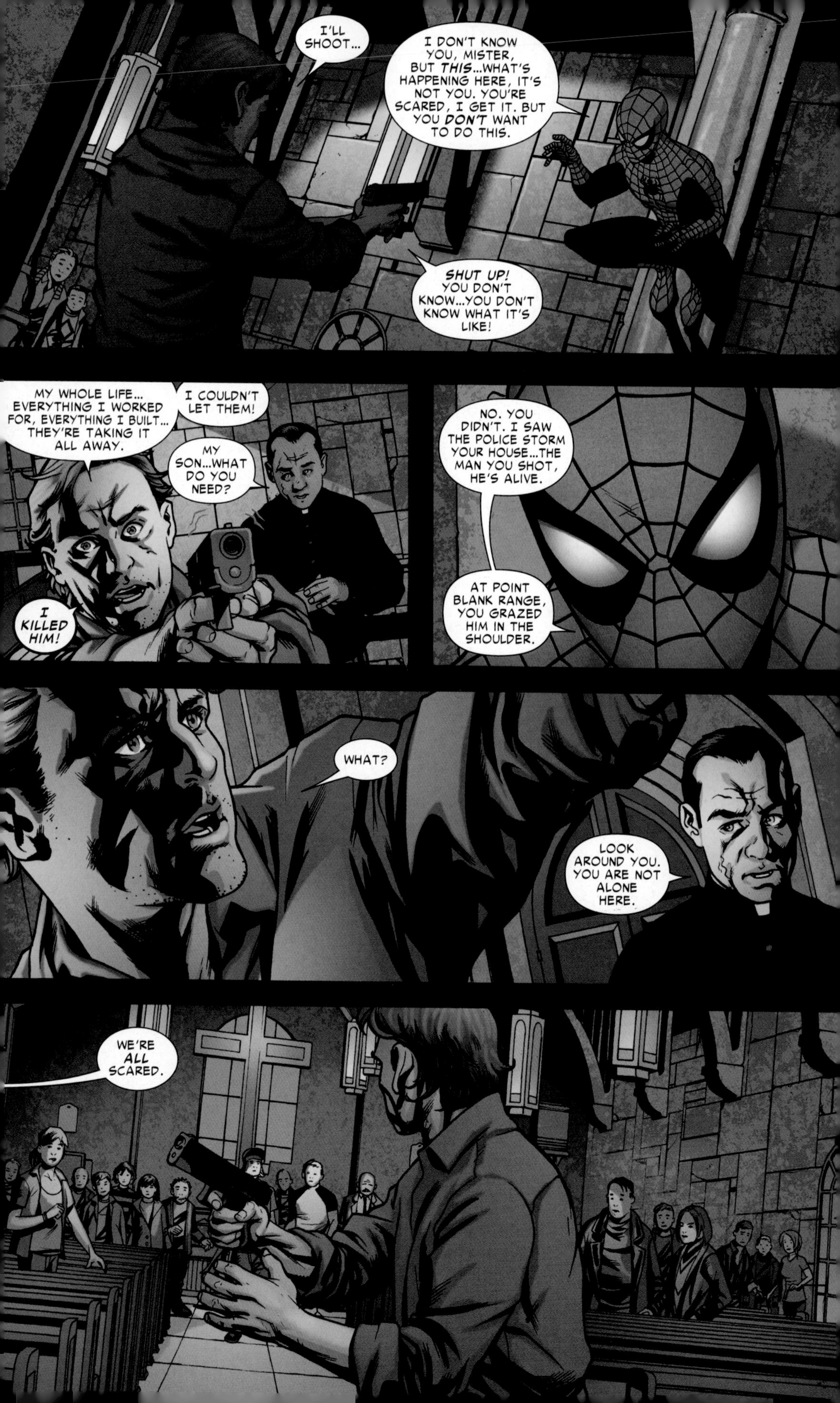
I'LL SHOOT...
I DON'T KNOW YOU, MISTER, BUT THIS...WHAT'S HAPPENING HERE, IT'S NOT YOU. YOU'RE SCARED, I GET IT. BUT YOU DON'T WANT TO DO THIS.
SHUT UP! YOU DON'T KNOW...YOU DON'T KNOW WHAT IT'S LIKE!
MY WHOLE LIFE... EVERYTHING I WORKED FOR, EVERYTHING I BUILT... THEY'RE TAKING IT ALL AWAY.
I COULDN'T LET THEM!
MY SON...WHAT DO YOU NEED?
I KILLED HIM!
NO. YOU DIDN'T. I SAW THE POLICE STORM YOUR HOUSE...THE MAN YOU SHOT, HE'S ALIVE.
AT POINT BLANK RANGE, YOU GRAZED HIM IN THE SHOULDER.
WHAT?
LOOK AROUND YOU. YOU ARE NOT ALONE HERE.
WE'RE ALL SCARED.

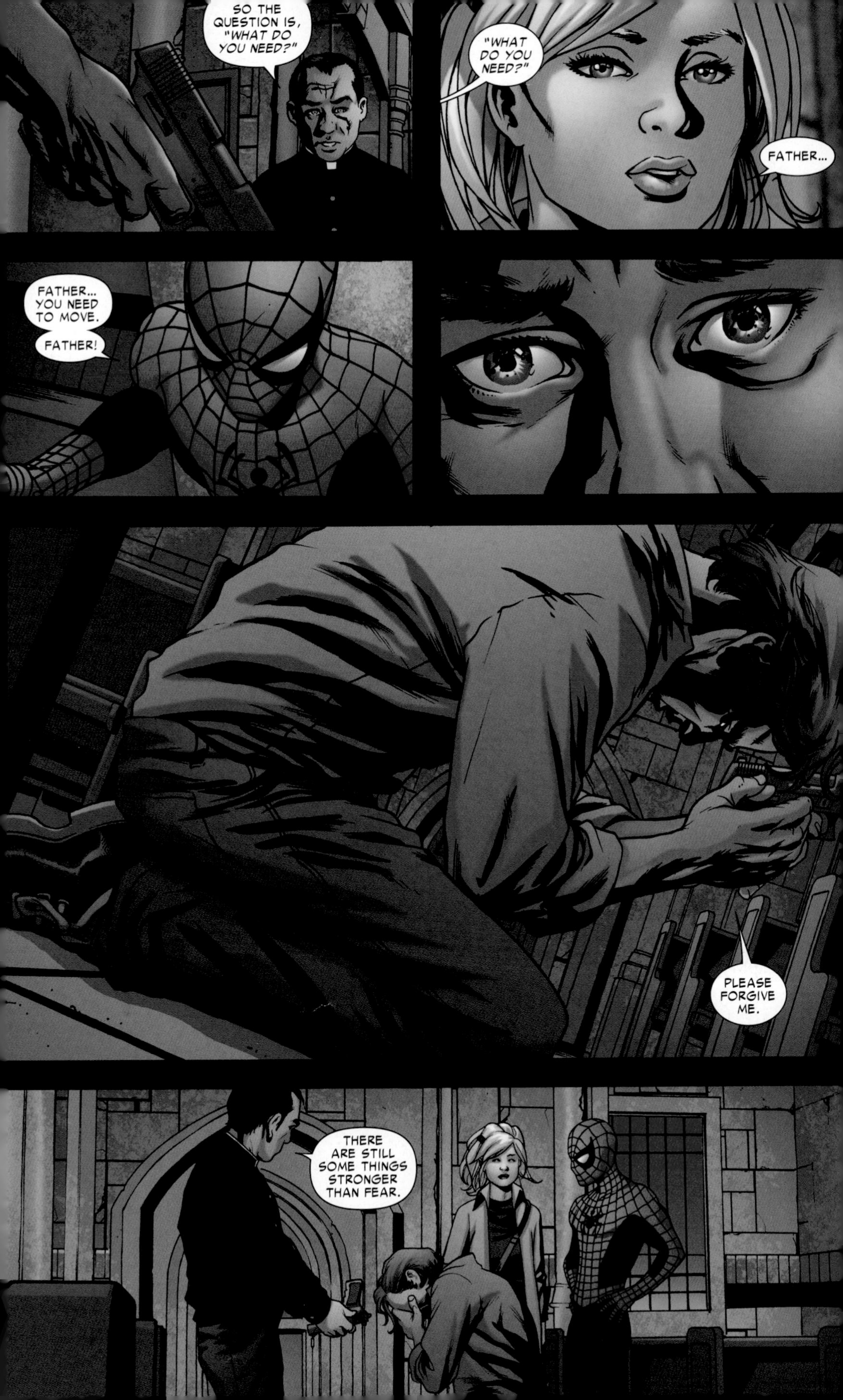
SO THE QUESTION IS, "WHAT DO YOU NEED?"
"WHAT DO YOU NEED?"
FATHER...
FATHER... YOU NEED TO MOVE.
FATHER!
PLEASE FORGIVE ME.
THERE ARE STILL SOME THINGS STRONGER THAN FEAR.

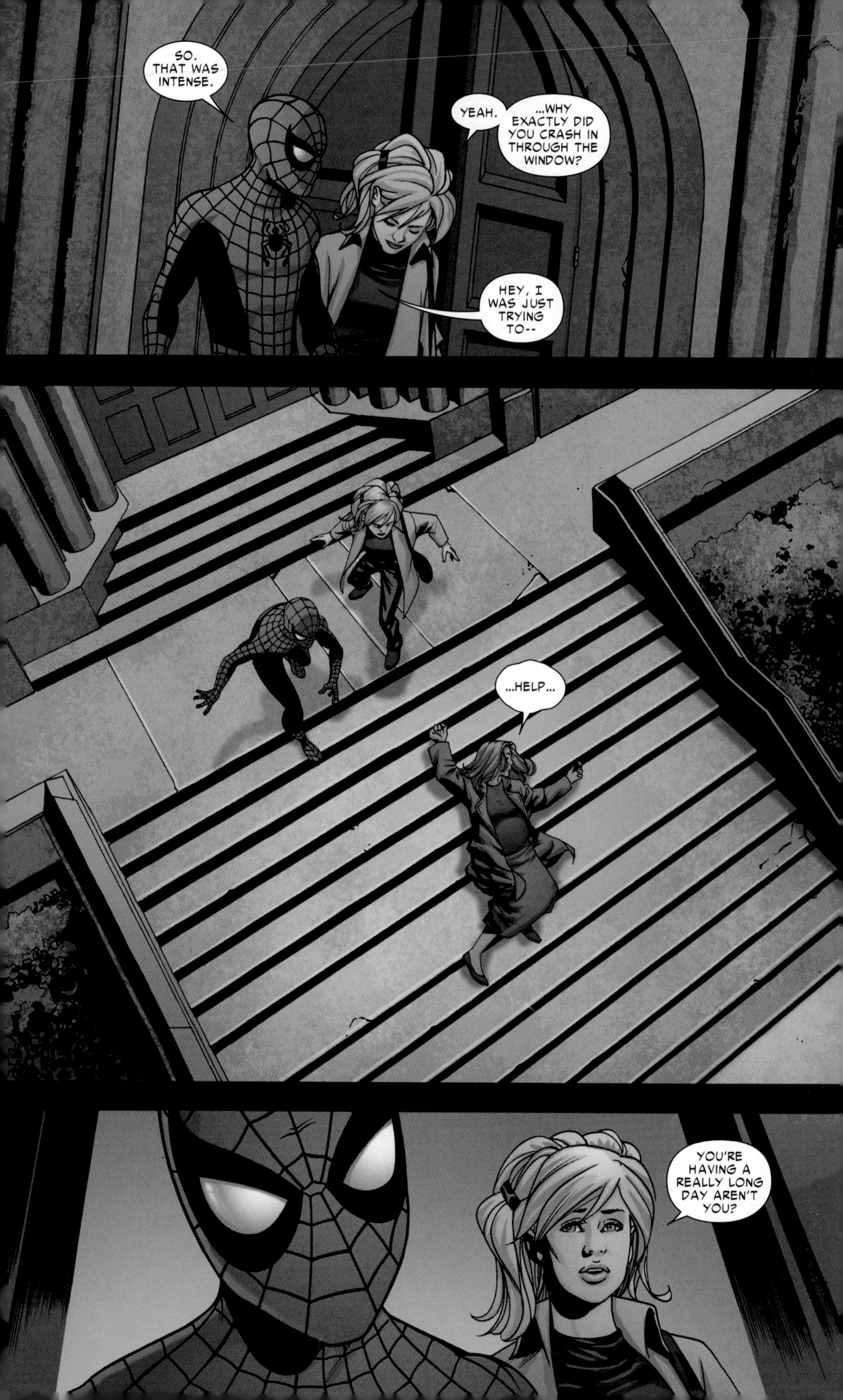
SO. THAT WAS INTENSE.
YEAH.
...WHY EXACTLY DID YOU CRASH IN THROUGH THE WINDOW?
HEY, I WAS JUST TRYING TO--
...HELP...
YOU'RE HAVING A REALLY LONG DAY AREN'T YOU?

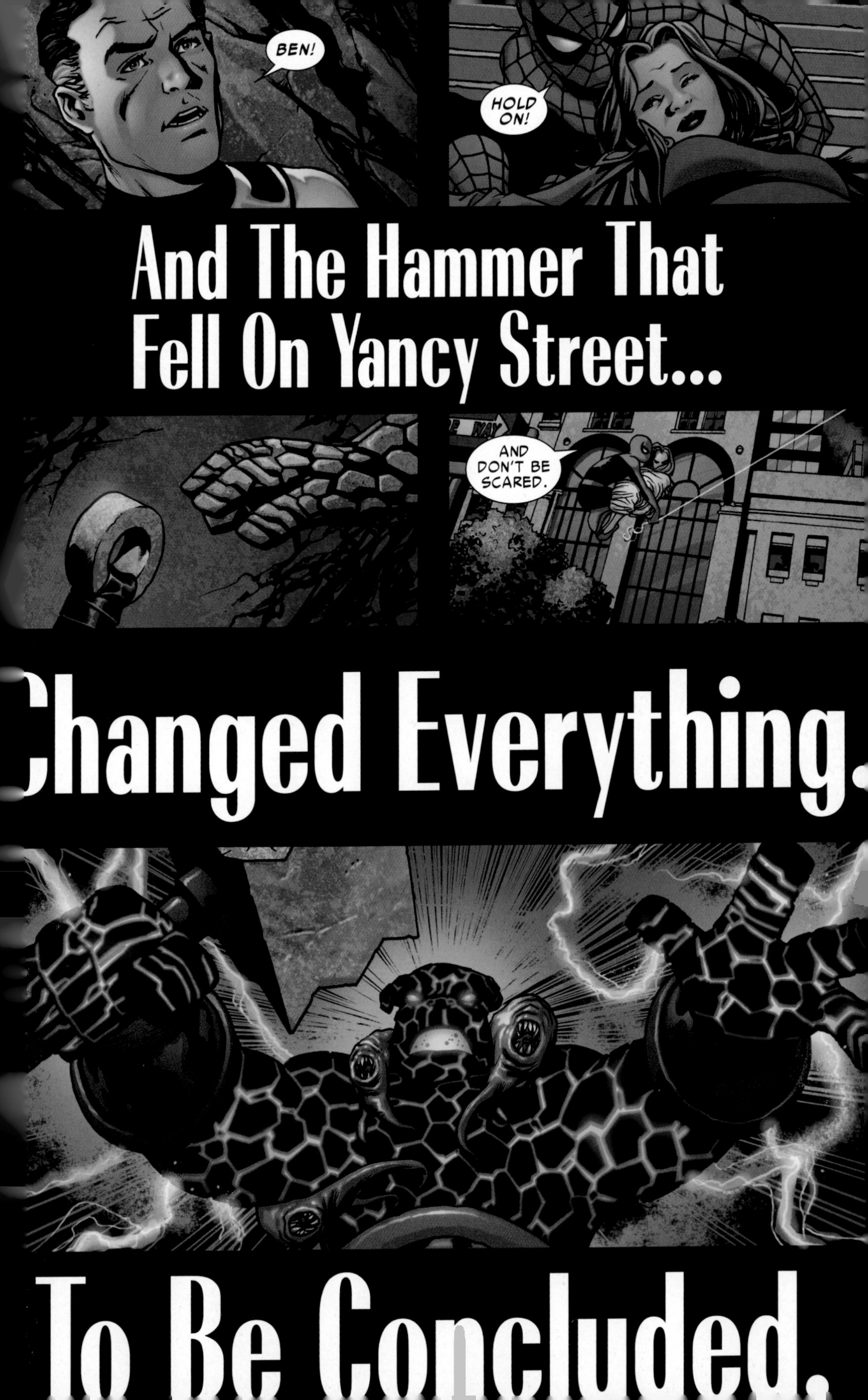
BEN!
HOLD ON!
And The Hammer That Fell On Yancy Street...
AND DON'T BE SCARED.
Changed Everything.
To Be Concluded.

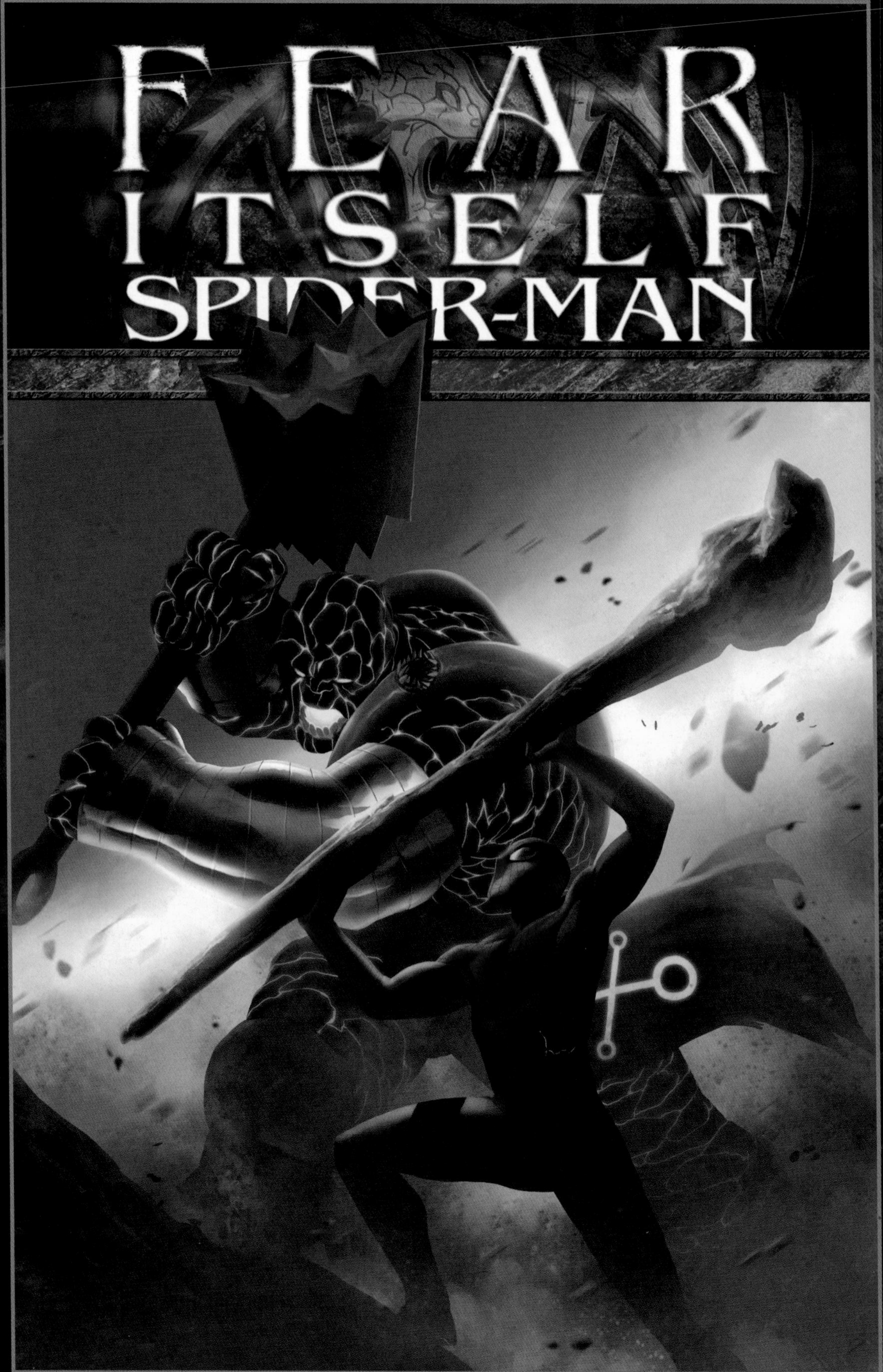
FEAR
ITSELF
SPIDER-MAN

DAY THREE

Hour Forty-One Of The Fear

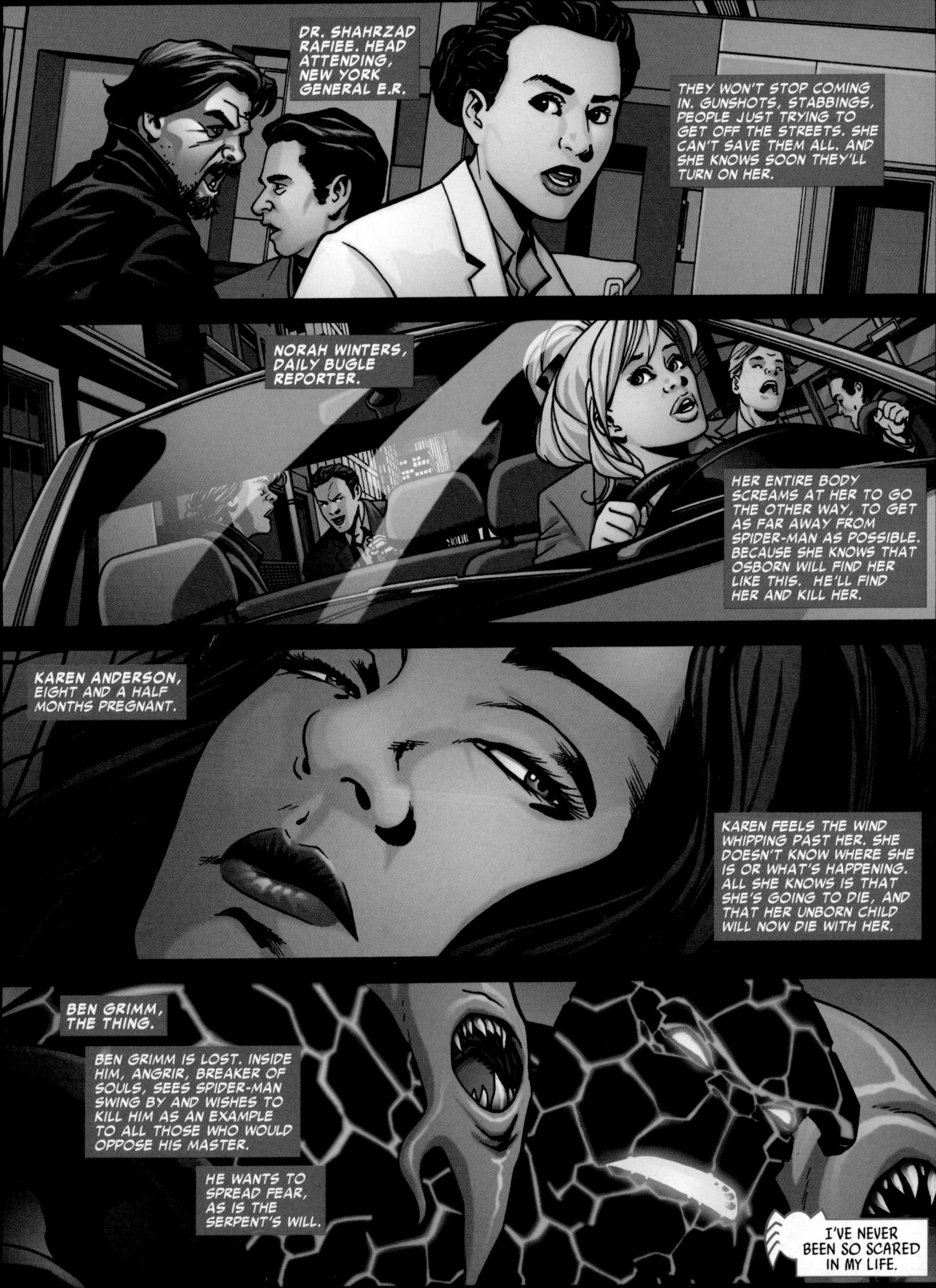
DR. SHAHRZAD RAFIEE. HEAD ATTENDING, NEW YORK GENERAL E.R.
THEY WON'T STOP COMING IN. GUNSHOTS, STABBINGS, PEOPLE JUST TRYING TO GET OFF THE STREETS. SHE CAN'T SAVE THEM ALL. AND SHE KNOWS SOON THEY'LL TURN ON HER.
NORAH WINTERS, DAILY BUGLE REPORTER.
HER ENTIRE BODY SCREAMS AT HER TO GO THE OTHER WAY, TO GET AS FAR AWAY FROM SPIDER-MAN AS POSSIBLE. BECAUSE SHE KNOWS THAT OSBORN WILL FIND HER LIKE THIS. HE'LL FIND HER AND KILL HER.
KAREN ANDERSON, EIGHT AND A HALF MONTHS PREGNANT.
KAREN FEELS THE WIND WHIPPING PAST HER. SHE DOESN'T KNOW WHERE SHE IS OR WHAT'S HAPPENING. ALL SHE KNOWS IS THAT SHE'S GOING TO DIE, AND THAT HER UNBORN CHILD WILL NOW DIE WITH HER.
BEN GRIMM, THE THING.
BEN GRIMM IS LOST. INSIDE HIM, ANGRIR, BREAKER OF SOULS, SEES SPIDER-MAN SWING BY AND WISHES TO KILL HIM AS AN EXAMPLE TO ALL THOSE WHO WOULD OPPOSE HIS MASTER.
HE WANTS TO SPREAD FEAR, AS IS THE SERPENT'S WILL.
I'VE NEVER BEEN SO SCARED IN MY LIFE.

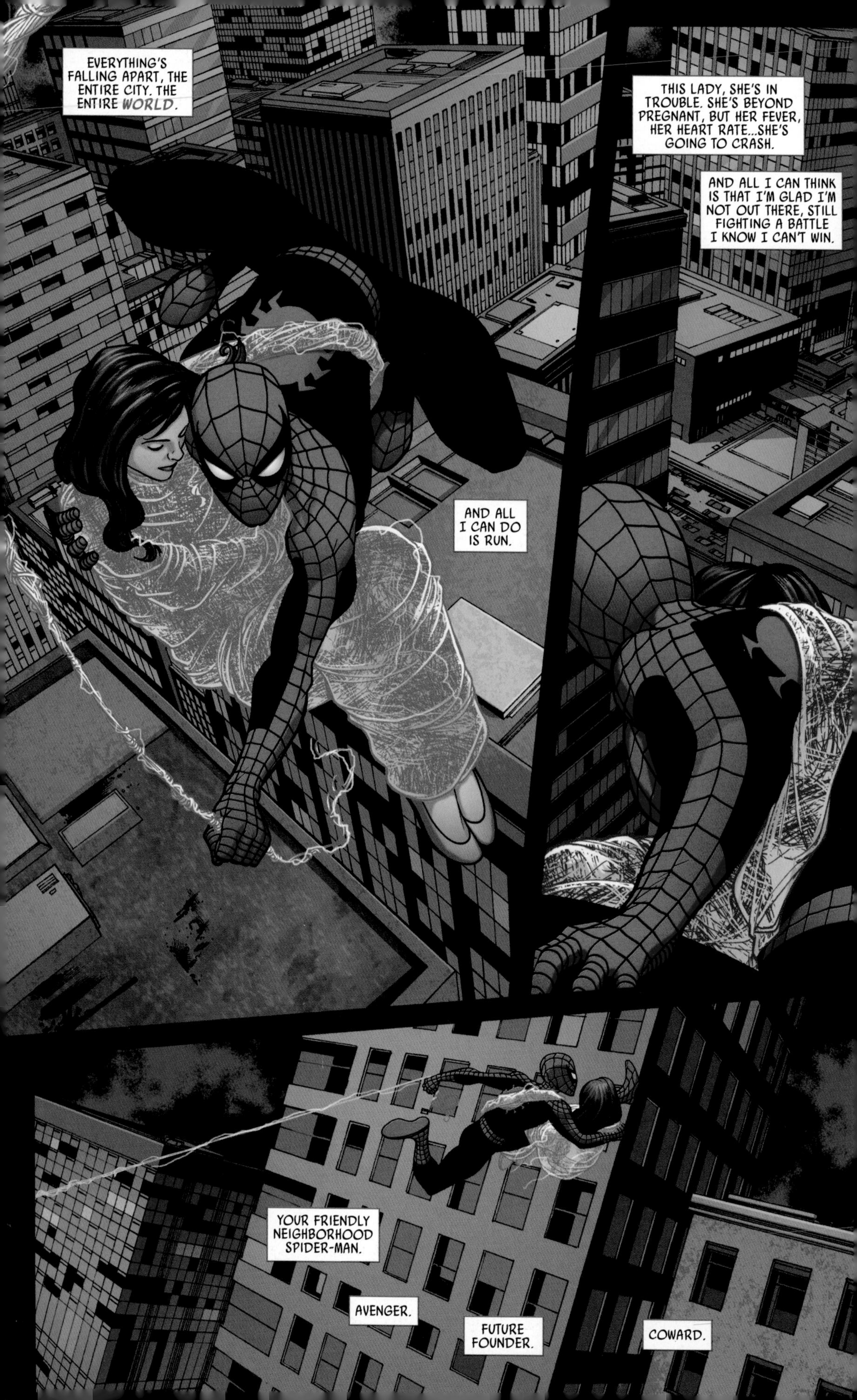
EVERYTHING'S FALLING APART, THE ENTIRE CITY. THE ENTIRE WORLD.
THIS LADY, SHE'S IN TROUBLE. SHE'S BEYOND PREGNANT, BUT HER FEVER, HER HEART RATE...SHE'S GOING TO CRASH.
AND ALL I CAN THINK IS THAT I'M GLAD I'M NOT OUT THERE, STILL FIGHTING A BATTLE I KNOW I CAN'T WIN.
AND ALL I CAN DO IS RUN.
YOUR FRIENDLY NEIGHBORHOOD SPIDER-MAN.
AVENGER.
FUTURE FOUNDER.
COWARD.

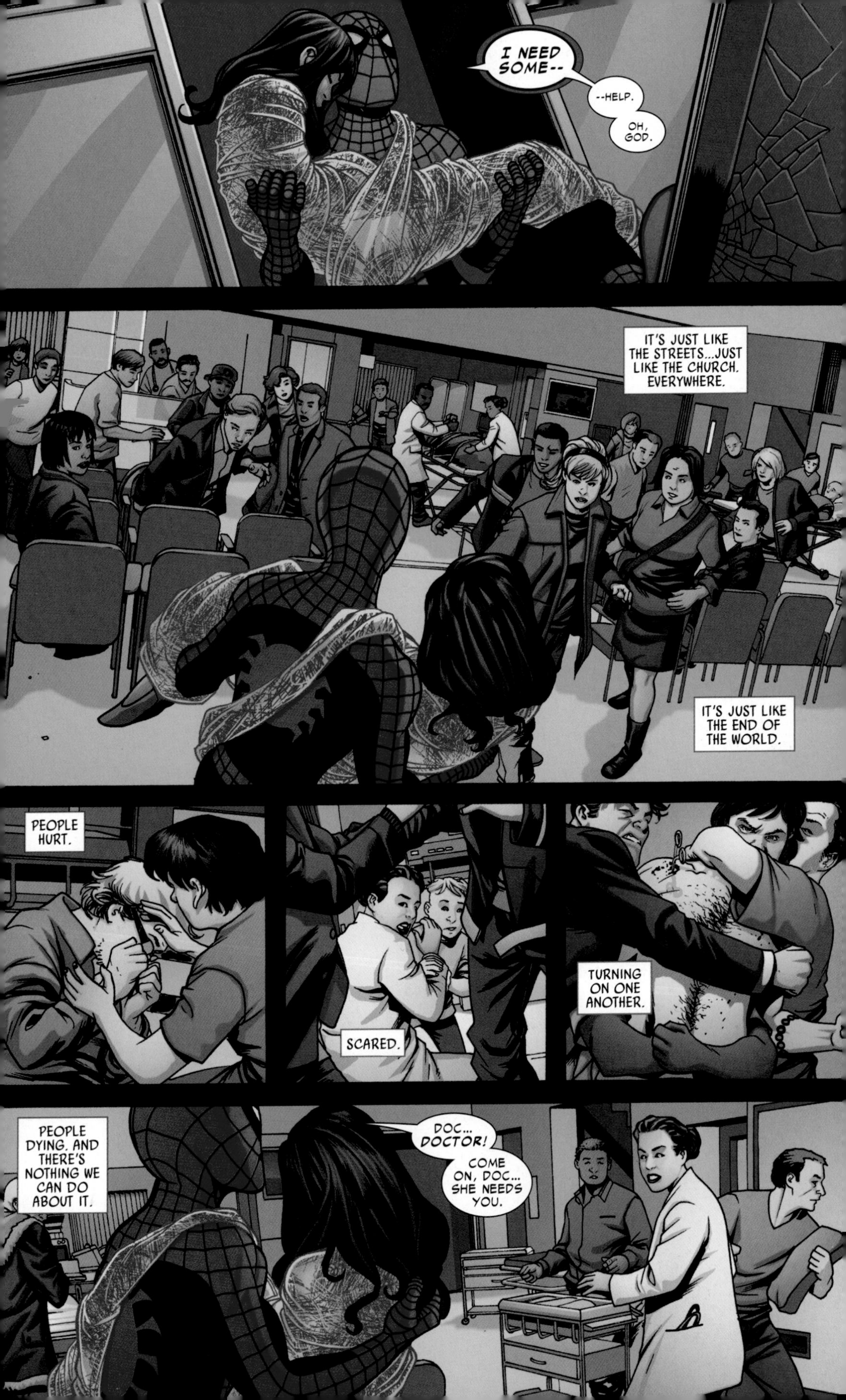
I NEED SOME--
--HELP.
OH, GOD.
IT'S JUST LIKE THE STREETS...JUST LIKE THE CHURCH. EVERYWHERE.
IT'S JUST LIKE THE END OF THE WORLD.
PEOPLE HURT.
SCARED.
TURNING ON ONE ANOTHER.
PEOPLE DYING. AND THERE'S NOTHING WE CAN DO ABOUT IT.
DOC... DOCTOR!
COME ON, DOC... SHE NEEDS YOU.

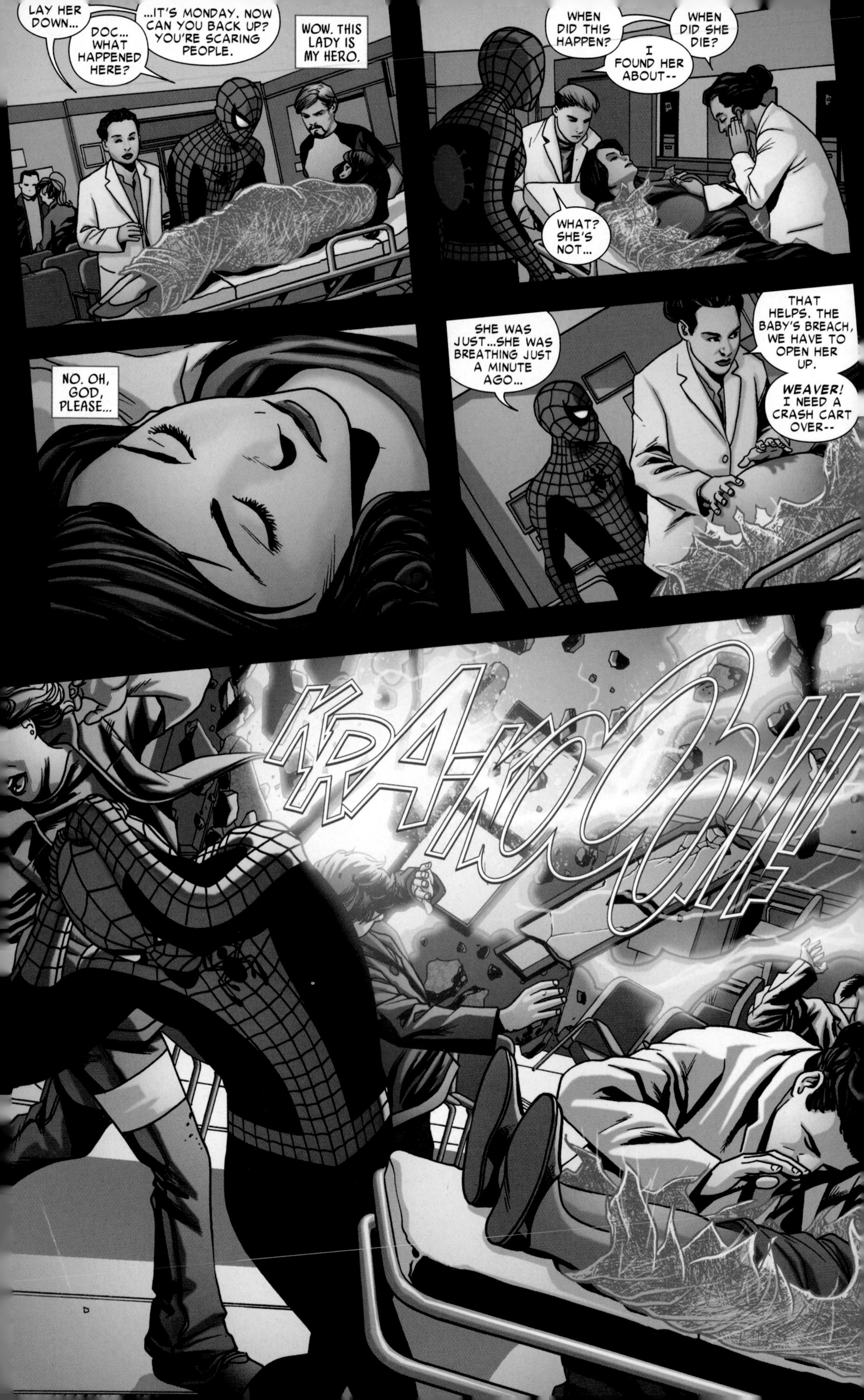
LAY HER DOWN...
DOC... WHAT HAPPENED HERE?
...IT'S MONDAY. NOW CAN YOU BACK UP? YOU'RE SCARING PEOPLE.
WOW. THIS LADY IS MY HERO.
WHEN DID THIS HAPPEN?
WHEN DID SHE DIE?
I FOUND HER ABOUT--
WHAT? SHE'S NOT...
NO. OH, GOD, PLEASE...
SHE WAS JUST...SHE WAS BREATHING JUST A MINUTE AGO...
THAT HELPS. THE BABY'S BREACH, WE HAVE TO OPEN HER UP.
WEAVER! I NEED A CRASH CART OVER--
KRAKOOOM!

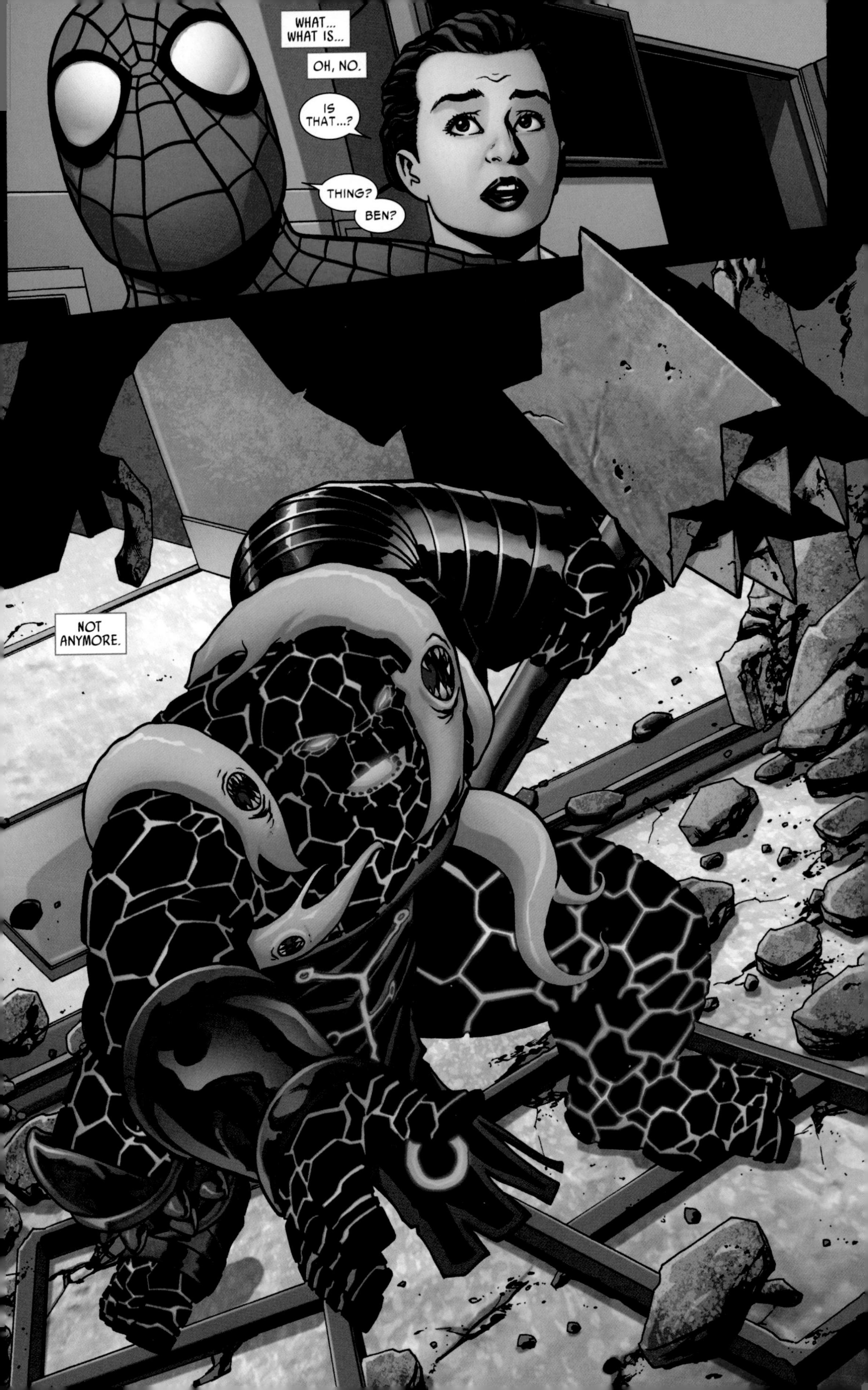
WHAT... WHAT IS...
OH, NO.
IS THAT...?
THING?
BEN?
NOT ANYMORE.

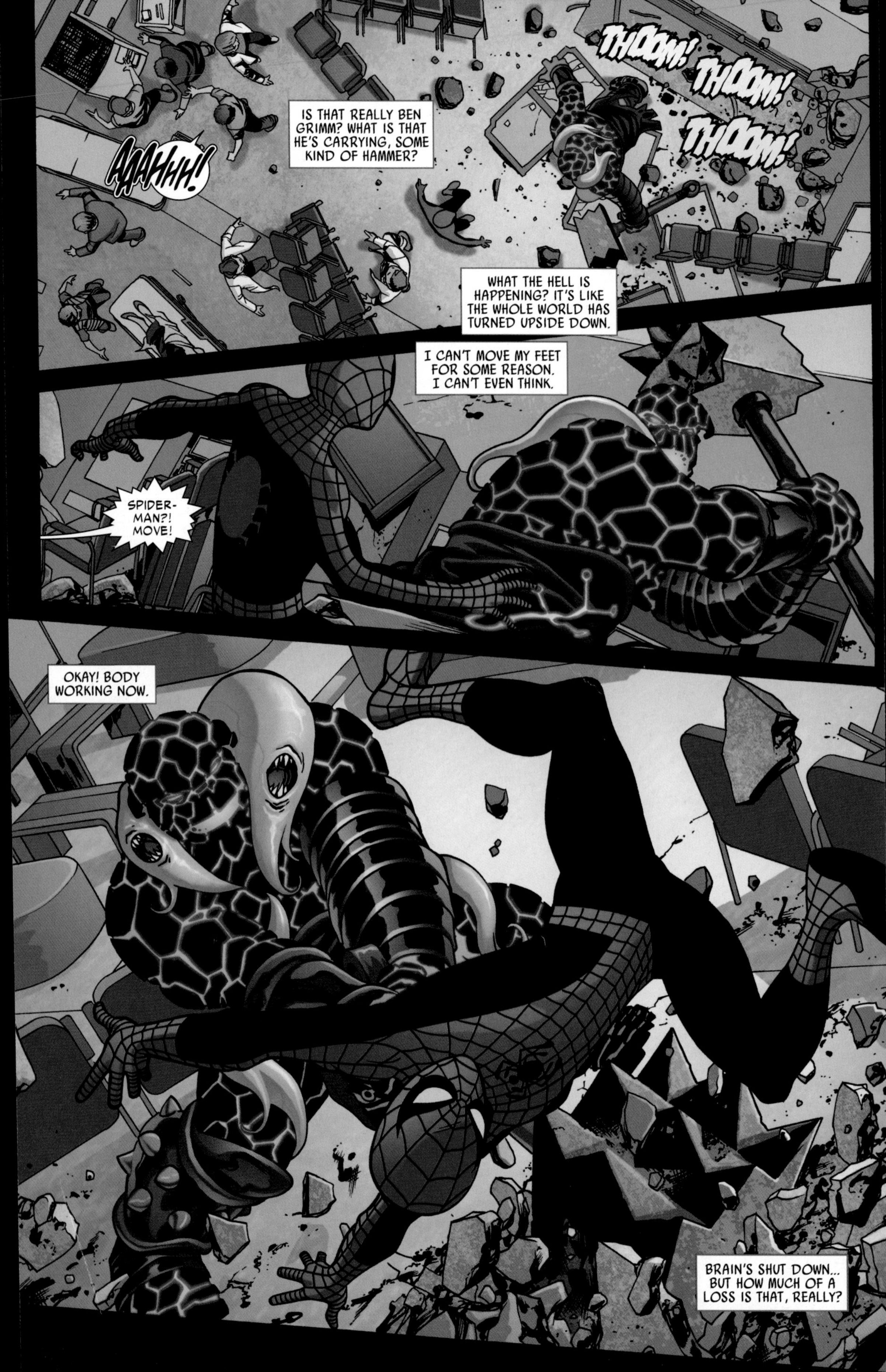
AAAHHH!
IS THAT REALLY BEN GRIMM? WHAT IS THAT HE'S CARRYING, SOME KIND OF HAMMER?
THOOM! THOOM! THOOM!
WHAT THE HELL IS HAPPENING? IT'S LIKE THE WHOLE WORLD HAS TURNED UPSIDE DOWN.
I CAN'T MOVE MY FEET FOR SOME REASON. I CAN'T EVEN THINK.
SPIDER-MAN?! MOVE!
OKAY! BODY WORKING NOW.
BRAIN'S SHUT DOWN... BUT HOW MUCH OF A LOSS IS THAT, REALLY?

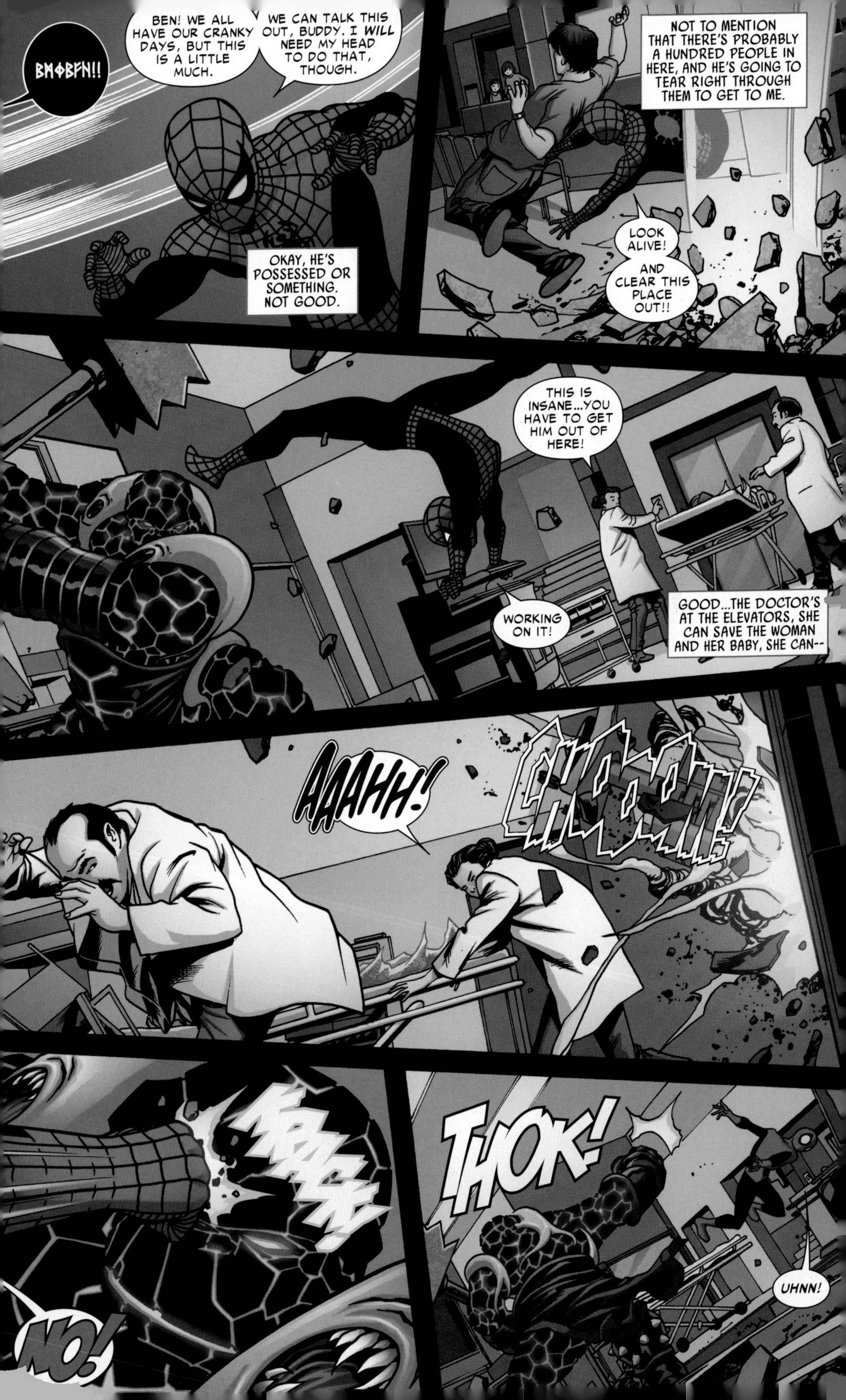

BMØBFN!!
BEN! WE ALL HAVE OUR CRANKY DAYS, BUT THIS IS A LITTLE MUCH.
WE CAN TALK THIS OUT, BUDDY. I *WILL* NEED MY HEAD TO DO THAT, THOUGH.
OKAY, HE'S POSSESSED OR SOMETHING. NOT GOOD.
NOT TO MENTION THAT THERE'S PROBABLY A HUNDRED PEOPLE IN HERE, AND HE'S GOING TO TEAR RIGHT THROUGH THEM TO GET TO ME.
LOOK ALIVE!
AND CLEAR THIS PLACE OUT!!
THIS IS INSANE...YOU HAVE TO GET HIM OUT OF HERE!
WORKING ON IT!
GOOD...THE DOCTOR'S AT THE ELEVATORS, SHE CAN SAVE THE WOMAN AND HER BABY, SHE CAN--
AAAHH!
THOK!
UHNN!
NO!

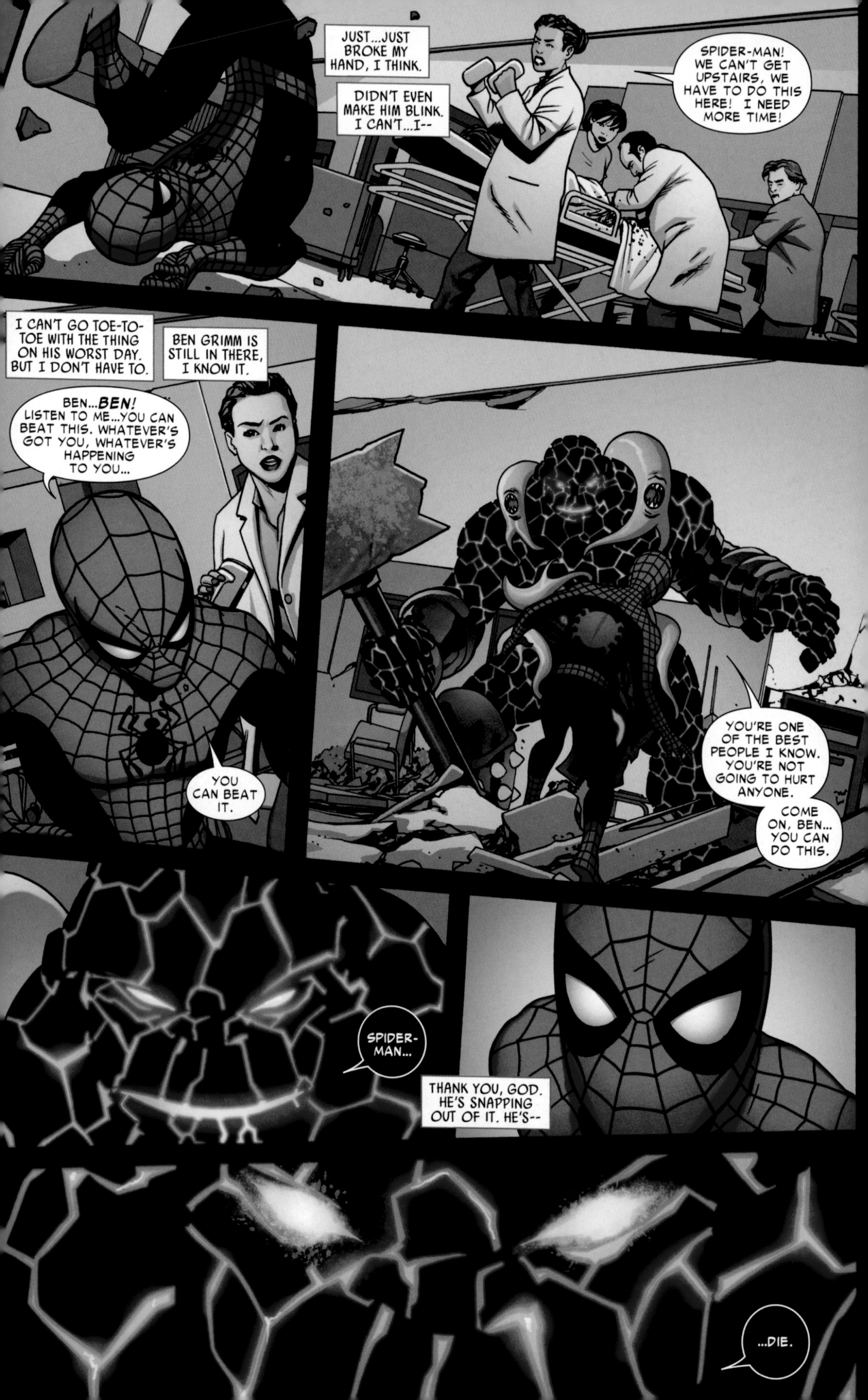
JUST...JUST BROKE MY HAND, I THINK.
DIDN'T EVEN MAKE HIM BLINK. I CAN'T...I--
SPIDER-MAN! WE CAN'T GET UPSTAIRS, WE HAVE TO DO THIS HERE! I NEED MORE TIME!
I CAN'T GO TOE-TO-TOE WITH THE THING ON HIS WORST DAY. BUT I DON'T HAVE TO.
BEN GRIMM IS STILL IN THERE, I KNOW IT.
BEN...BEN! LISTEN TO ME...YOU CAN BEAT THIS. WHATEVER'S GOT YOU, WHATEVER'S HAPPENING TO YOU...
YOU CAN BEAT IT.
YOU'RE ONE OF THE BEST PEOPLE I KNOW. YOU'RE NOT GOING TO HURT ANYONE.
COME ON, BEN... YOU CAN DO THIS.
SPIDER-MAN...
THANK YOU, GOD. HE'S SNAPPING OUT OF IT. HE'S--
...DIE.

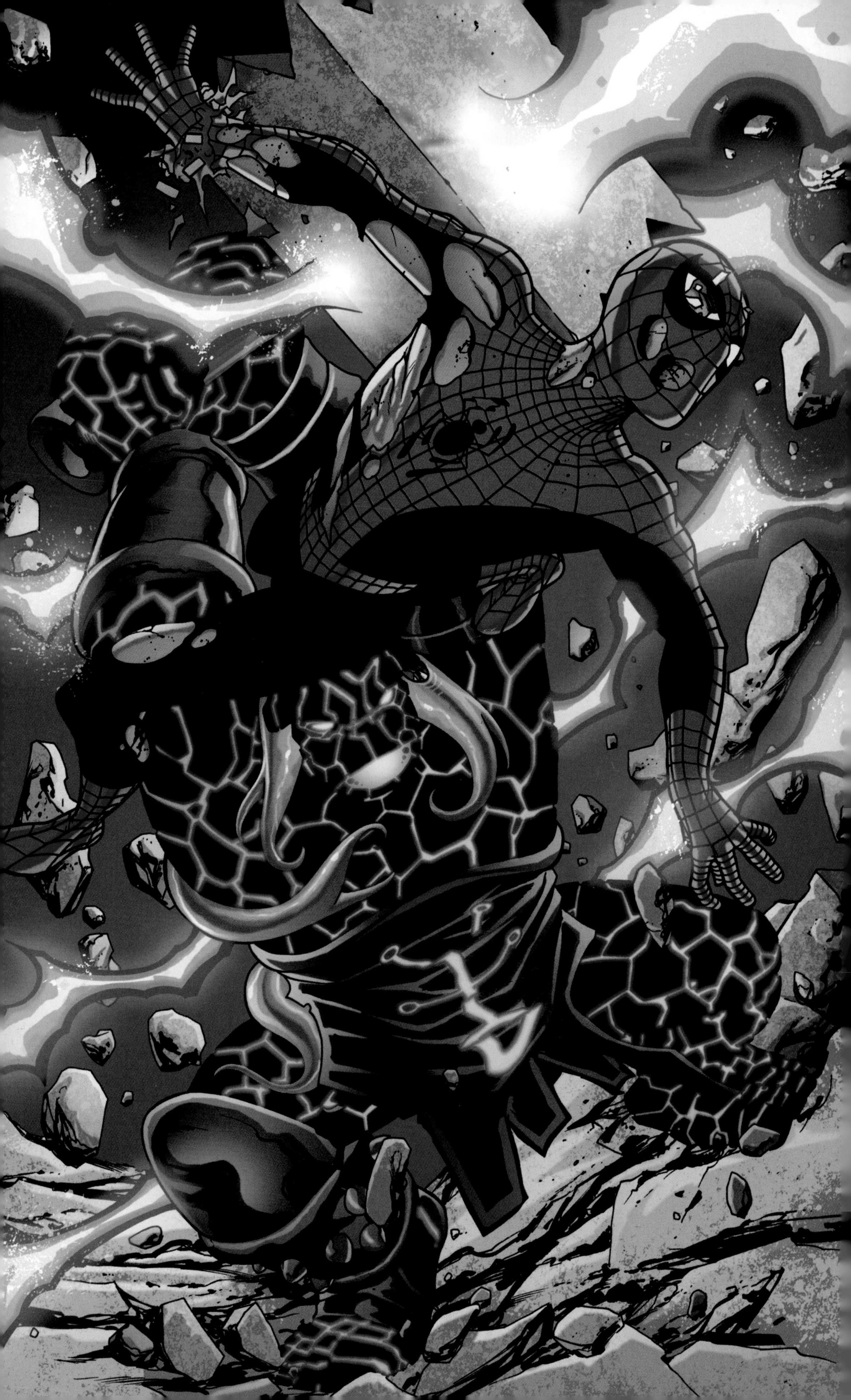

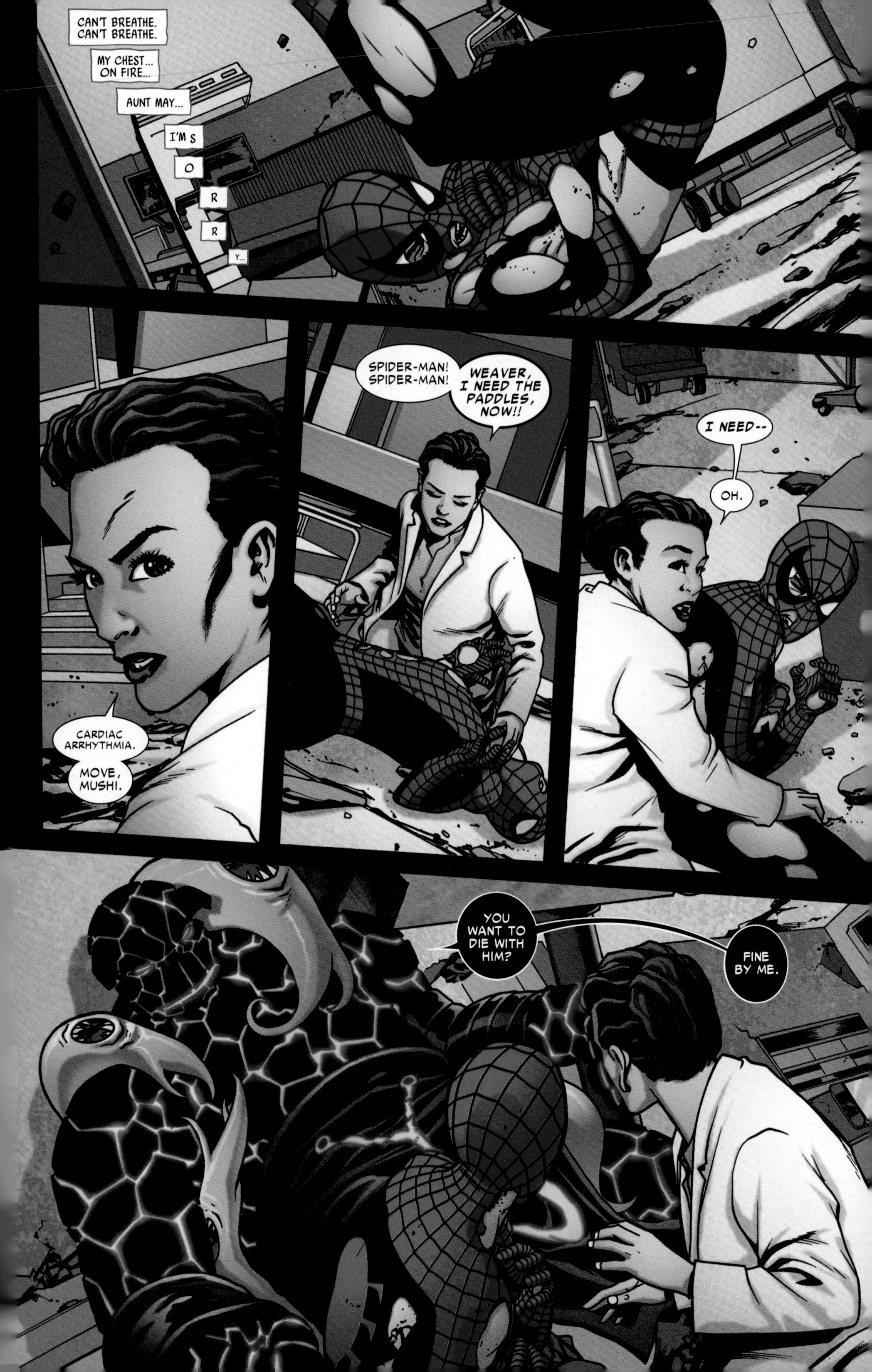
CAN'T BREATHE. CAN'T BREATHE.
MY CHEST... ON FIRE...
AUNT MAY...
I'M S
O
R
R
Y...
CARDIAC ARRHYTHMIA.
MOVE, MUSHI.
SPIDER-MAN! SPIDER-MAN!
WEAVER, I NEED THE PADDLES, NOW!!
I NEED--
OH.
YOU WANT TO DIE WITH HIM?
FINE BY ME.

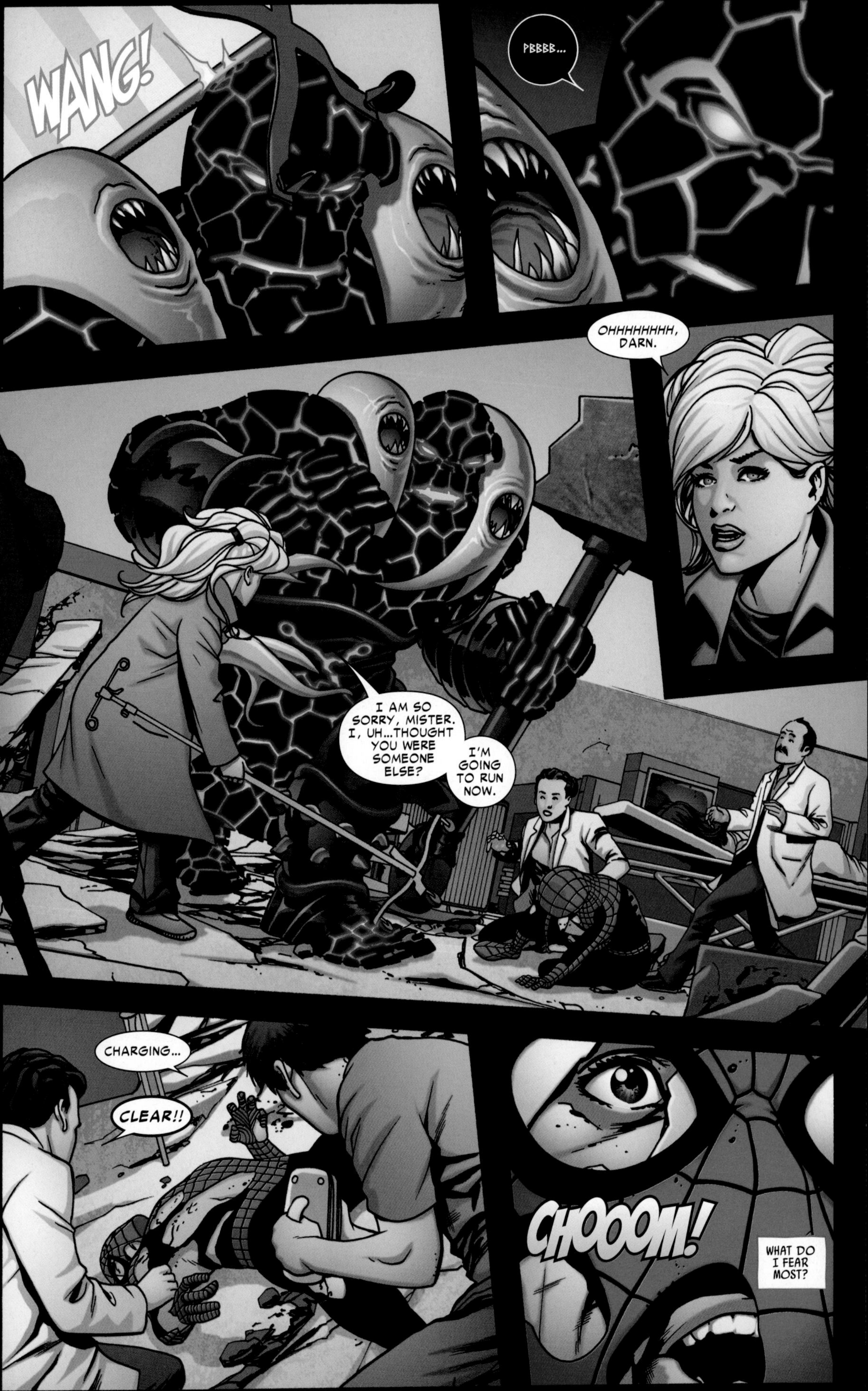
WANG!
PBBBB...
OHHHHHHHH, DARN.
I AM SO SORRY, MISTER. I, UH...THOUGHT YOU WERE SOMEONE ELSE?
I'M GOING TO RUN NOW.
CHARGING...
CLEAR!!
CHOOOM!
WHAT DO I FEAR MOST?

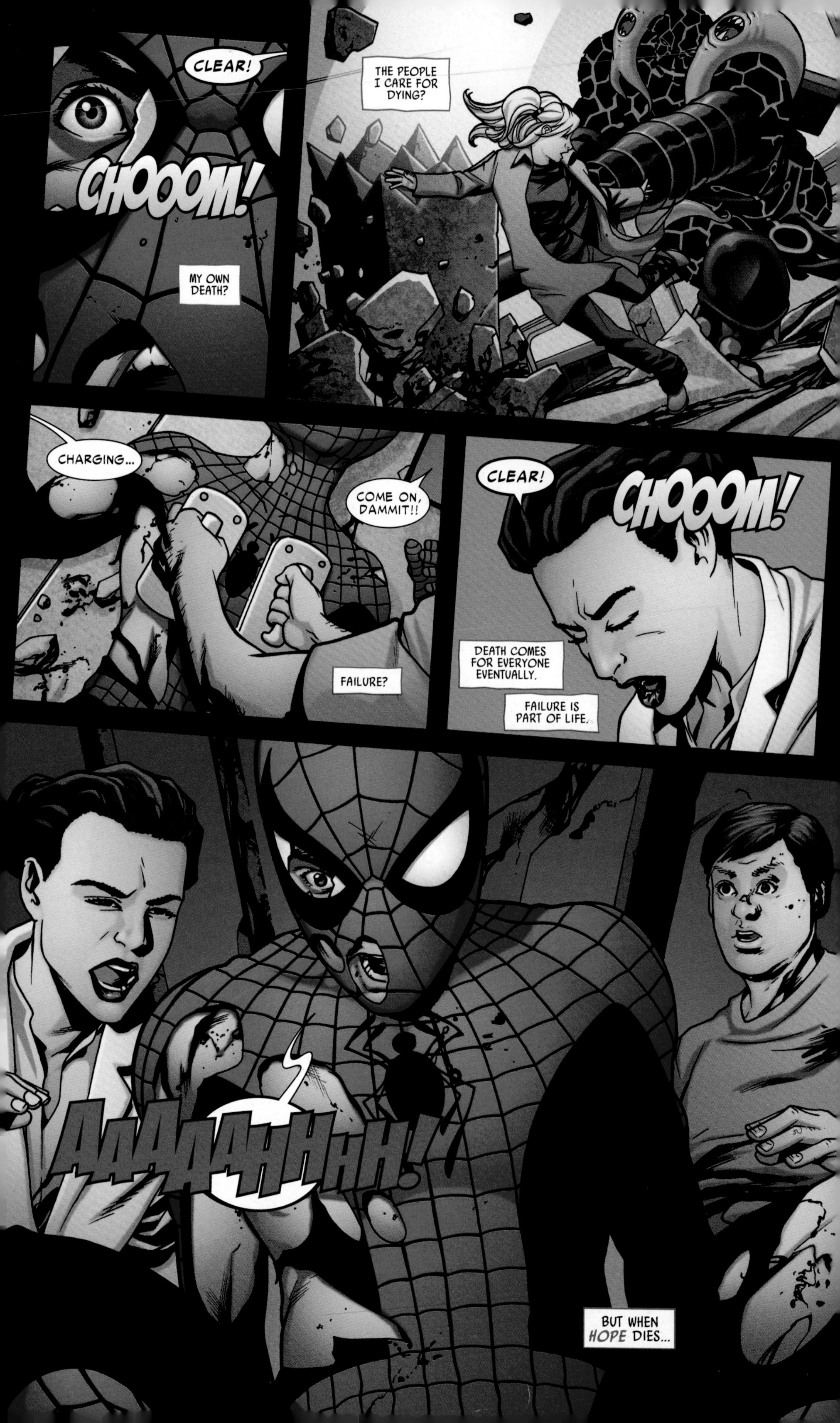
CLEAR!
CHOOOM!
MY OWN DEATH?
THE PEOPLE I CARE FOR DYING?
CHARGING...
COME ON, DAMMIT!!
FAILURE?
CLEAR!
CHOOOM!
DEATH COMES FOR EVERYONE EVENTUALLY.
FAILURE IS PART OF LIFE.
AAAAAHHHH!!
BUT WHEN *HOPE* DIES...

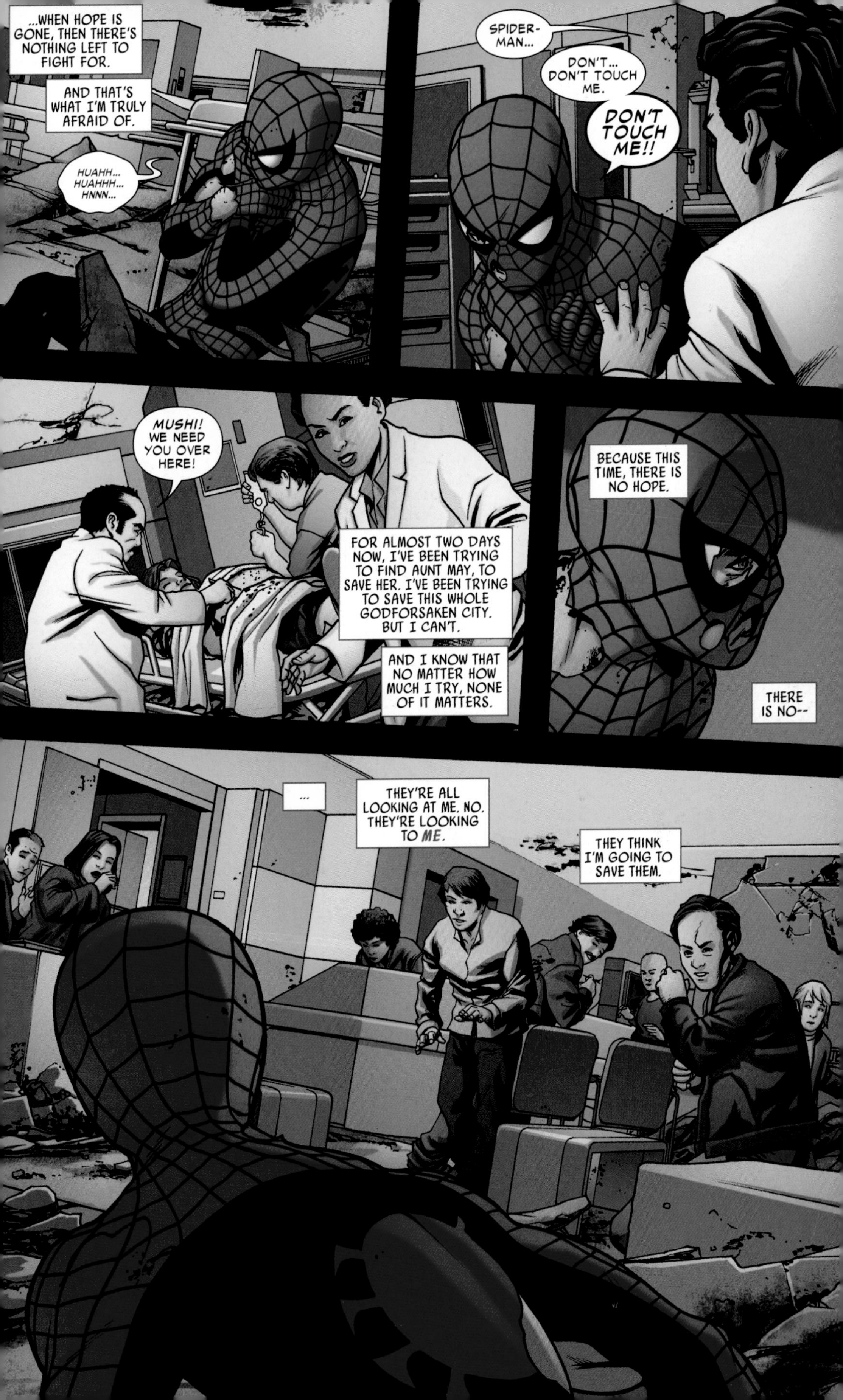
...WHEN HOPE IS GONE, THEN THERE'S NOTHING LEFT TO FIGHT FOR.
AND THAT'S WHAT I'M TRULY AFRAID OF.
HUAHH... HUAHHH... HNNN...
SPIDER-MAN...
DON'T... DON'T TOUCH ME.
DON'T TOUCH ME!!
MUSHI! WE NEED YOU OVER HERE!
FOR ALMOST TWO DAYS NOW, I'VE BEEN TRYING TO FIND AUNT MAY, TO SAVE HER. I'VE BEEN TRYING TO SAVE THIS WHOLE GODFORSAKEN CITY. BUT I CAN'T.
AND I KNOW THAT NO MATTER HOW MUCH I TRY, NONE OF IT MATTERS.
BECAUSE THIS TIME, THERE IS NO HOPE.
THERE IS NO--
...
THEY'RE ALL LOOKING AT ME. NO. THEY'RE LOOKING TO *ME*.
THEY THINK I'M GOING TO SAVE THEM.

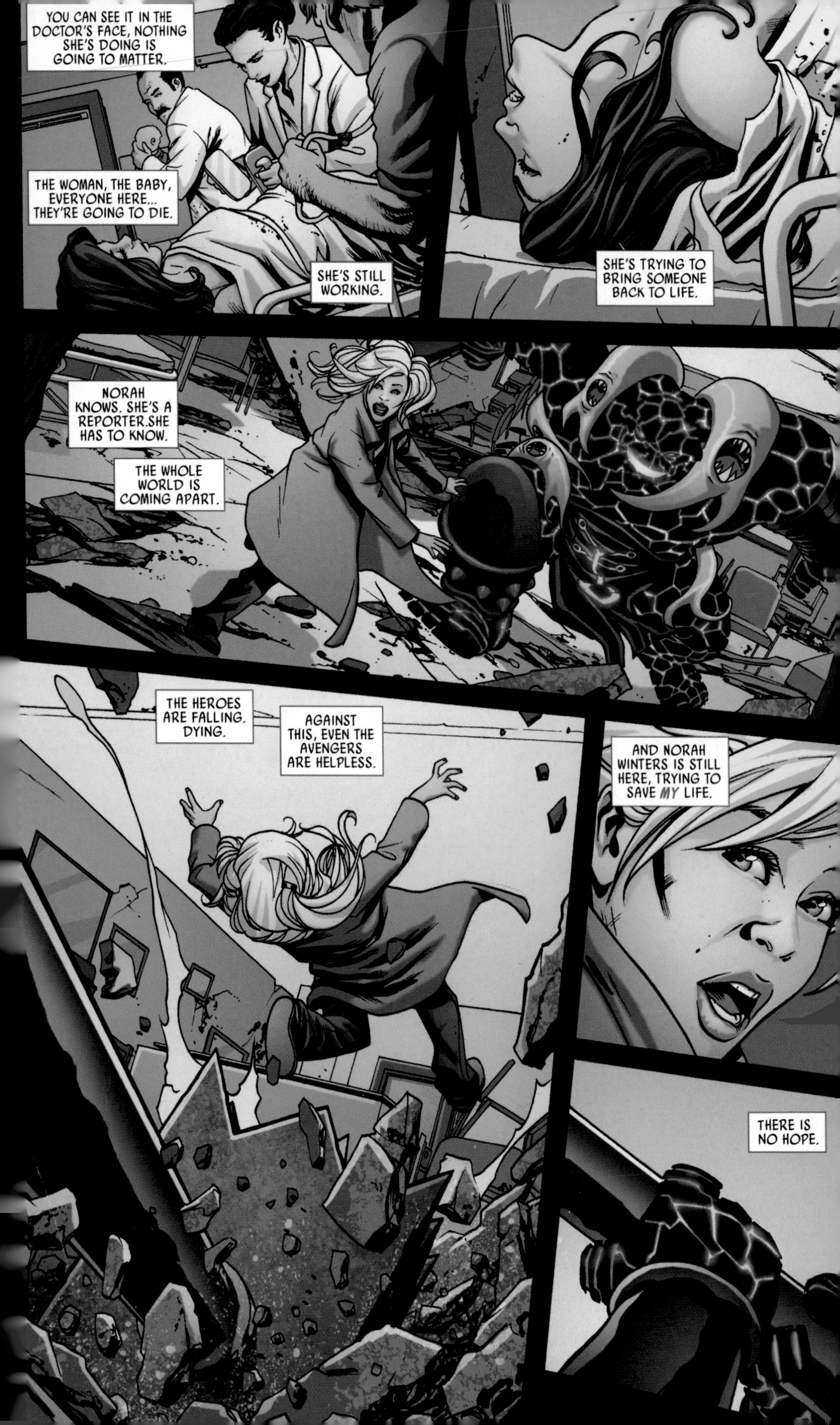
YOU CAN SEE IT IN THE DOCTOR'S FACE, NOTHING SHE'S DOING IS GOING TO MATTER.
THE WOMAN, THE BABY, EVERYONE HERE... THEY'RE GOING TO DIE.
SHE'S STILL WORKING.
SHE'S TRYING TO BRING SOMEONE BACK TO LIFE.
NORAH KNOWS. SHE'S A REPORTER.SHE HAS TO KNOW.
THE WHOLE WORLD IS COMING APART.
THE HEROES ARE FALLING. DYING.
AGAINST THIS, EVEN THE AVENGERS ARE HELPLESS.
AND NORAH WINTERS IS STILL HERE, TRYING TO SAVE MY LIFE.
THERE IS NO HOPE.

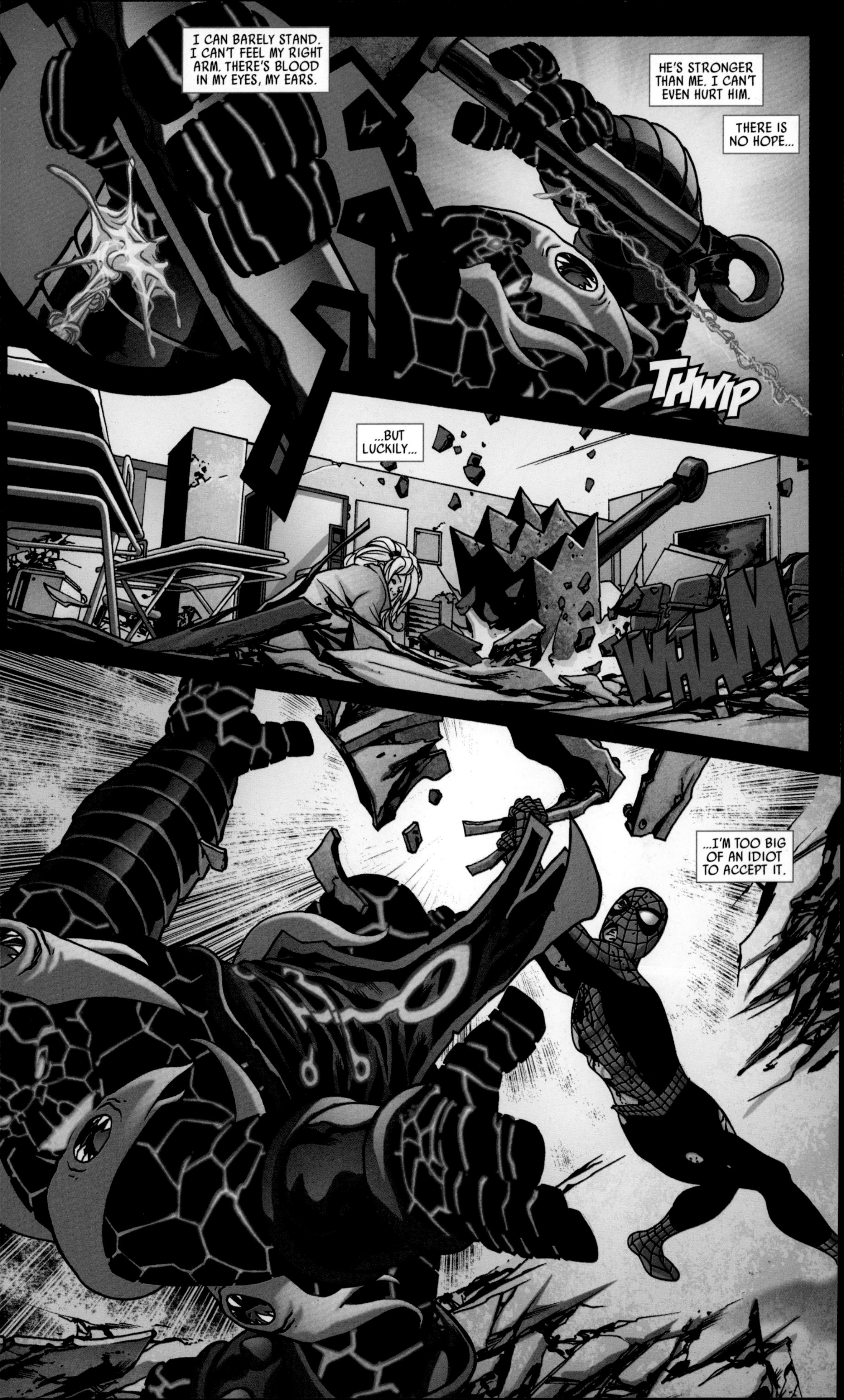
I CAN BARELY STAND. I CAN'T FEEL MY RIGHT ARM. THERE'S BLOOD IN MY EYES, MY EARS.
HE'S STRONGER THAN ME. I CAN'T EVEN HURT HIM.
THERE IS NO HOPE...
THWIP
...BUT LUCKILY...
WHAM
...I'M TOO BIG OF AN IDIOT TO ACCEPT IT.

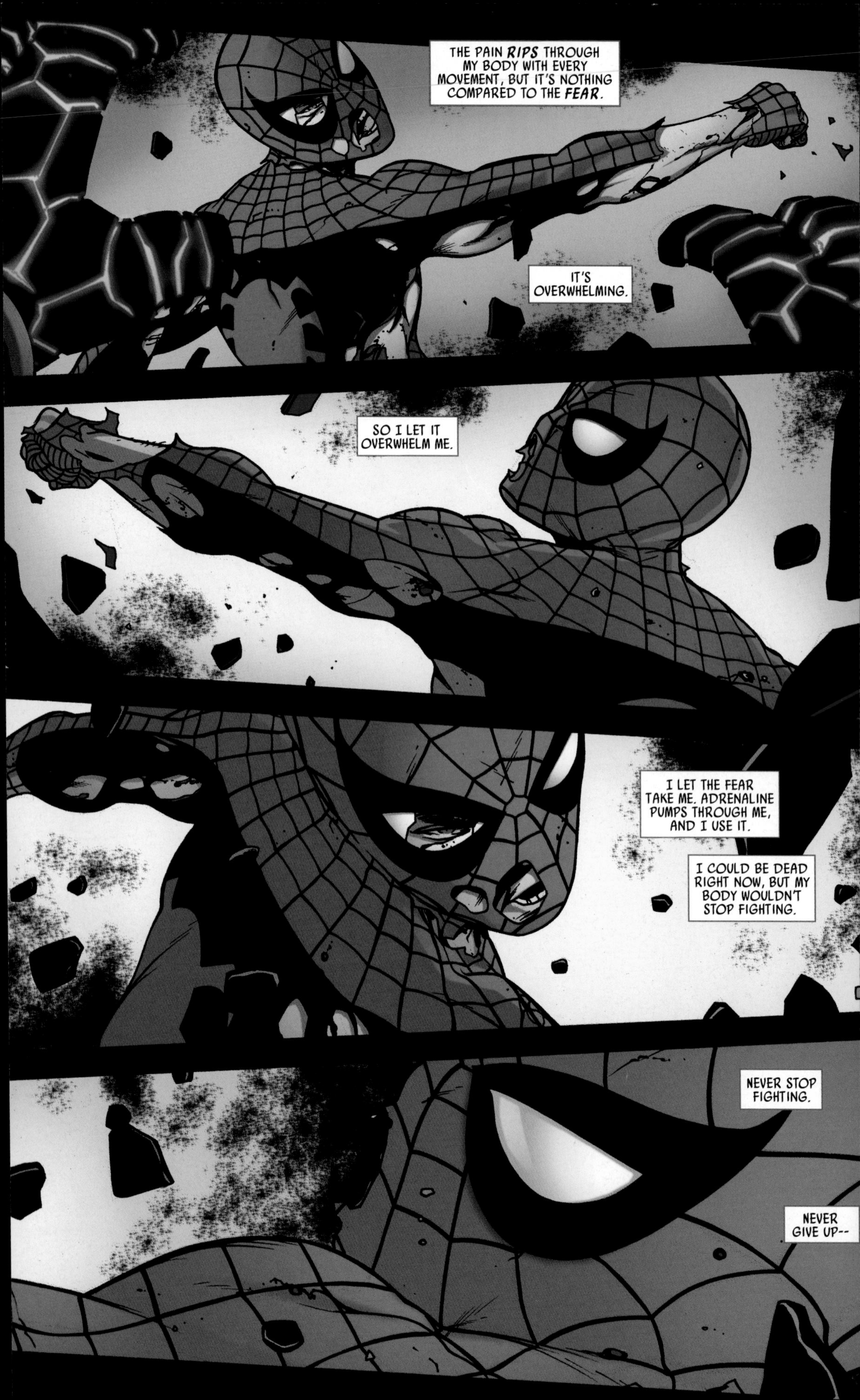
THE PAIN RIPS THROUGH MY BODY WITH EVERY MOVEMENT, BUT IT'S NOTHING COMPARED TO THE FEAR.
IT'S OVERWHELMING.
SO I LET IT OVERWHELM ME.
I LET THE FEAR TAKE ME. ADRENALINE PUMPS THROUGH ME, AND I USE IT.
I COULD BE DEAD RIGHT NOW, BUT MY BODY WOULDN'T STOP FIGHTING.
NEVER STOP FIGHTING.
NEVER GIVE UP--

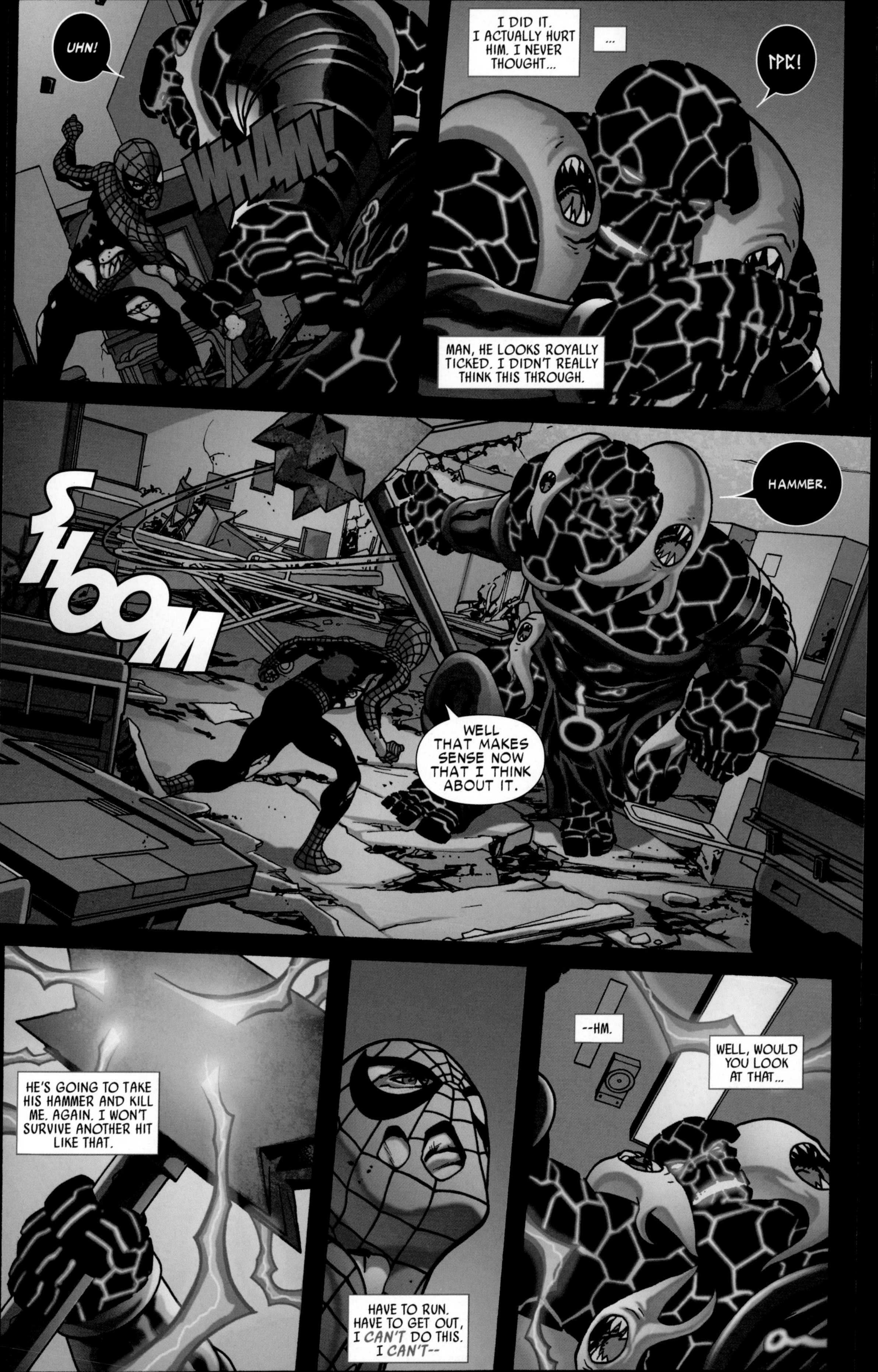
UHN!
WHAM!
I DID IT. I ACTUALLY HURT HIM. I NEVER THOUGHT...
...
MAN, HE LOOKS ROYALLY TICKED. I DIDN'T REALLY THINK THIS THROUGH.
HAMMER.
SHOOM
WELL THAT MAKES SENSE NOW THAT I THINK ABOUT IT.
HE'S GOING TO TAKE HIS HAMMER AND KILL ME. AGAIN. I WON'T SURVIVE ANOTHER HIT LIKE THAT.
HAVE TO RUN. HAVE TO GET OUT, I CAN'T DO THIS. I CAN'T--
--HM.
WELL, WOULD YOU LOOK AT THAT...

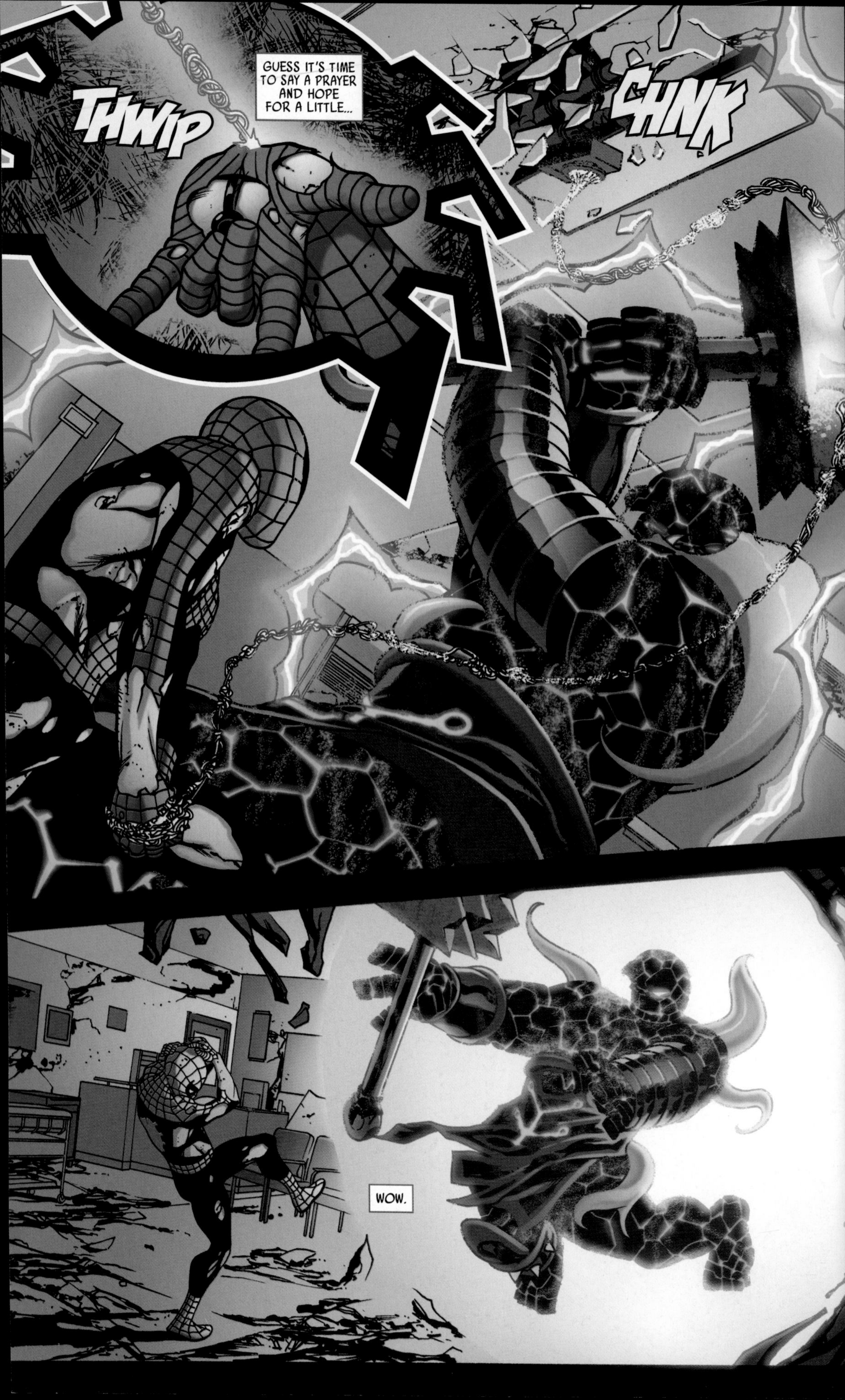
THWIP
GUESS IT'S TIME TO SAY A PRAYER AND HOPE FOR A LITTLE...
CHNK
WOW.

WHATEVER'S HAPPENING, NO MATTER HOW MUCH OF A GRIP IT'S GOT ON HIM, BEN GRIMM IS STILL IN THERE.

PLEASE LET HIM BE IN THERE.

PLEASE BEN...JUST FOR A SECOND...

HRR... HURRR...

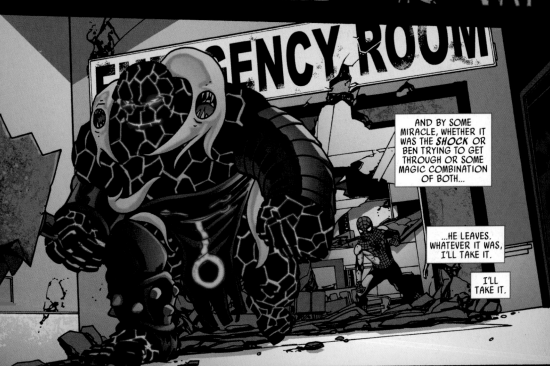

AND BY SOME MIRACLE, WHETHER IT WAS THE *SHOCK* OR BEN TRYING TO GET THROUGH OR SOME MAGIC COMBINATION OF BOTH...

...HE LEAVES. WHATEVER IT WAS, I'LL TAKE IT.

I'LL TAKE IT.

SPIDER-MAN... YOU DID IT. YOU DID IT...

YOU SAVED US.

...WHAT? THE FLOOR'S IN TROUBLE?

FLOOR... IN TROUBLE. MUST RESCUE...

THUD!

OH.

Hour Forty-Eight Of The Fear

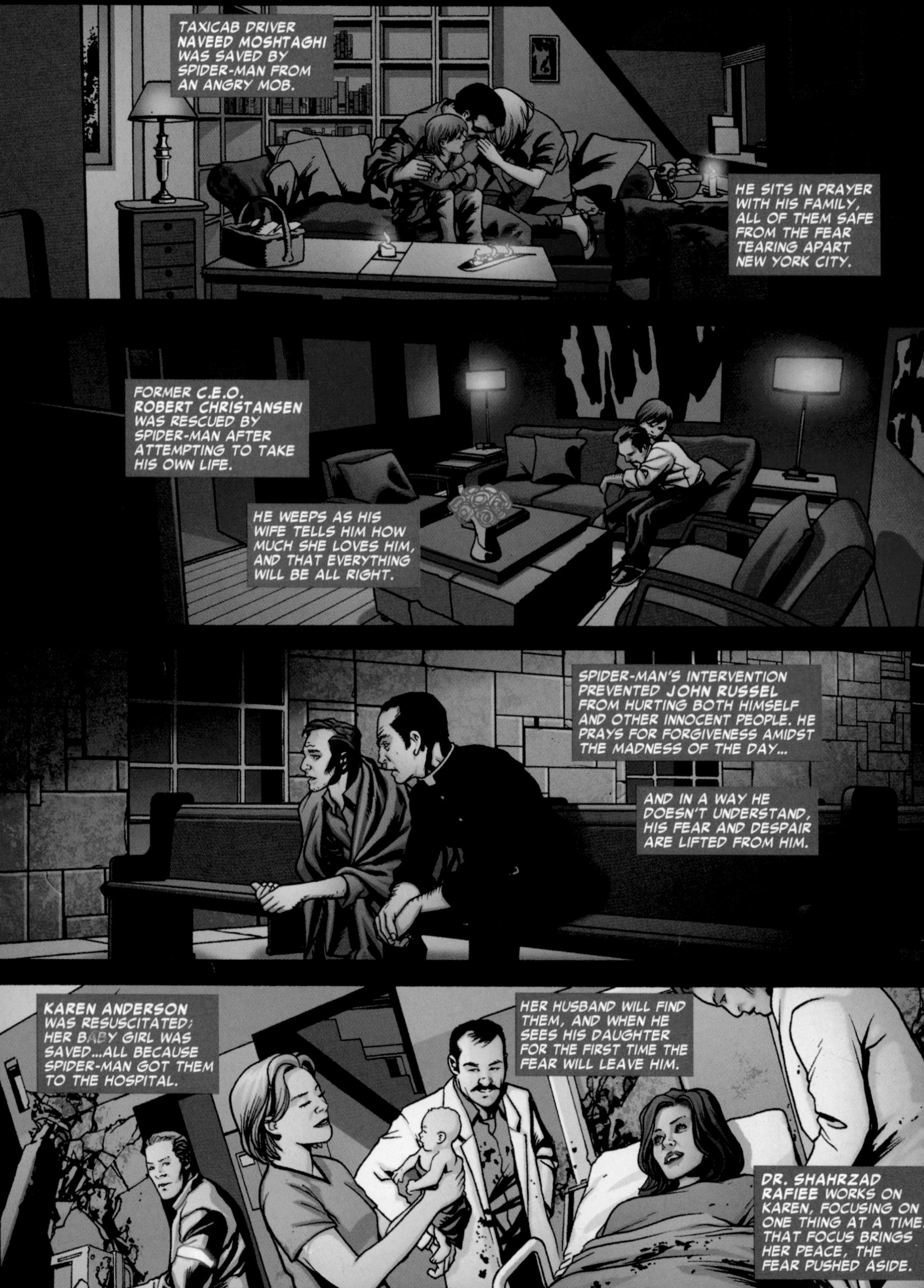
TAXICAB DRIVER NAVEED MOSHTAGHI WAS SAVED BY SPIDER-MAN FROM AN ANGRY MOB.
HE SITS IN PRAYER WITH HIS FAMILY, ALL OF THEM SAFE FROM THE FEAR TEARING APART NEW YORK CITY.
FORMER C.E.O. ROBERT CHRISTANSEN WAS RESCUED BY SPIDER-MAN AFTER ATTEMPTING TO TAKE HIS OWN LIFE.
HE WEEPS AS HIS WIFE TELLS HIM HOW MUCH SHE LOVES HIM, AND THAT EVERYTHING WILL BE ALL RIGHT.
SPIDER-MAN'S INTERVENTION PREVENTED JOHN RUSSEL FROM HURTING BOTH HIMSELF AND OTHER INNOCENT PEOPLE. HE PRAYS FOR FORGIVENESS AMIDST THE MADNESS OF THE DAY...
AND IN A WAY HE DOESN'T UNDERSTAND, HIS FEAR AND DESPAIR ARE LIFTED FROM HIM.
KAREN ANDERSON WAS RESUSCITATED; HER BABY GIRL WAS SAVED...ALL BECAUSE SPIDER-MAN GOT THEM TO THE HOSPITAL.
HER HUSBAND WILL FIND THEM, AND WHEN HE SEES HIS DAUGHTER FOR THE FIRST TIME THE FEAR WILL LEAVE HIM.
DR. SHAHRZAD RAFIEE WORKS ON KAREN, FOCUSING ON ONE THING AT A TIME. THAT FOCUS BRINGS HER PEACE, THE FEAR PUSHED ASIDE.

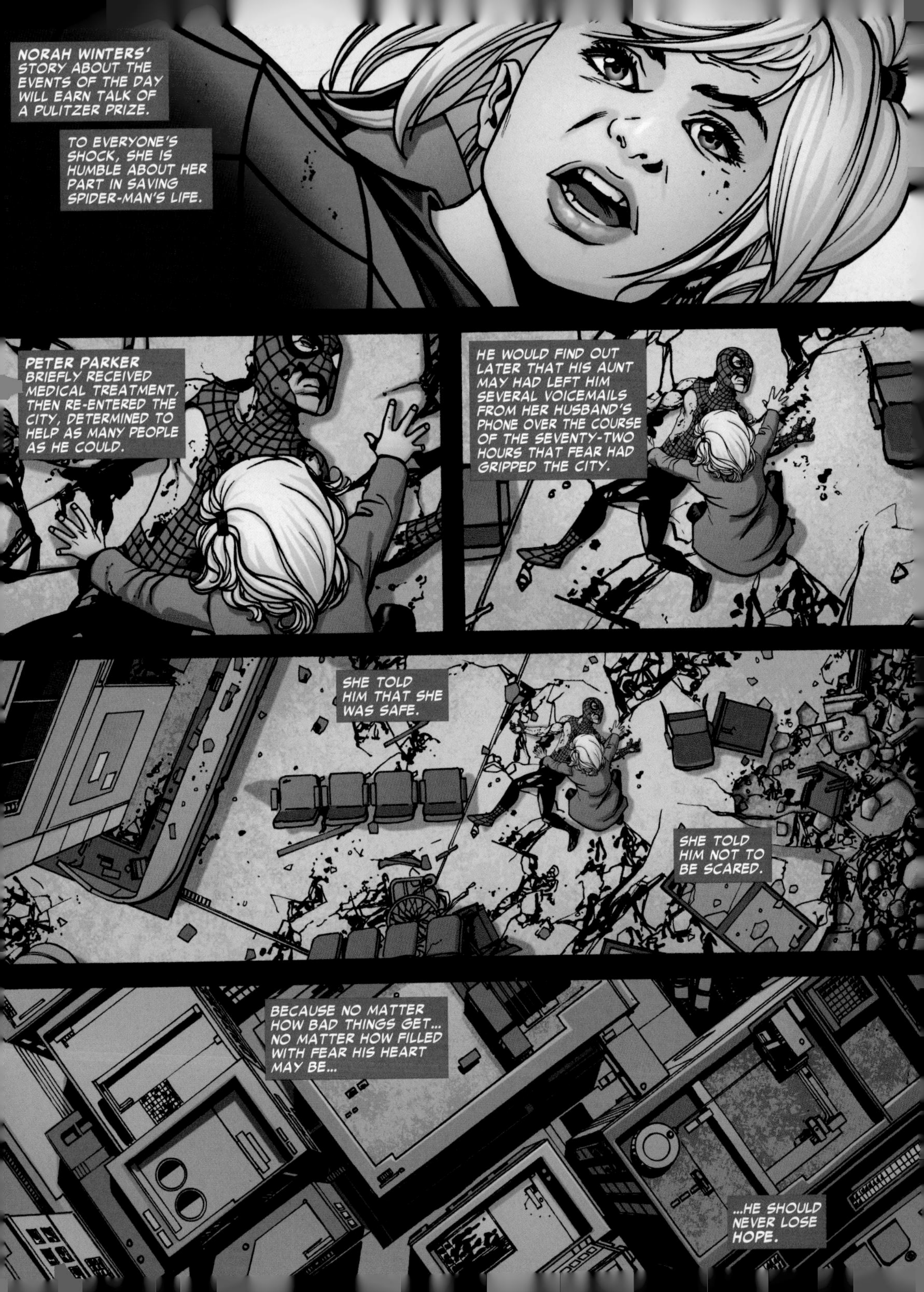
NORAH WINTERS' STORY ABOUT THE EVENTS OF THE DAY WILL EARN TALK OF A PULITZER PRIZE.
TO EVERYONE'S SHOCK, SHE IS HUMBLE ABOUT HER PART IN SAVING SPIDER-MAN'S LIFE.
PETER PARKER BRIEFLY RECEIVED MEDICAL TREATMENT, THEN RE-ENTERED THE CITY, DETERMINED TO HELP AS MANY PEOPLE AS HE COULD.
HE WOULD FIND OUT LATER THAT HIS AUNT MAY HAD LEFT HIM SEVERAL VOICEMAILS FROM HER HUSBAND'S PHONE OVER THE COURSE OF THE SEVENTY-TWO HOURS THAT FEAR HAD GRIPPED THE CITY.
SHE TOLD HIM THAT SHE WAS SAFE.
SHE TOLD HIM NOT TO BE SCARED.
BECAUSE NO MATTER HOW BAD THINGS GET... NO MATTER HOW FILLED WITH FEAR HIS HEART MAY BE...
...HE SHOULD NEVER LOSE HOPE.

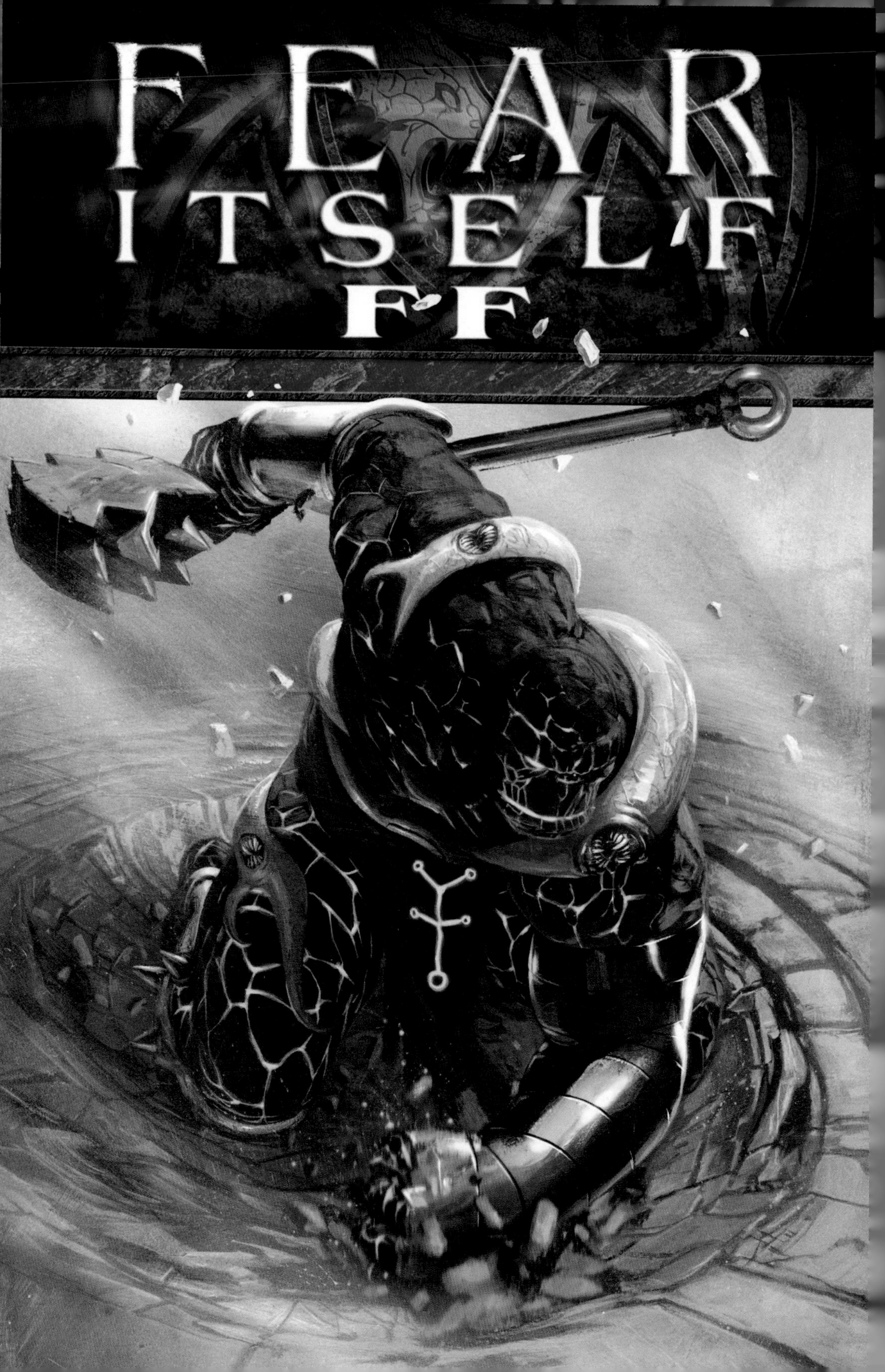
FEAR ITSELF
FF

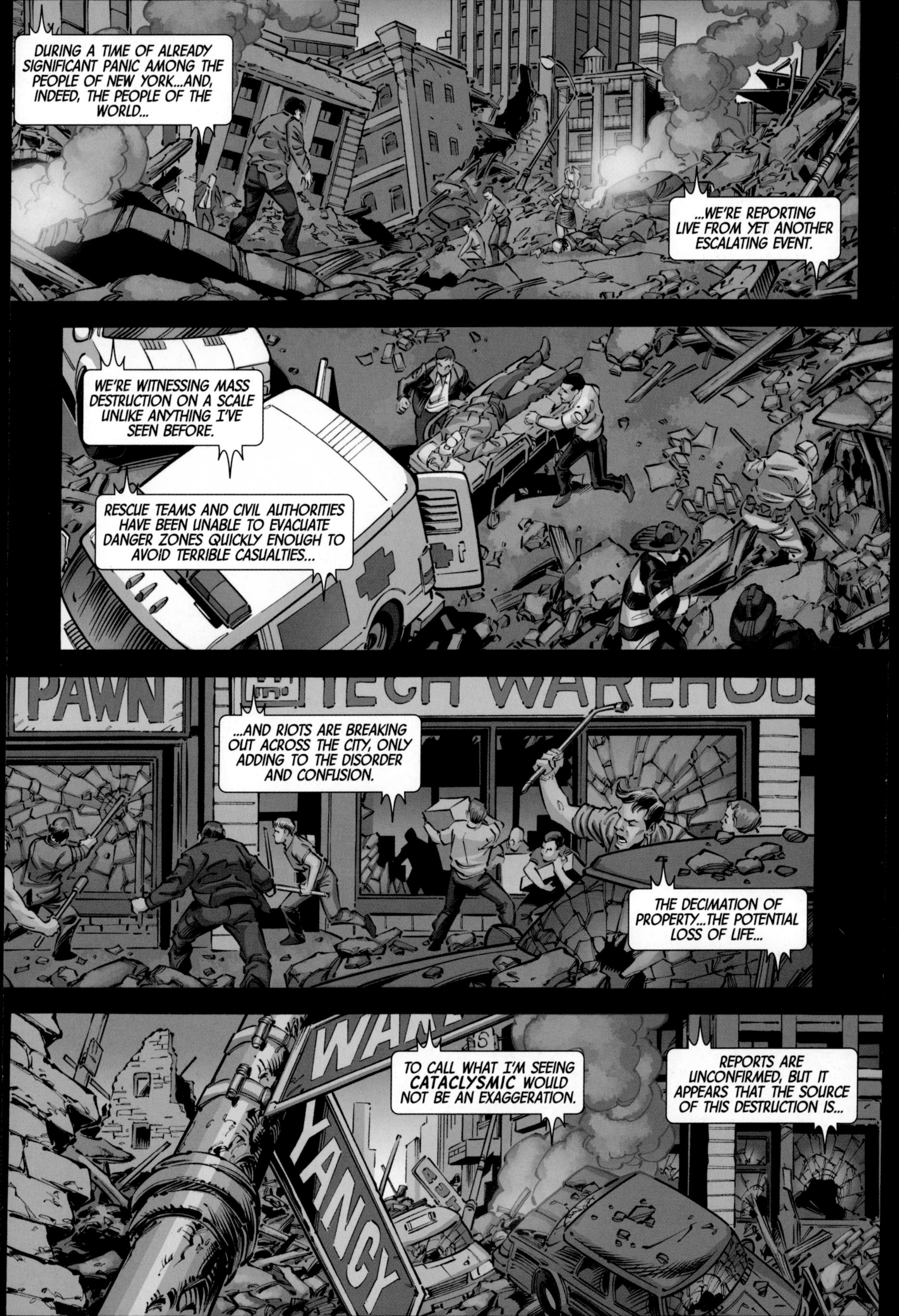
DURING A TIME OF ALREADY SIGNIFICANT PANIC AMONG THE PEOPLE OF NEW YORK...AND, INDEED, THE PEOPLE OF THE WORLD...
...WE'RE REPORTING LIVE FROM YET ANOTHER ESCALATING EVENT.
WE'RE WITNESSING MASS DESTRUCTION ON A SCALE UNLIKE ANYTHING I'VE SEEN BEFORE.
RESCUE TEAMS AND CIVIL AUTHORITIES HAVE BEEN UNABLE TO EVACUATE DANGER ZONES QUICKLY ENOUGH TO AVOID TERRIBLE CASUALTIES...
PAWN
...AND RIOTS ARE BREAKING OUT ACROSS THE CITY, ONLY ADDING TO THE DISORDER AND CONFUSION.
THE DECIMATION OF PROPERTY...THE POTENTIAL LOSS OF LIFE...
TO CALL WHAT I'M SEEING **CATACLYSMIC** WOULD NOT BE AN EXAGGERATION.
REPORTS ARE UNCONFIRMED, BUT IT APPEARS THAT THE SOURCE OF THIS DESTRUCTION IS...

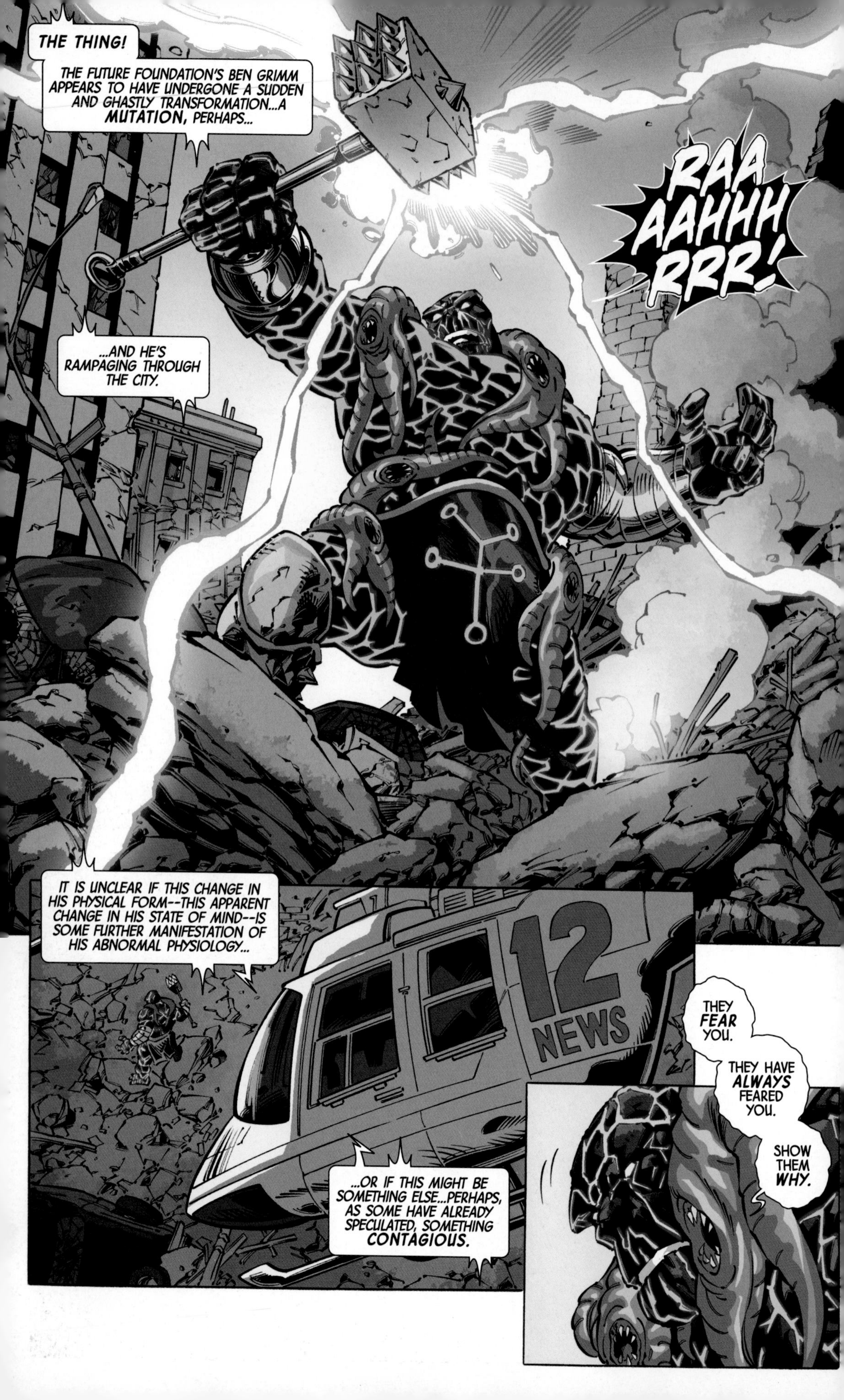
THE THING!
THE FUTURE FOUNDATION'S BEN GRIMM APPEARS TO HAVE UNDERGONE A SUDDEN AND GHASTLY TRANSFORMATION...A MUTATION, PERHAPS...
RAAAAHHHRRR!
...AND HE'S RAMPAGING THROUGH THE CITY.
IT IS UNCLEAR IF THIS CHANGE IN HIS PHYSICAL FORM--THIS APPARENT CHANGE IN HIS STATE OF MIND--IS SOME FURTHER MANIFESTATION OF HIS ABNORMAL PHYSIOLOGY...
12 NEWS
...OR IF THIS MIGHT BE SOMETHING ELSE...PERHAPS, AS SOME HAVE ALREADY SPECULATED, SOMETHING CONTAGIOUS.
THEY FEAR YOU.
THEY HAVE ALWAYS FEARED YOU.
SHOW THEM WHY.

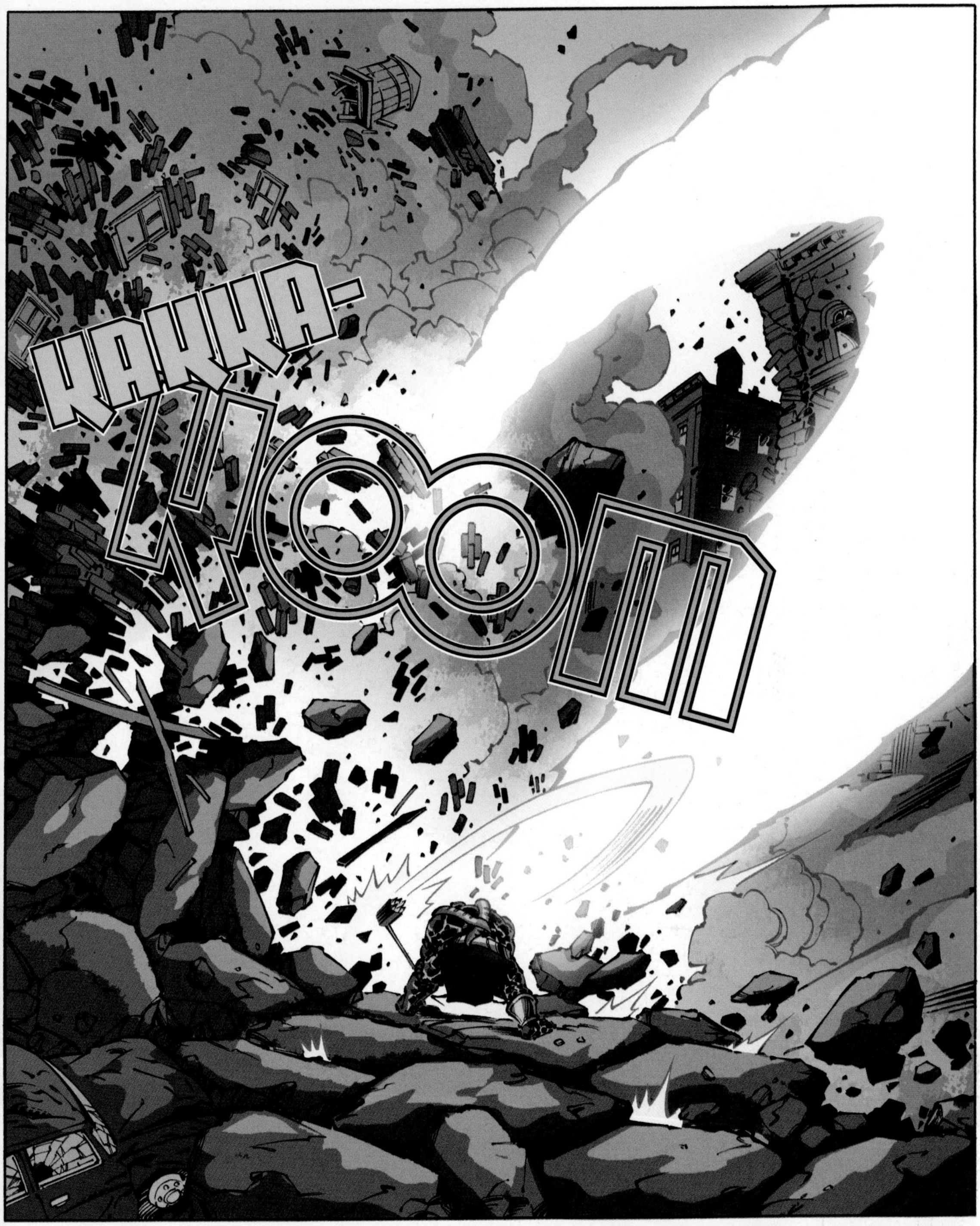
KAKKA-
KOOM

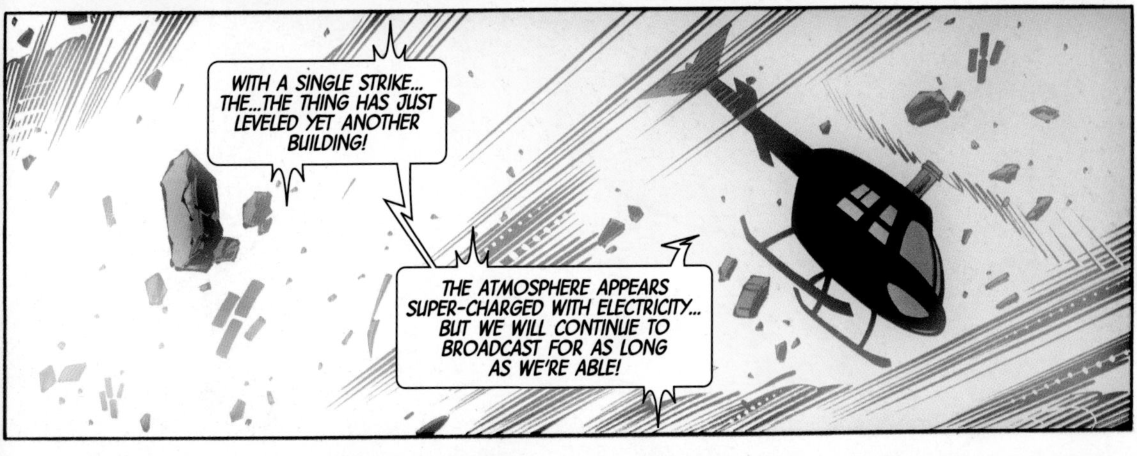
WITH A SINGLE STRIKE... THE...THE THING HAS JUST LEVELED YET ANOTHER BUILDING!
THE ATMOSPHERE APPEARS SUPER-CHARGED WITH ELECTRICITY... BUT WE WILL CONTINUE TO BROADCAST FOR AS LONG AS WE'RE ABLE!

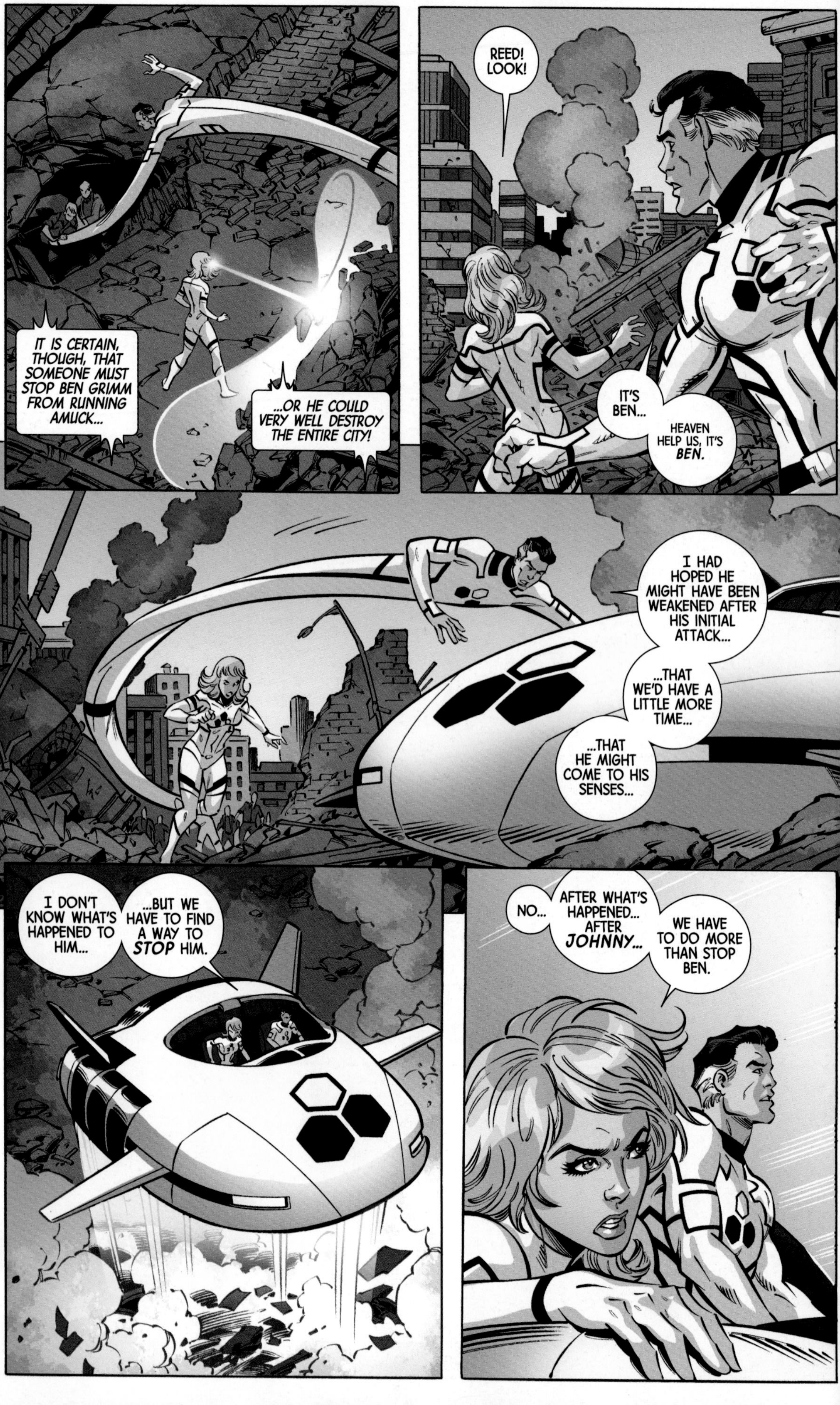
IT IS CERTAIN, THOUGH, THAT SOMEONE MUST STOP BEN GRIMM FROM RUNNING AMUCK...
...OR HE COULD VERY WELL DESTROY THE ENTIRE CITY!
REED! LOOK!
IT'S BEN...
HEAVEN HELP US, IT'S BEN.
I HAD HOPED HE MIGHT HAVE BEEN WEAKENED AFTER HIS INITIAL ATTACK...
...THAT WE'D HAVE A LITTLE MORE TIME...
...THAT HE MIGHT COME TO HIS SENSES...
I DON'T KNOW WHAT'S HAPPENED TO HIM...
...BUT WE HAVE TO FIND A WAY TO STOP HIM.
NO...
AFTER WHAT'S HAPPENED... AFTER JOHNNY...
WE HAVE TO DO MORE THAN STOP BEN.

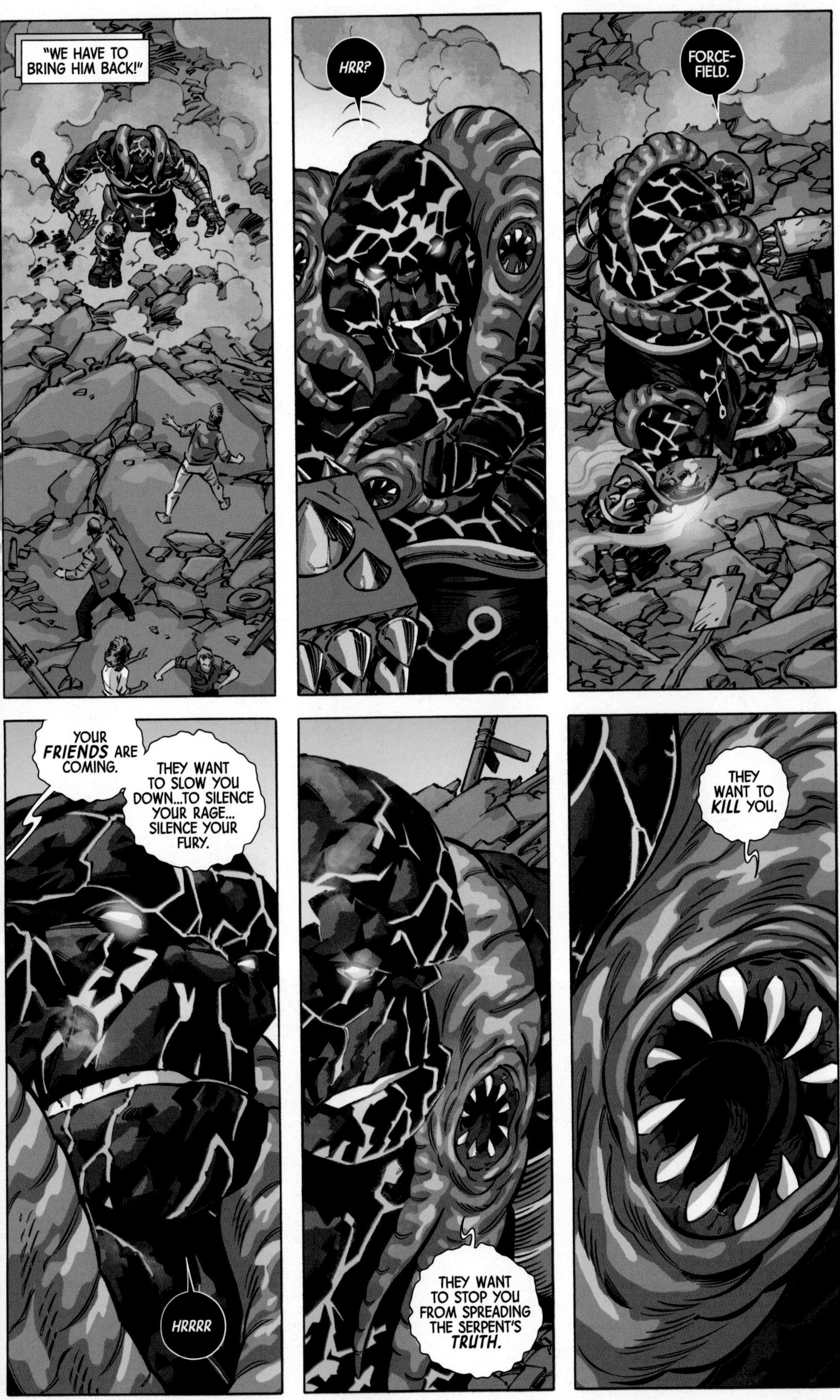
"WE HAVE TO BRING HIM BACK!"
HRR?
FORCE-FIELD.
YOUR FRIENDS ARE COMING.
THEY WANT TO SLOW YOU DOWN...TO SILENCE YOUR RAGE... SILENCE YOUR FURY.
HRRRR
THEY WANT TO STOP YOU FROM SPREADING THE SERPENT'S TRUTH.
THEY WANT TO KILL YOU.

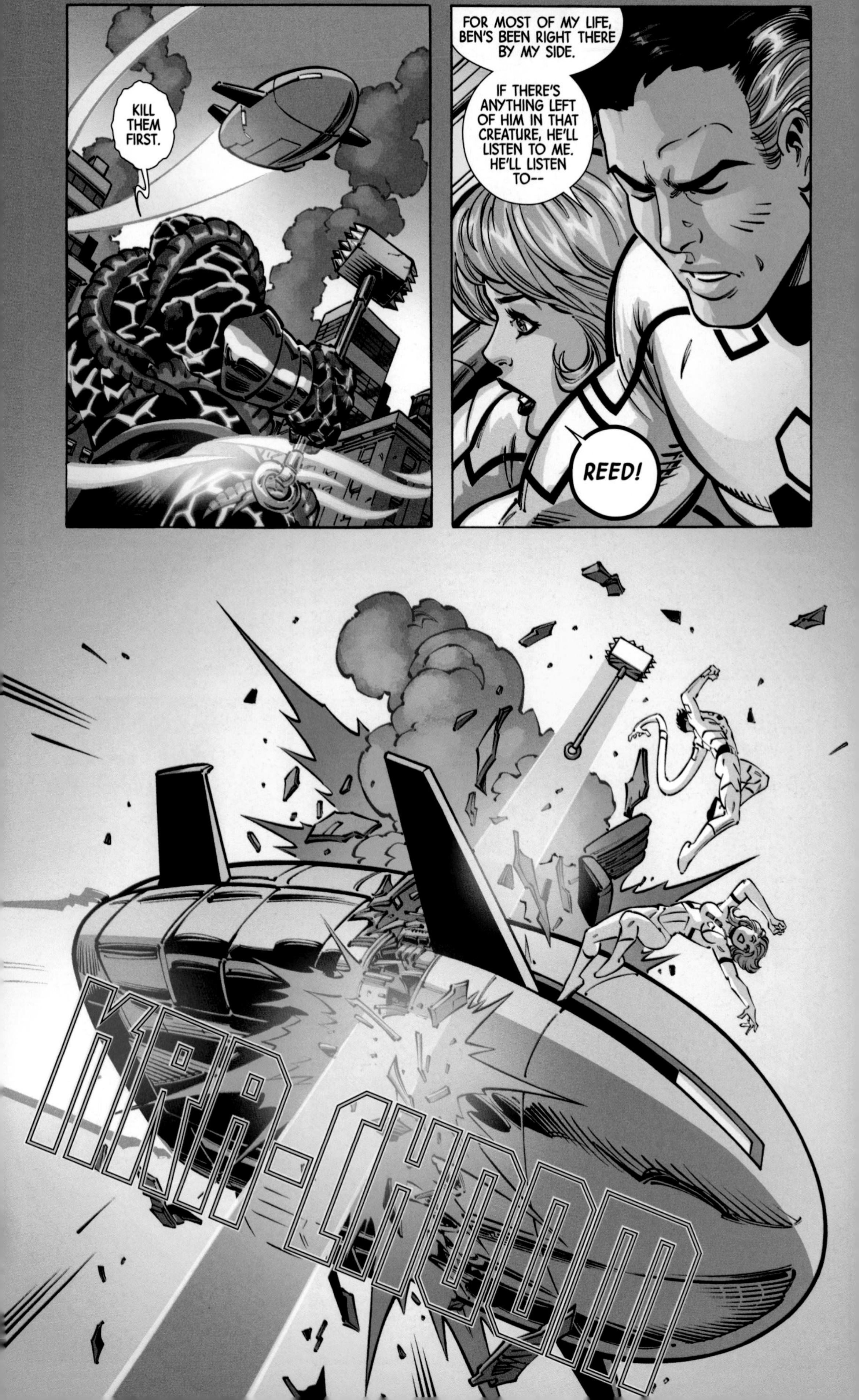
KILL THEM FIRST.
FOR MOST OF MY LIFE, BEN'S BEEN RIGHT THERE BY MY SIDE.
IF THERE'S ANYTHING LEFT OF HIM IN THAT CREATURE, HE'LL LISTEN TO ME. HE'LL LISTEN TO--
REED!
KRA-CHOOM

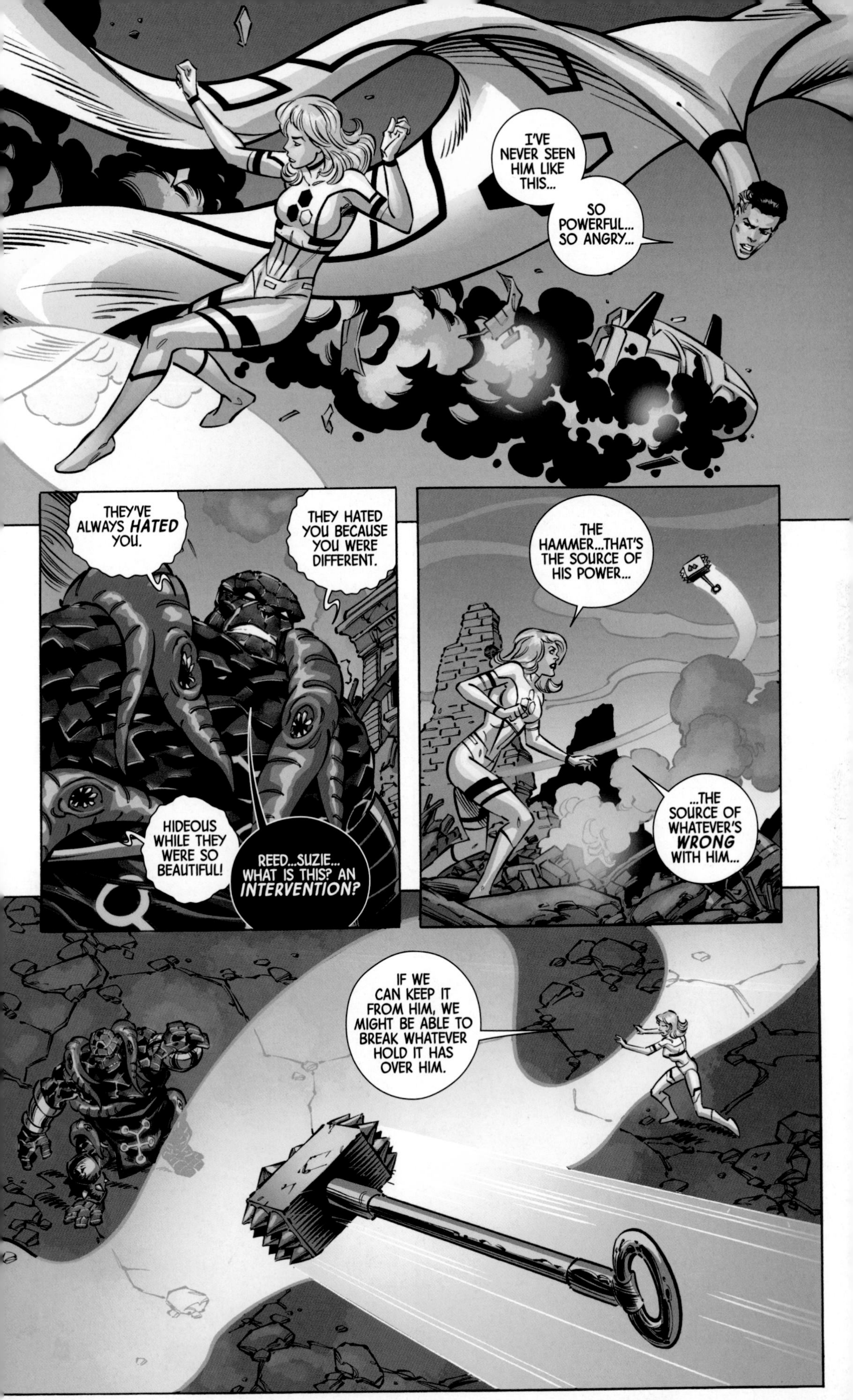

I'VE NEVER SEEN HIM LIKE THIS...
SO POWERFUL... SO ANGRY...
THEY'VE ALWAYS *HATED* YOU.
THEY HATED YOU BECAUSE YOU WERE DIFFERENT.
HIDEOUS WHILE THEY WERE SO BEAUTIFUL!
REED...SUZIE... WHAT IS THIS? AN *INTERVENTION?*
THE HAMMER...THAT'S THE SOURCE OF HIS POWER...
...THE SOURCE OF WHATEVER'S *WRONG* WITH HIM...
IF WE CAN KEEP IT FROM HIM, WE MIGHT BE ABLE TO BREAK WHATEVER HOLD IT HAS OVER HIM.

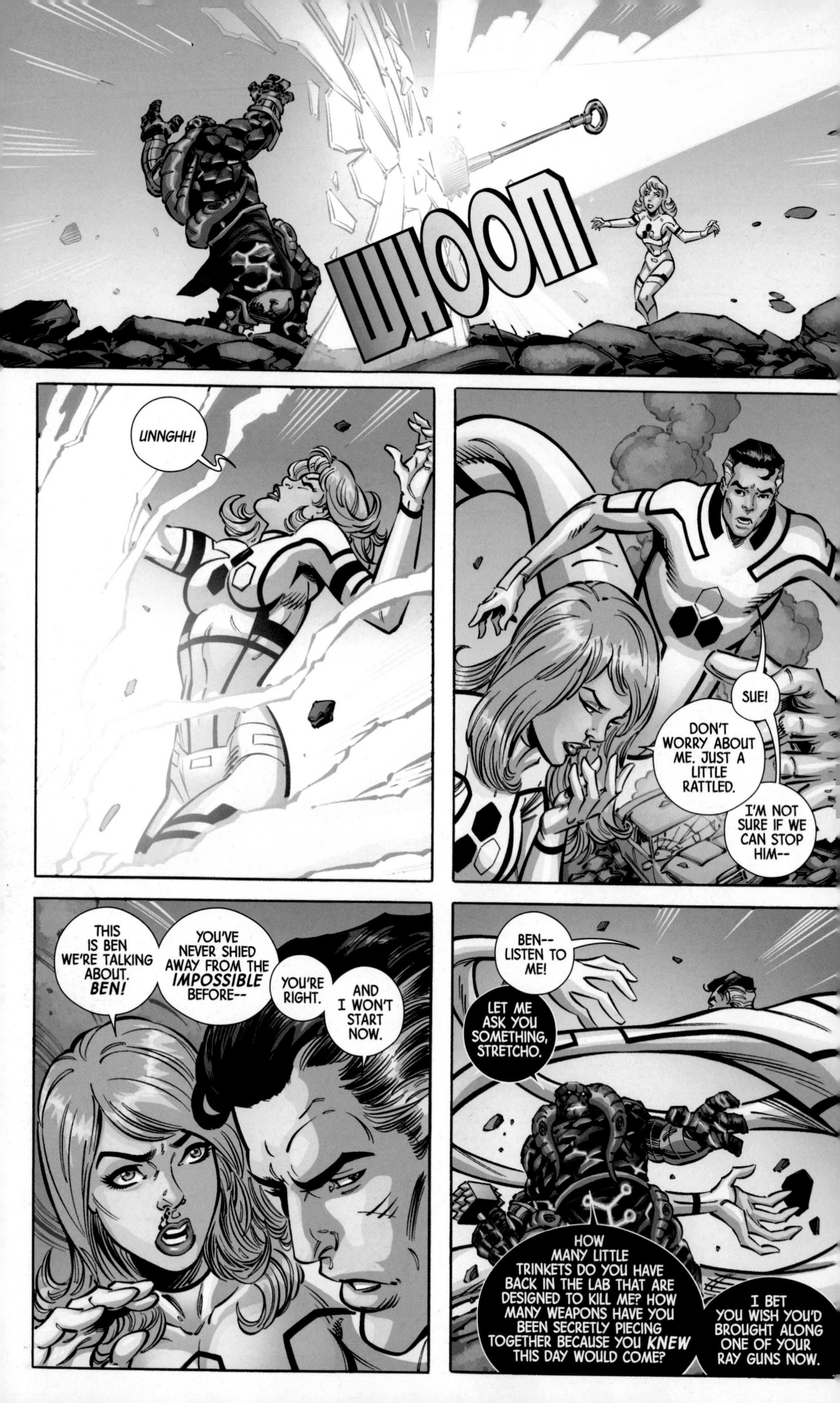
WHOOM
UNNGHH!
SUE!
DON'T WORRY ABOUT ME. JUST A LITTLE RATTLED.
I'M NOT SURE IF WE CAN STOP HIM--
THIS IS BEN WE'RE TALKING ABOUT. BEN!
YOU'VE NEVER SHIED AWAY FROM THE IMPOSSIBLE BEFORE--
YOU'RE RIGHT.
AND I WON'T START NOW.
BEN-- LISTEN TO ME!
LET ME ASK YOU SOMETHING, STRETCHO.
HOW MANY LITTLE TRINKETS DO YOU HAVE BACK IN THE LAB THAT ARE DESIGNED TO KILL ME? HOW MANY WEAPONS HAVE YOU BEEN SECRETLY PIECING TOGETHER BECAUSE YOU KNEW THIS DAY WOULD COME?
I BET YOU WISH YOU'D BROUGHT ALONG ONE OF YOUR RAY GUNS NOW.

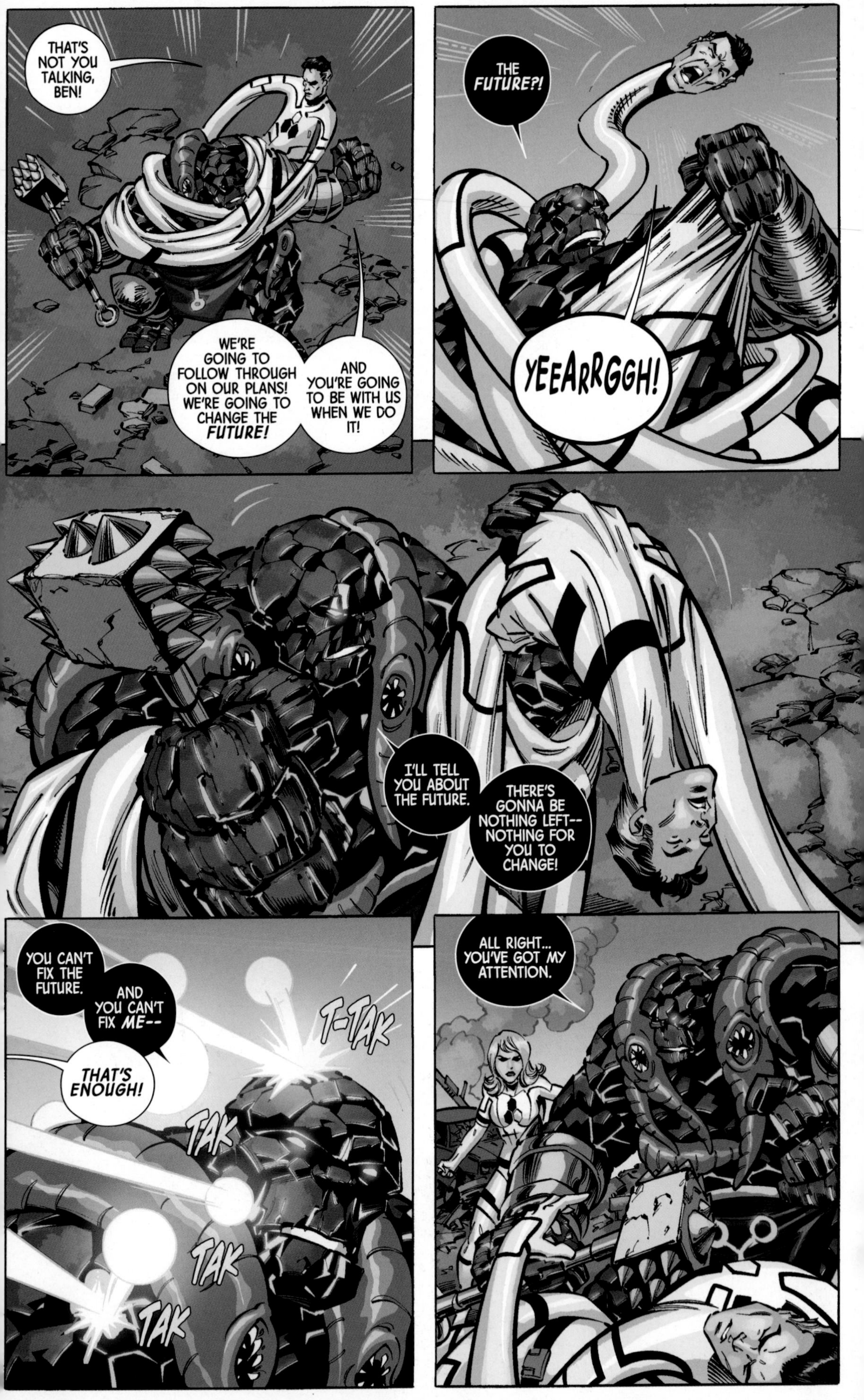
THAT'S NOT YOU TALKING, BEN!
WE'RE GOING TO FOLLOW THROUGH ON OUR PLANS! WE'RE GOING TO CHANGE THE *FUTURE!*
AND YOU'RE GOING TO BE WITH US WHEN WE DO IT!
THE *FUTURE?!*
YEEARRGGH!
I'LL TELL YOU ABOUT THE FUTURE.
THERE'S GONNA BE NOTHING LEFT-- NOTHING FOR YOU TO CHANGE!
YOU CAN'T FIX THE FUTURE.
AND YOU CAN'T FIX *ME*--
THAT'S ENOUGH!
T-TAK
TAK
TAK
TAK
ALL RIGHT... YOU'VE GOT MY ATTENTION.

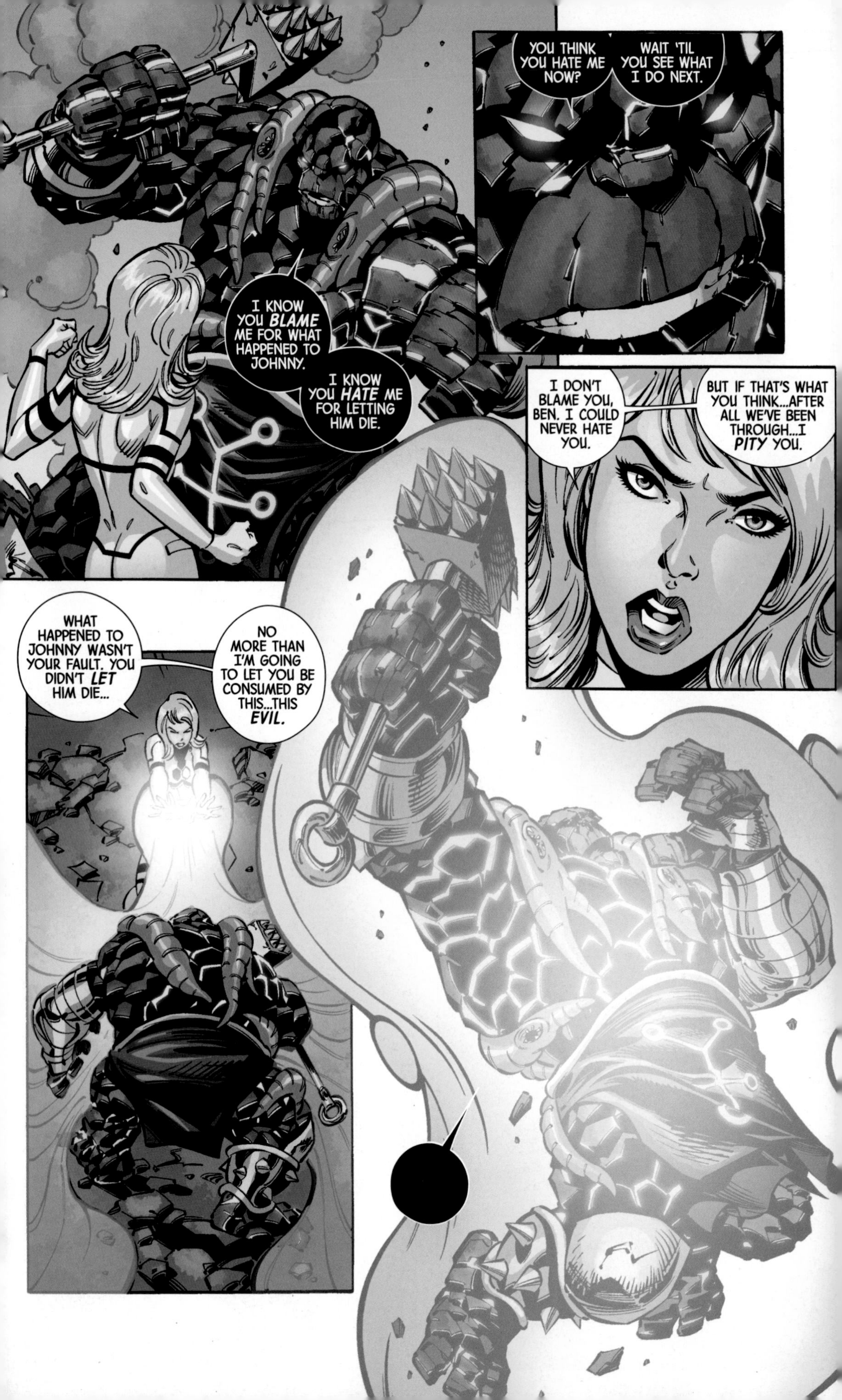
YOU THINK YOU HATE ME NOW?
WAIT 'TIL YOU SEE WHAT I DO NEXT.
I KNOW YOU *BLAME* ME FOR WHAT HAPPENED TO JOHNNY.
I KNOW YOU *HATE* ME FOR LETTING HIM DIE.
I DON'T BLAME YOU, BEN. I COULD NEVER HATE YOU.
BUT IF THAT'S WHAT YOU THINK...AFTER ALL WE'VE BEEN THROUGH...I *PITY* YOU.
WHAT HAPPENED TO JOHNNY WASN'T YOUR FAULT. YOU DIDN'T *LET* HIM DIE...
NO MORE THAN I'M GOING TO LET YOU BE CONSUMED BY THIS...THIS *EVIL.*

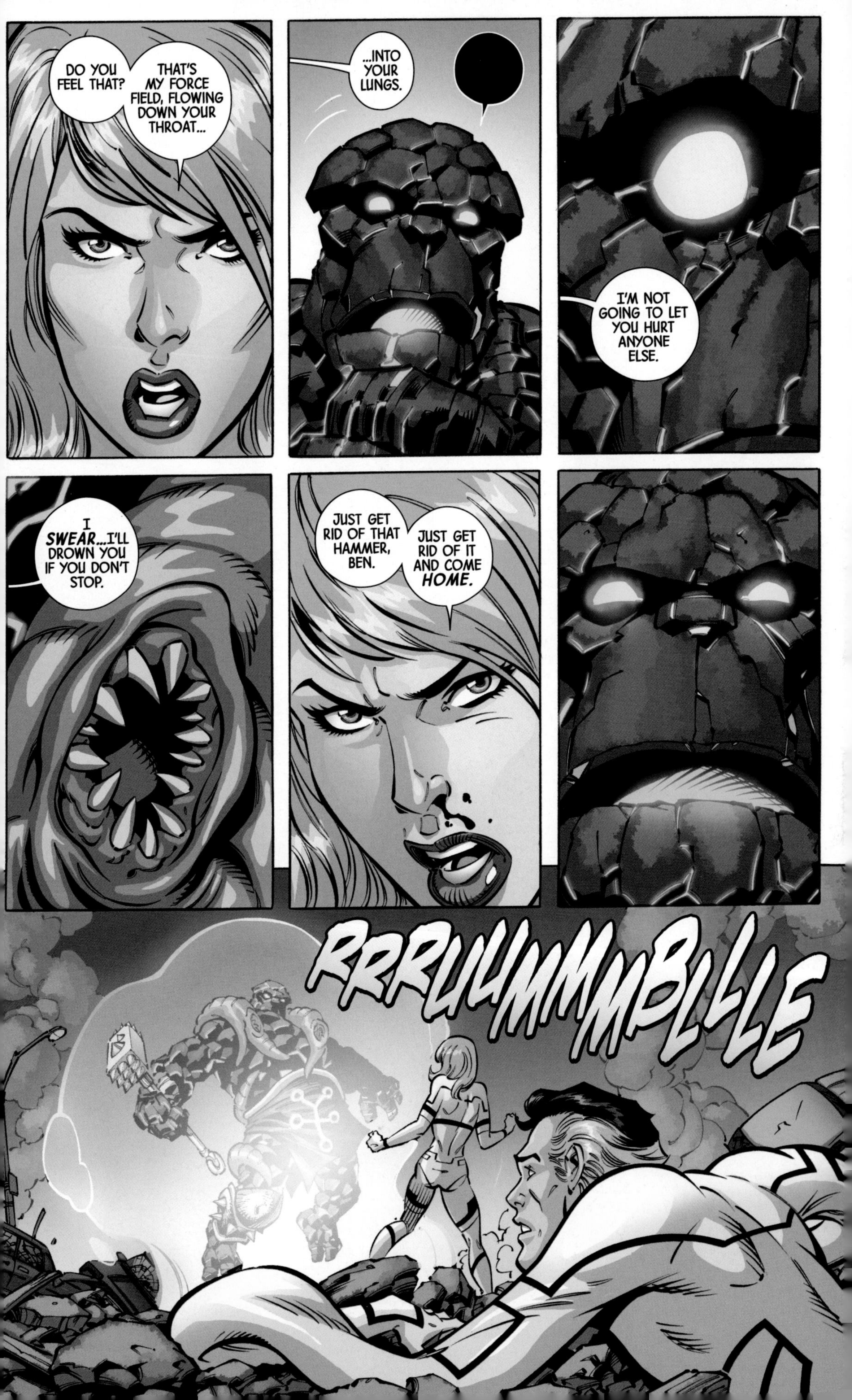
DO YOU FEEL THAT?
THAT'S MY FORCE FIELD, FLOWING DOWN YOUR THROAT...
...INTO YOUR LUNGS.
I'M NOT GOING TO LET YOU HURT ANYONE ELSE.
I SWEAR...I'LL DROWN YOU IF YOU DON'T STOP.
JUST GET RID OF THAT HAMMER, BEN.
JUST GET RID OF IT AND COME HOME.
RRRUUMMMBLLLE

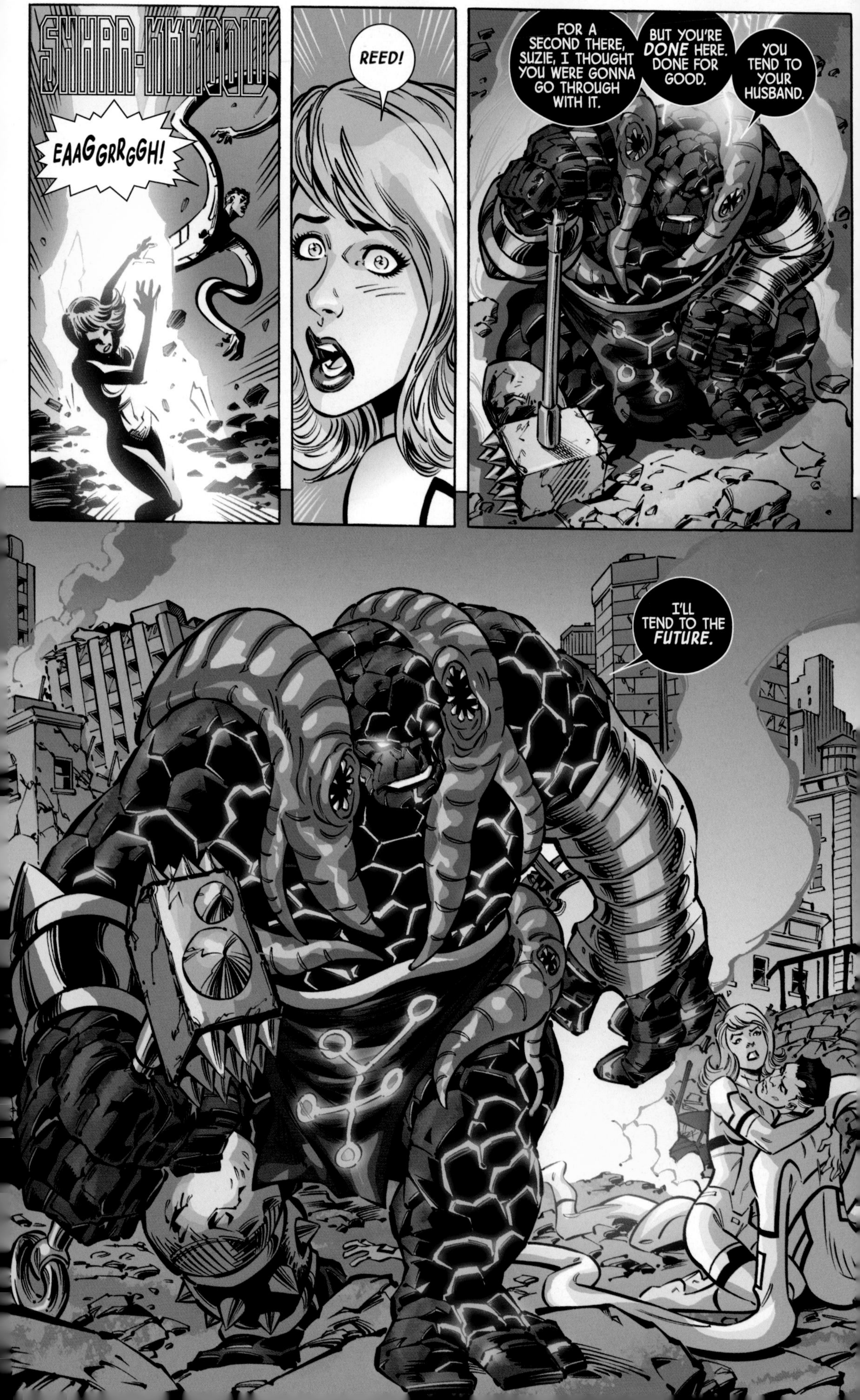
SHHRA-KKKOOW
EAAGGRRGGH!
REED!
FOR A SECOND THERE, SUZIE, I THOUGHT YOU WERE GONNA GO THROUGH WITH IT.
BUT YOU'RE DONE HERE. DONE FOR GOOD.
YOU TEND TO YOUR HUSBAND.
I'LL TEND TO THE FUTURE.

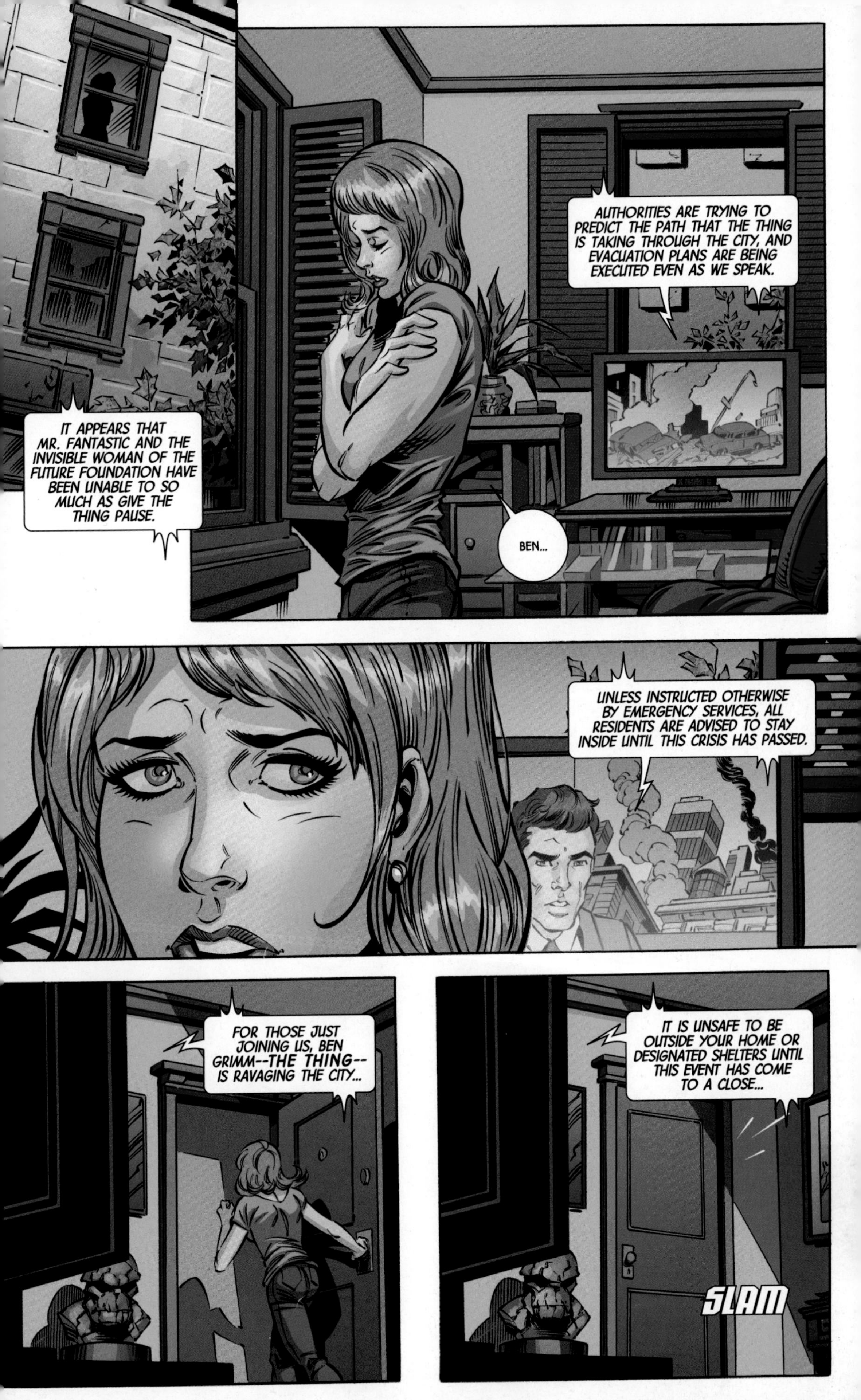
AUTHORITIES ARE TRYING TO PREDICT THE PATH THAT THE THING IS TAKING THROUGH THE CITY, AND EVACUATION PLANS ARE BEING EXECUTED EVEN AS WE SPEAK.
IT APPEARS THAT MR. FANTASTIC AND THE INVISIBLE WOMAN OF THE FUTURE FOUNDATION HAVE BEEN UNABLE TO SO MUCH AS GIVE THE THING PAUSE.
BEN...
UNLESS INSTRUCTED OTHERWISE BY EMERGENCY SERVICES, ALL RESIDENTS ARE ADVISED TO STAY INSIDE UNTIL THIS CRISIS HAS PASSED.
FOR THOSE JUST JOINING US, BEN GRIMM--THE THING--IS RAVAGING THE CITY...
IT IS UNSAFE TO BE OUTSIDE YOUR HOME OR DESIGNATED SHELTERS UNTIL THIS EVENT HAS COME TO A CLOSE...
SLAM

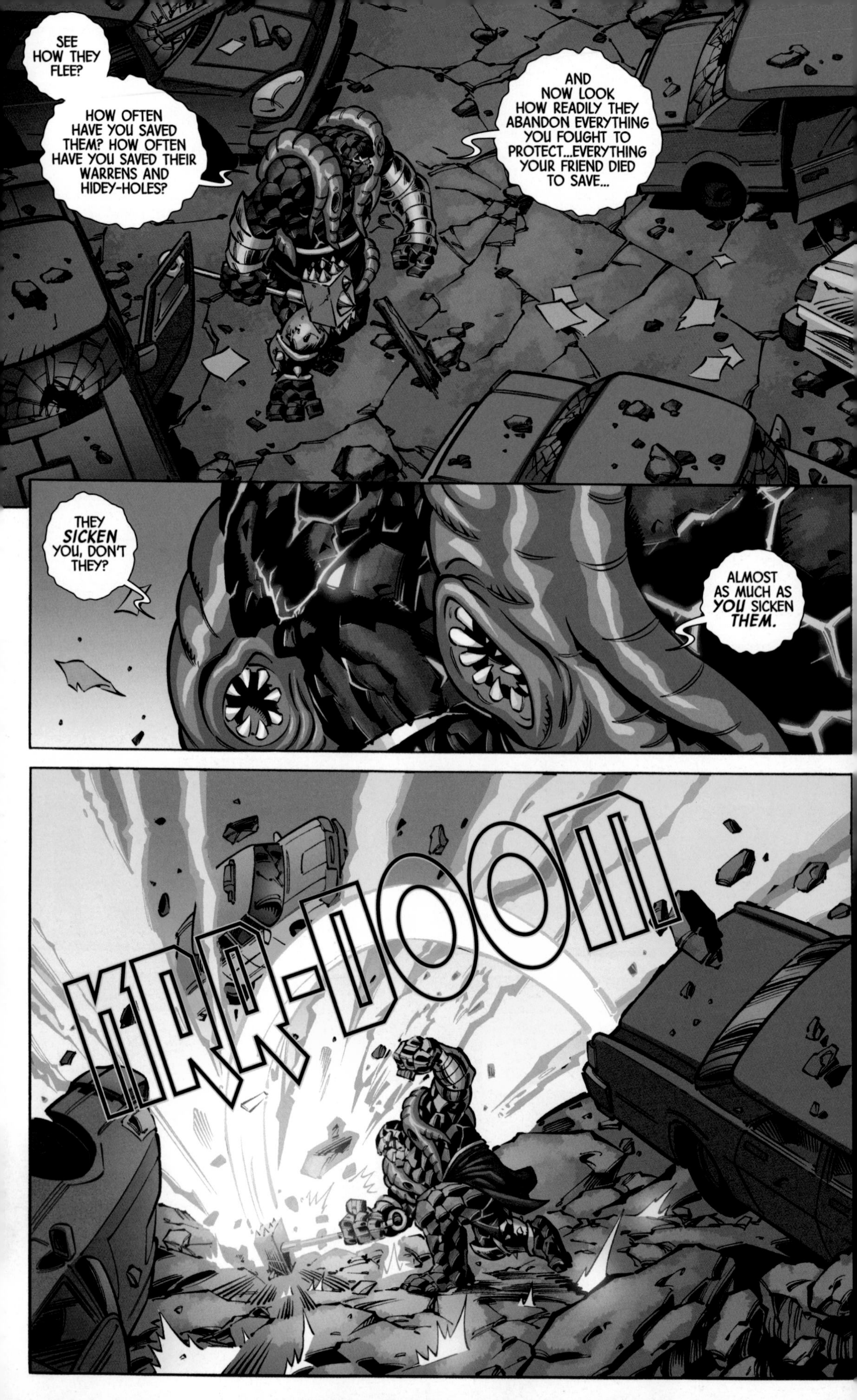
SEE HOW THEY FLEE?
HOW OFTEN HAVE YOU SAVED THEM? HOW OFTEN HAVE YOU SAVED THEIR WARRENS AND HIDEY-HOLES?
AND NOW LOOK HOW READILY THEY ABANDON EVERYTHING YOU FOUGHT TO PROTECT...EVERYTHING YOUR FRIEND DIED TO SAVE...
THEY *SICKEN* YOU, DON'T THEY?
ALMOST AS MUCH AS *YOU* SICKEN *THEM.*
KRA-DOOM

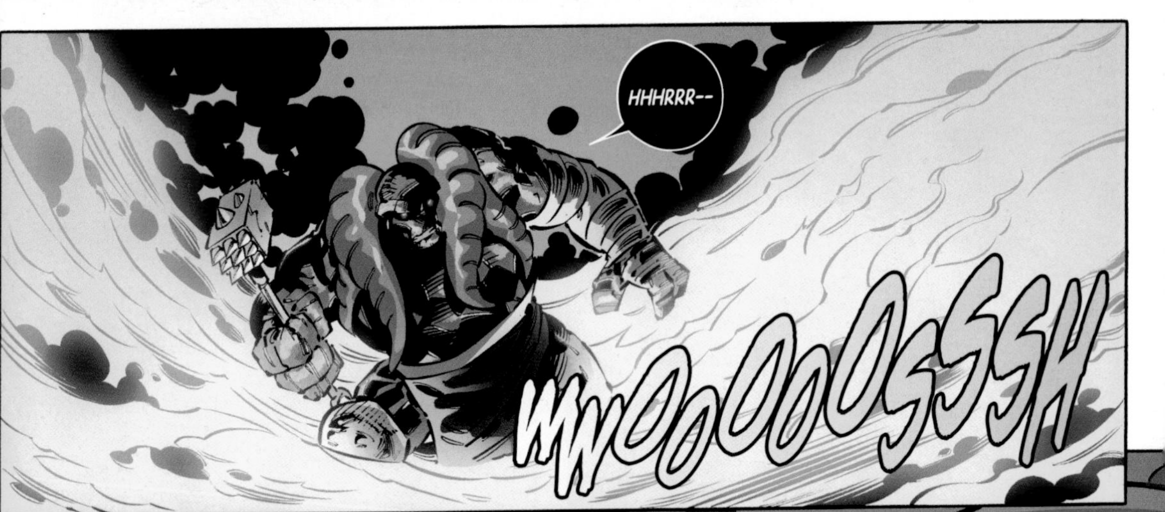
HHHRRR--
WWOOOOOOSSSH

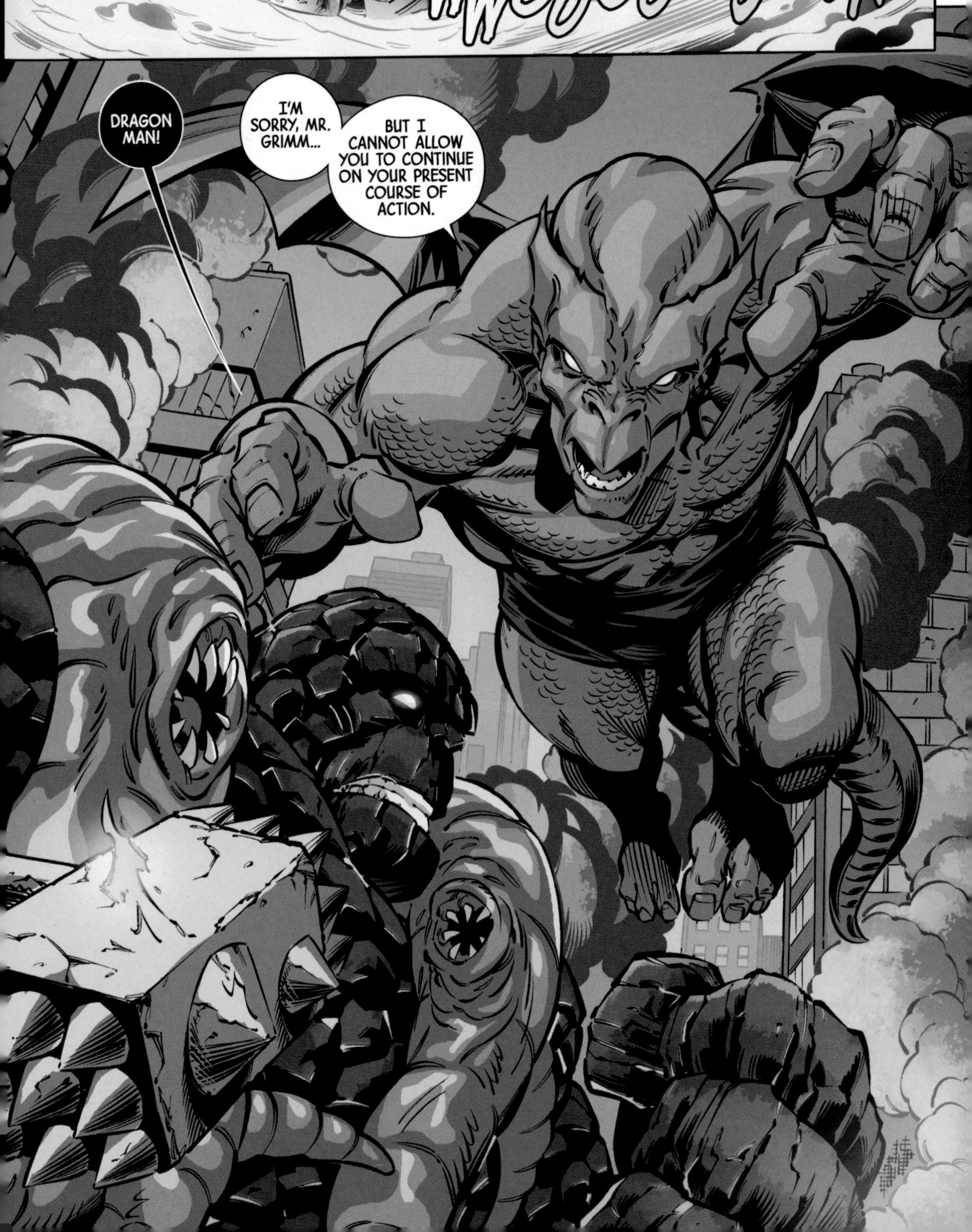
DRAGON MAN!
I'M SORRY, MR. GRIMM...
BUT I CANNOT ALLOW YOU TO CONTINUE ON YOUR PRESENT COURSE OF ACTION.

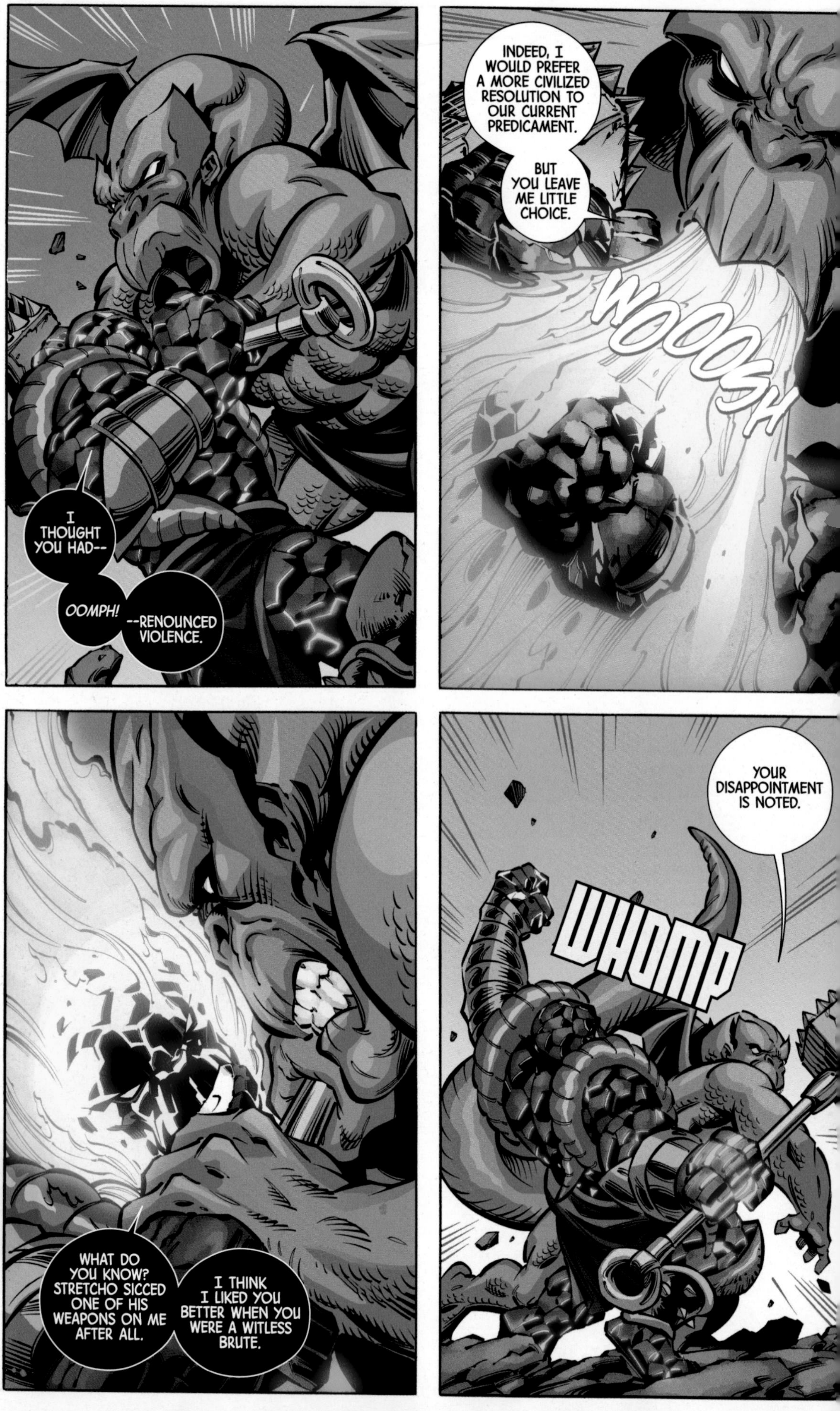

I THOUGHT YOU HAD--
OOMPH!
--RENOUNCED VIOLENCE.
INDEED, I WOULD PREFER A MORE CIVILIZED RESOLUTION TO OUR CURRENT PREDICAMENT.
BUT YOU LEAVE ME LITTLE CHOICE.
WOOOSH
WHAT DO YOU KNOW? STRETCHO SICCED ONE OF HIS WEAPONS ON ME AFTER ALL.
I THINK I LIKED YOU BETTER WHEN YOU WERE A WITLESS BRUTE.
YOUR DISAPPOINTMENT IS NOTED.
WHOMP

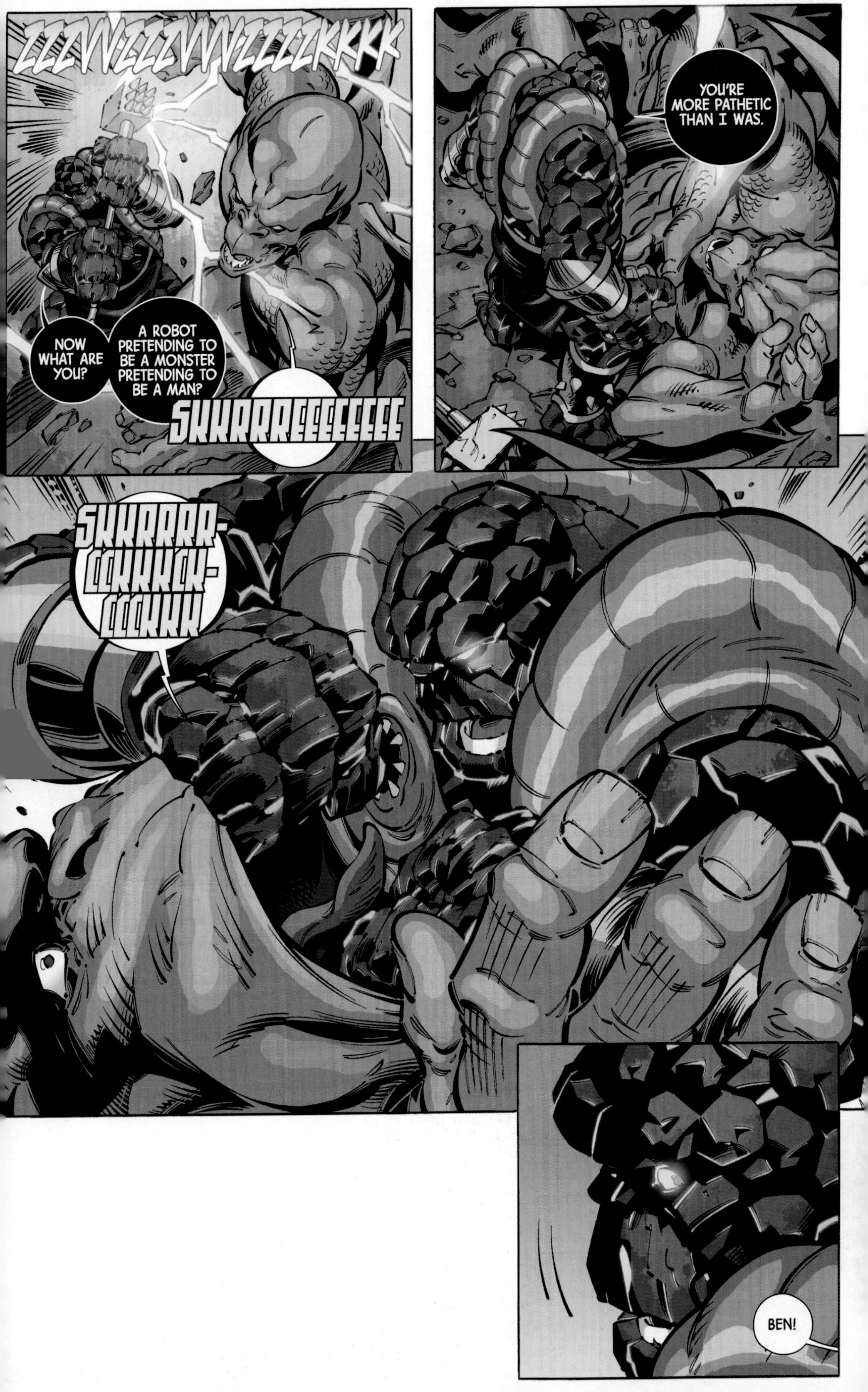
ZZZVVVZZZZVVVVZZZZZKKKK
NOW WHAT ARE YOU?
A ROBOT PRETENDING TO BE A MONSTER PRETENDING TO BE A MAN?
SKRRRREEEEEEEEE
YOU'RE MORE PATHETIC THAN I WAS.
SKRRRRR-CCRRRCK-CCCRRR
BEN!

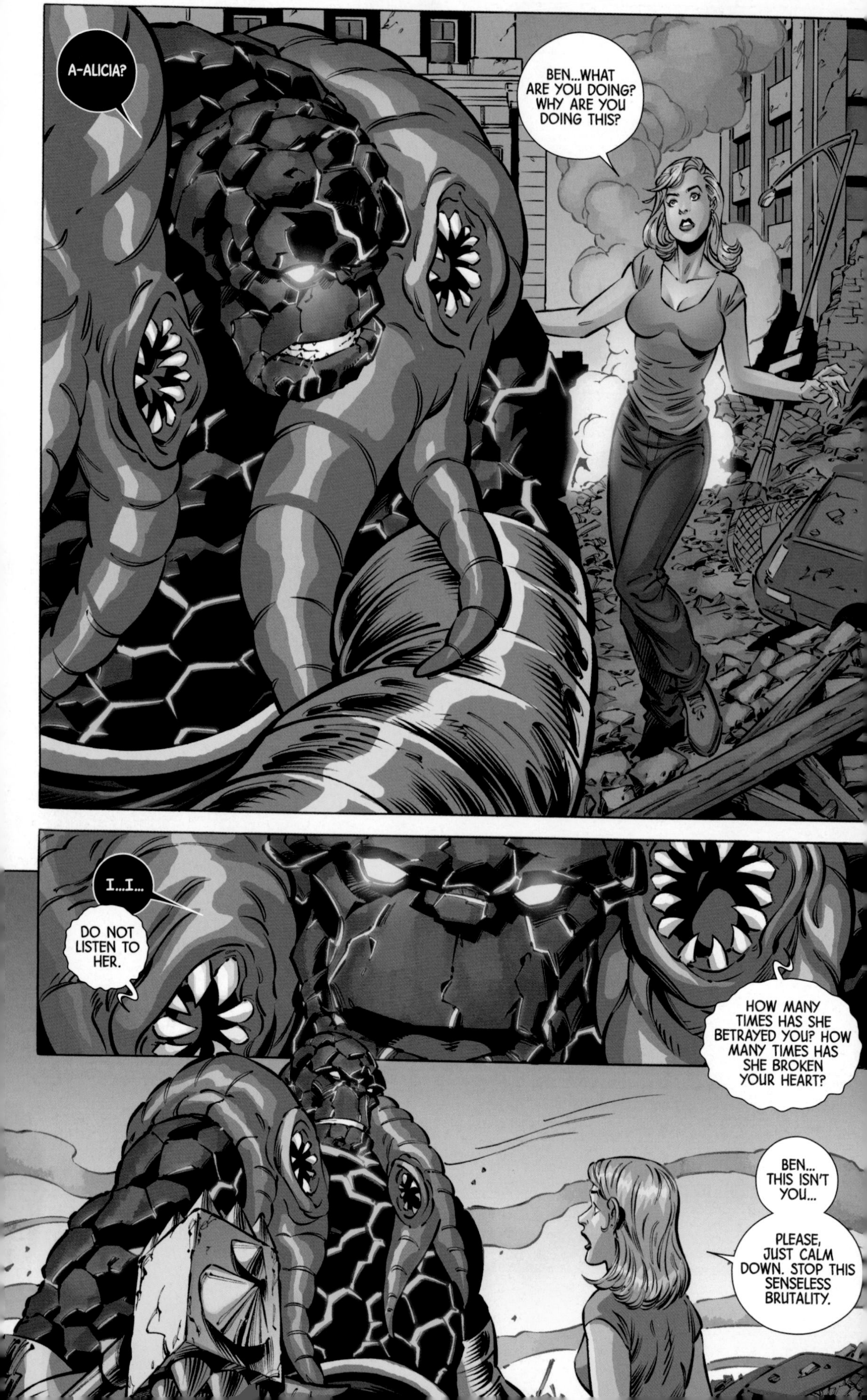
A-ALICIA?
BEN...WHAT ARE YOU DOING? WHY ARE YOU DOING THIS?
I...I...
DO NOT LISTEN TO HER.
HOW MANY TIMES HAS SHE BETRAYED YOU? HOW MANY TIMES HAS SHE BROKEN YOUR HEART?
BEN... THIS ISN'T YOU...
PLEASE, JUST CALM DOWN. STOP THIS SENSELESS BRUTALITY.

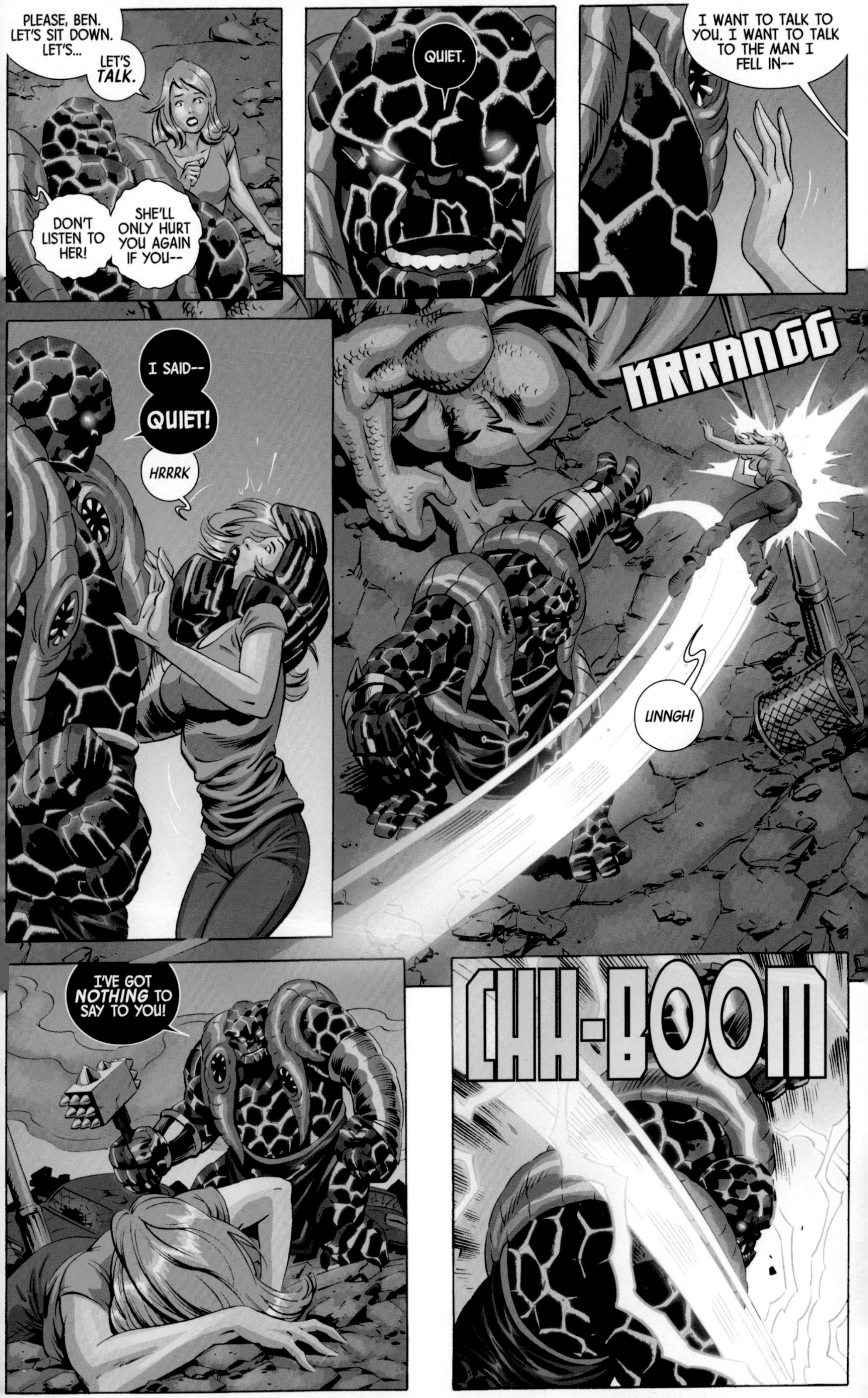
PLEASE, BEN. LET'S SIT DOWN. LET'S...
LET'S TALK.
DON'T LISTEN TO HER!
SHE'LL ONLY HURT YOU AGAIN IF YOU--
QUIET.
I WANT TO TALK TO YOU. I WANT TO TALK TO THE MAN I FELL IN--
I SAID--
QUIET!
HRRRK
KRRANGG
UNNGH!
I'VE GOT NOTHING TO SAY TO YOU!
CHH-BOOM

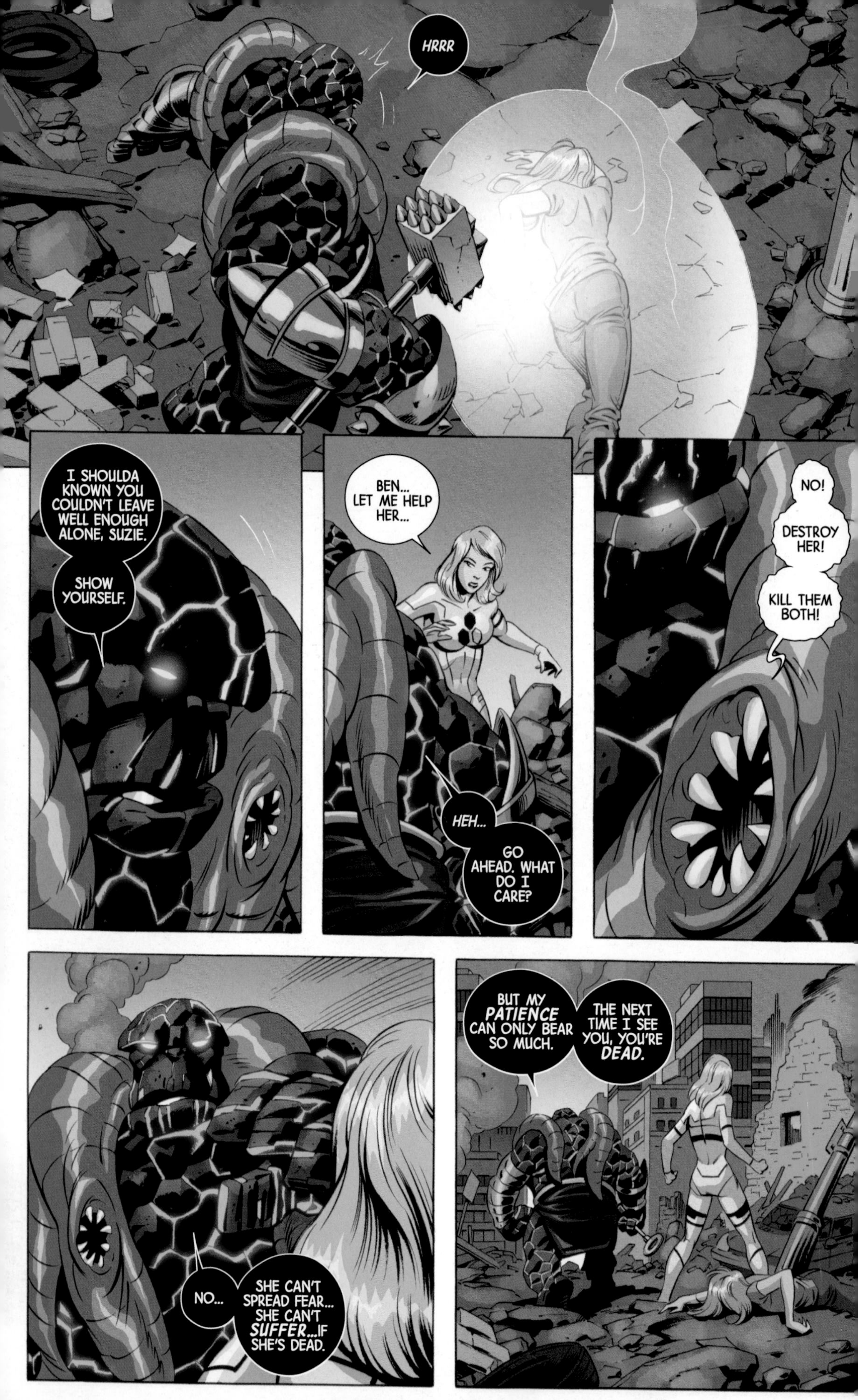
HRRR
I SHOULDA KNOWN YOU COULDN'T LEAVE WELL ENOUGH ALONE, SUZIE.
SHOW YOURSELF.
BEN... LET ME HELP HER...
HEH...
GO AHEAD. WHAT DO I CARE?
NO!
DESTROY HER!
KILL THEM BOTH!
NO...
SHE CAN'T SPREAD FEAR... SHE CAN'T SUFFER...IF SHE'S DEAD.
BUT MY PATIENCE CAN ONLY BEAR SO MUCH.
THE NEXT TIME I SEE YOU, YOU'RE DEAD.

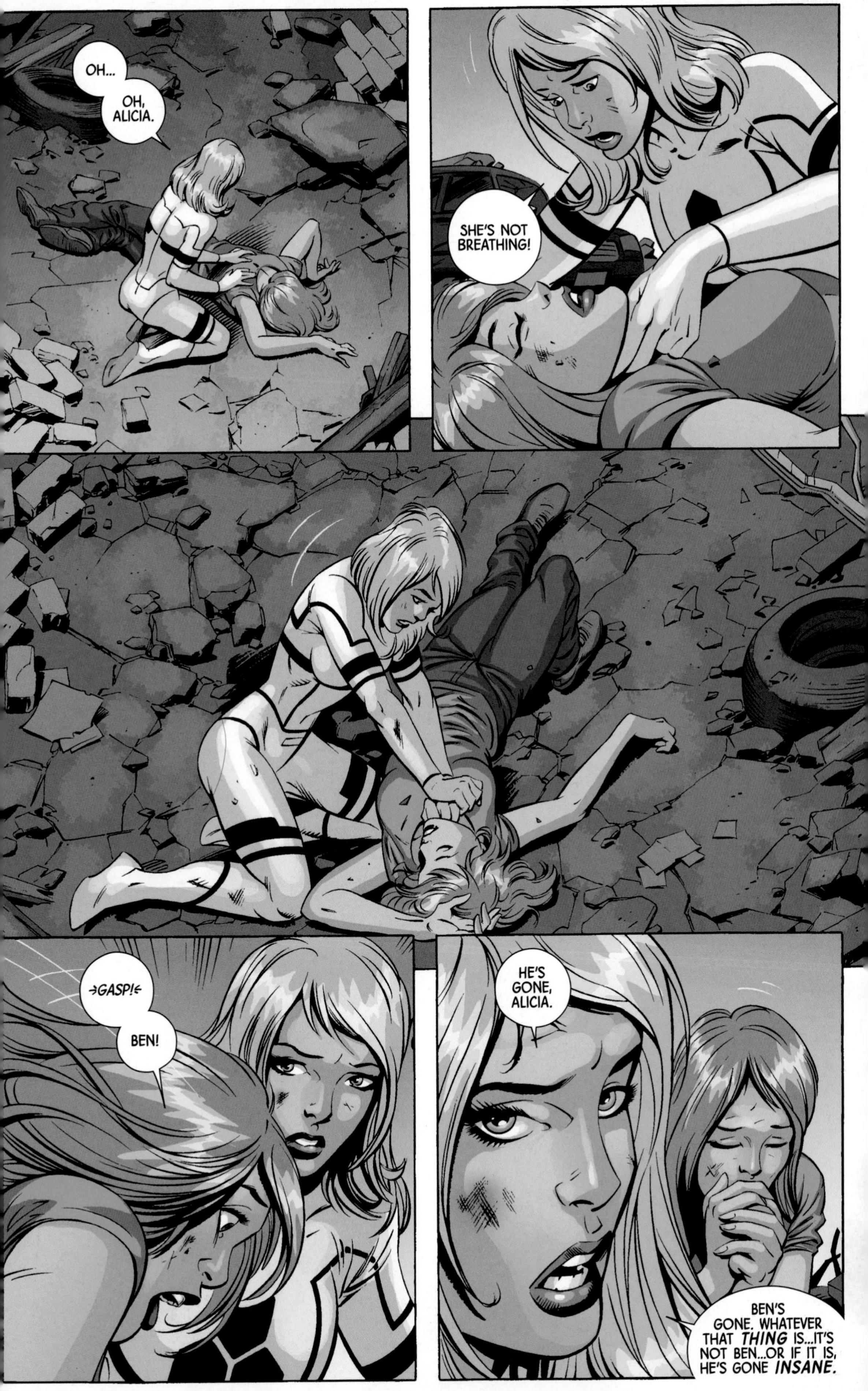
OH...
OH, ALICIA.
SHE'S NOT BREATHING!
→GASP!←
BEN!
HE'S GONE, ALICIA.
BEN'S GONE. WHATEVER THAT *THING* IS...IT'S NOT BEN...OR IF IT IS, HE'S GONE *INSANE.*

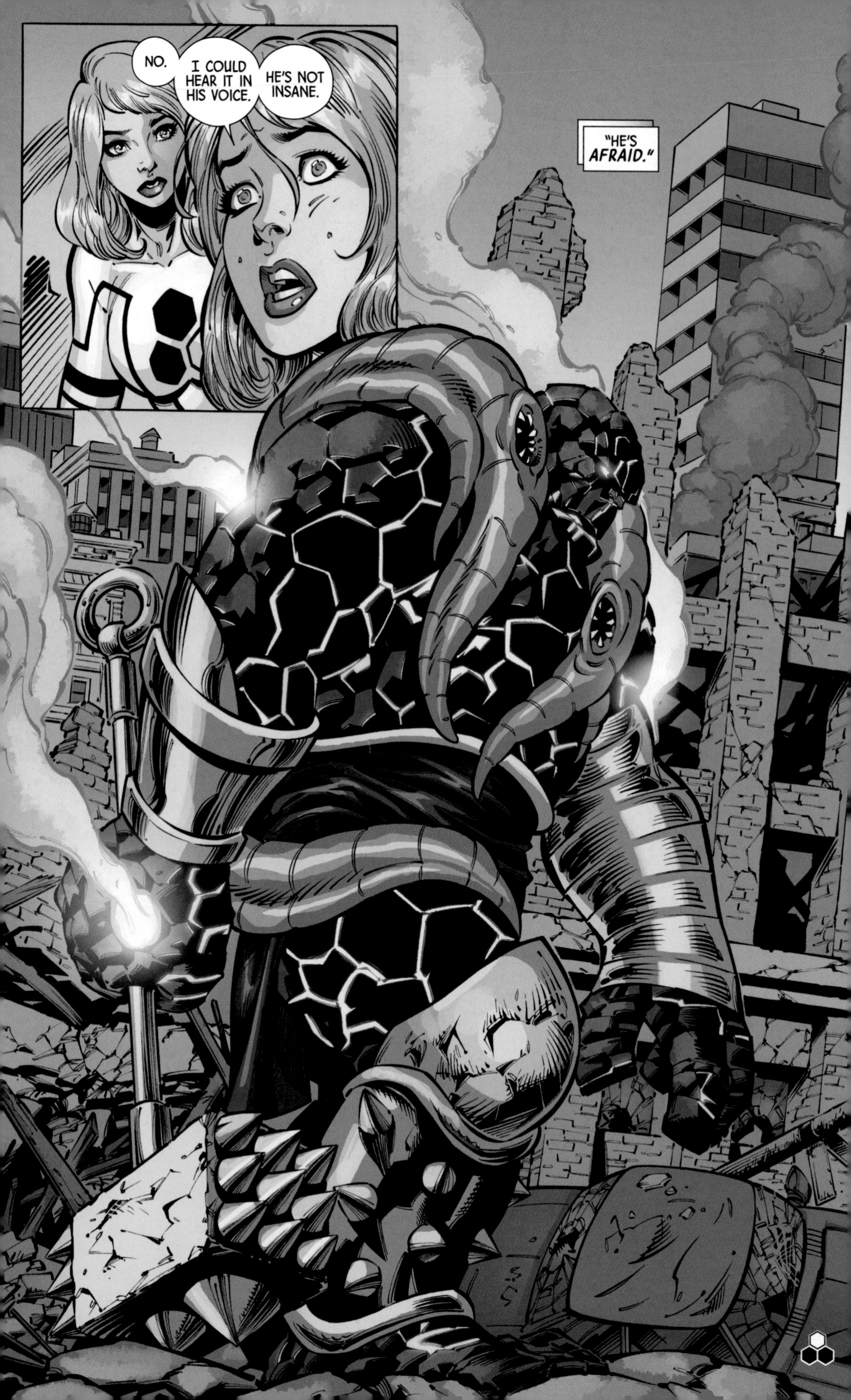
NO.
I COULD HEAR IT IN HIS VOICE.
HE'S NOT INSANE.
"HE'S AFRAID."

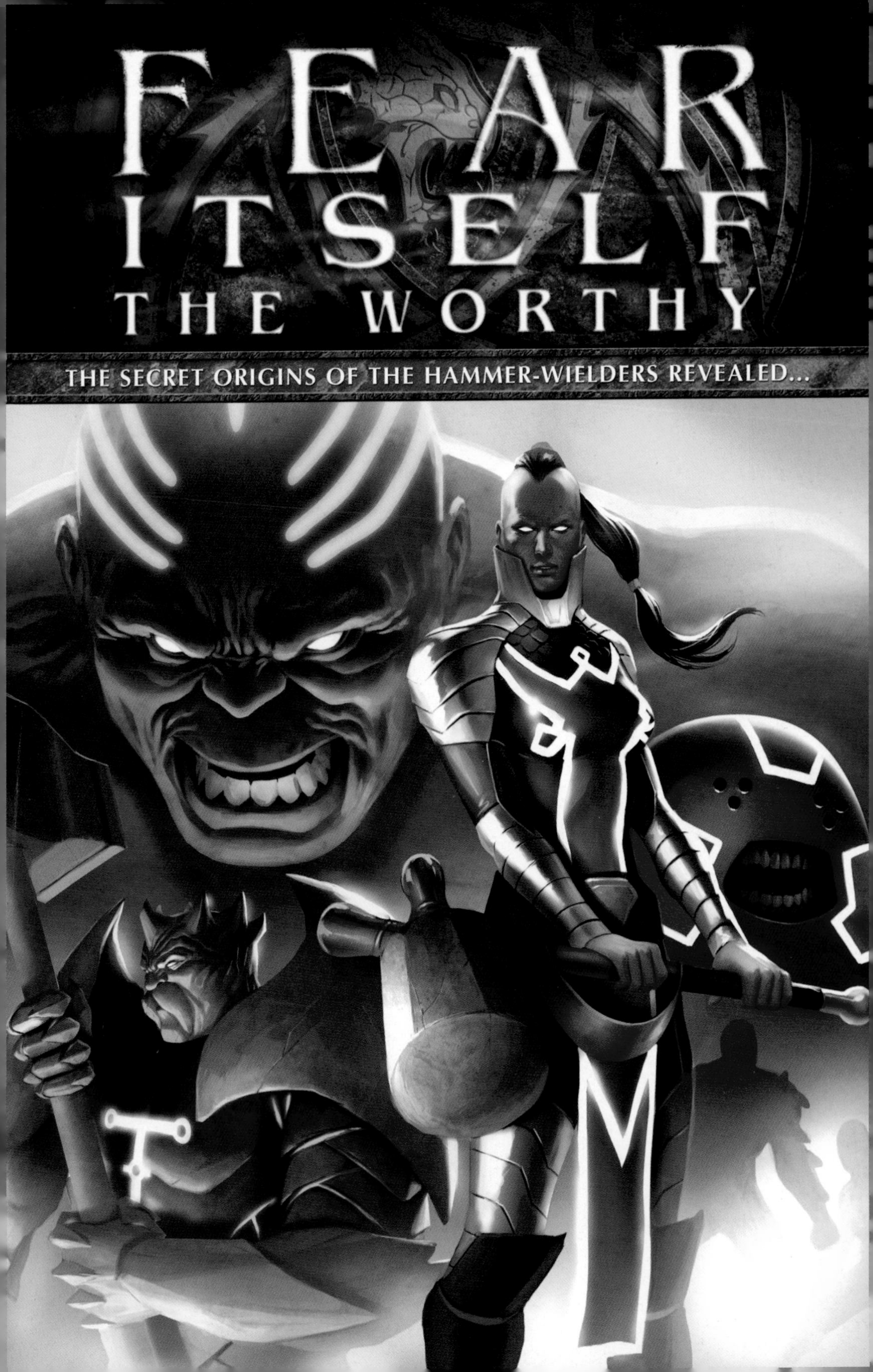
FEAR ITSELF
THE WORTHY
THE SECRET ORIGINS OF THE HAMMER-WIELDERS REVEALED...

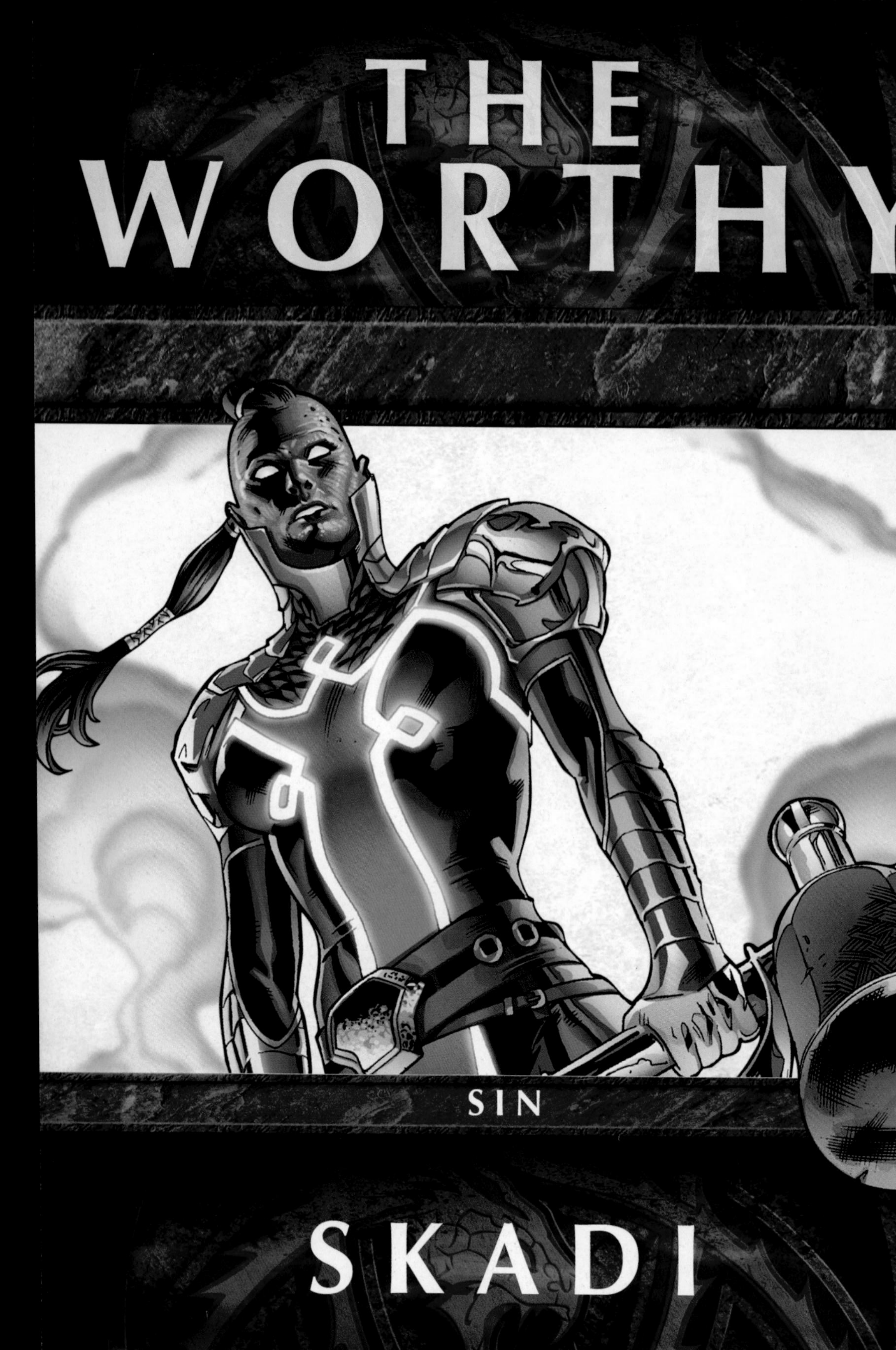
THE
WORTHY
SIN
SKADI

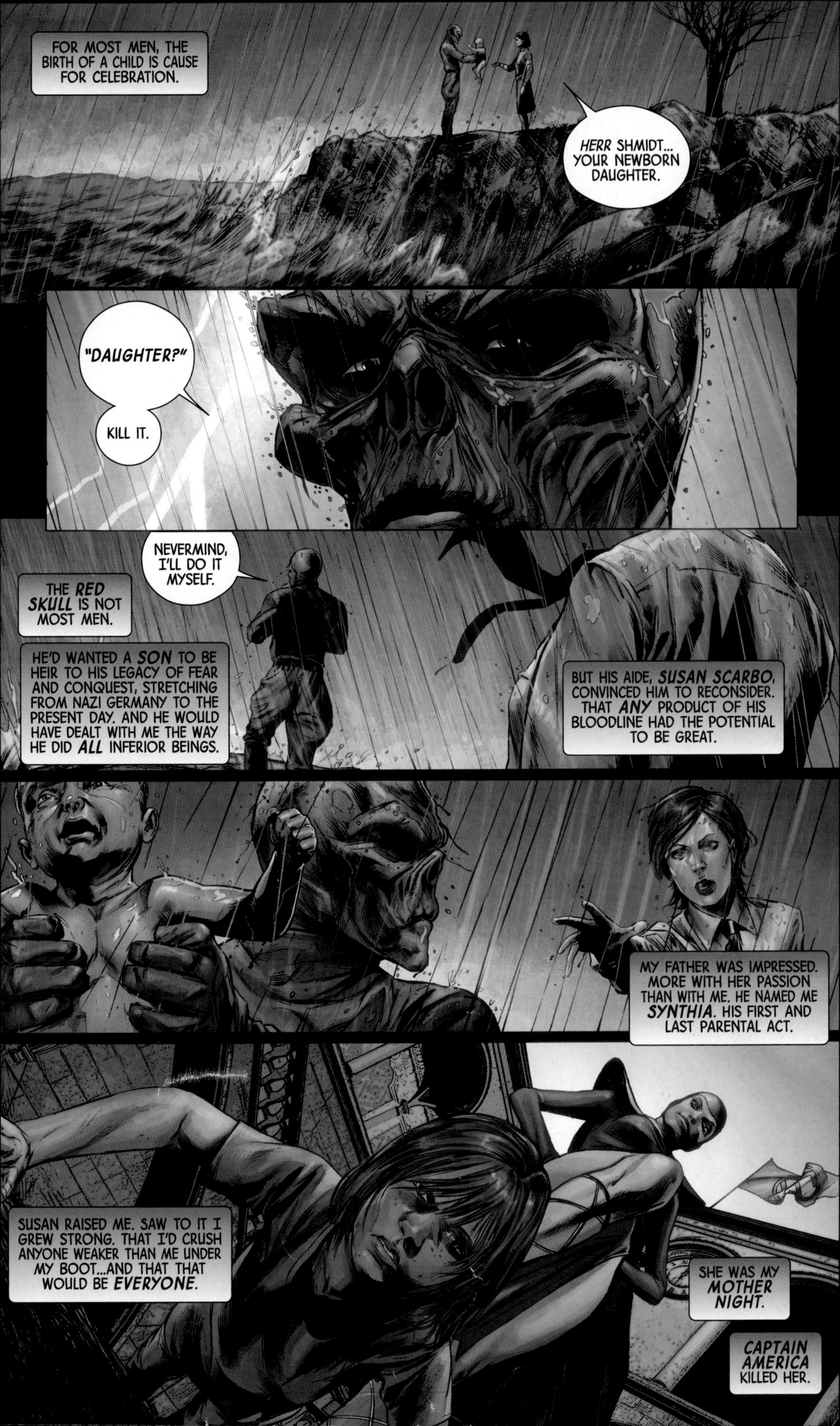

FOR MOST MEN, THE BIRTH OF A CHILD IS CAUSE FOR CELEBRATION.
HERR SHMIDT... YOUR NEWBORN DAUGHTER.
"*DAUGHTER?*"
KILL IT.
NEVERMIND, I'LL DO IT MYSELF.
THE ***RED SKULL*** IS NOT MOST MEN.
HE'D WANTED A ***SON*** TO BE HEIR TO HIS LEGACY OF FEAR AND CONQUEST, STRETCHING FROM NAZI GERMANY TO THE PRESENT DAY. AND HE WOULD HAVE DEALT WITH ME THE WAY HE DID ***ALL*** INFERIOR BEINGS.
BUT HIS AIDE, ***SUSAN SCARBO***, CONVINCED HIM TO RECONSIDER. THAT ***ANY*** PRODUCT OF HIS BLOODLINE HAD THE POTENTIAL TO BE GREAT.
MY FATHER WAS IMPRESSED. MORE WITH HER PASSION THAN WITH ME. HE NAMED ME ***SYNTHIA***. HIS FIRST AND LAST PARENTAL ACT.
SUSAN RAISED ME. SAW TO IT I GREW STRONG. THAT I'D CRUSH ANYONE WEAKER THAN ME UNDER MY BOOT...AND THAT THAT WOULD BE ***EVERYONE***.
SHE WAS MY ***MOTHER NIGHT***.
CAPTAIN AMERICA KILLED HER.

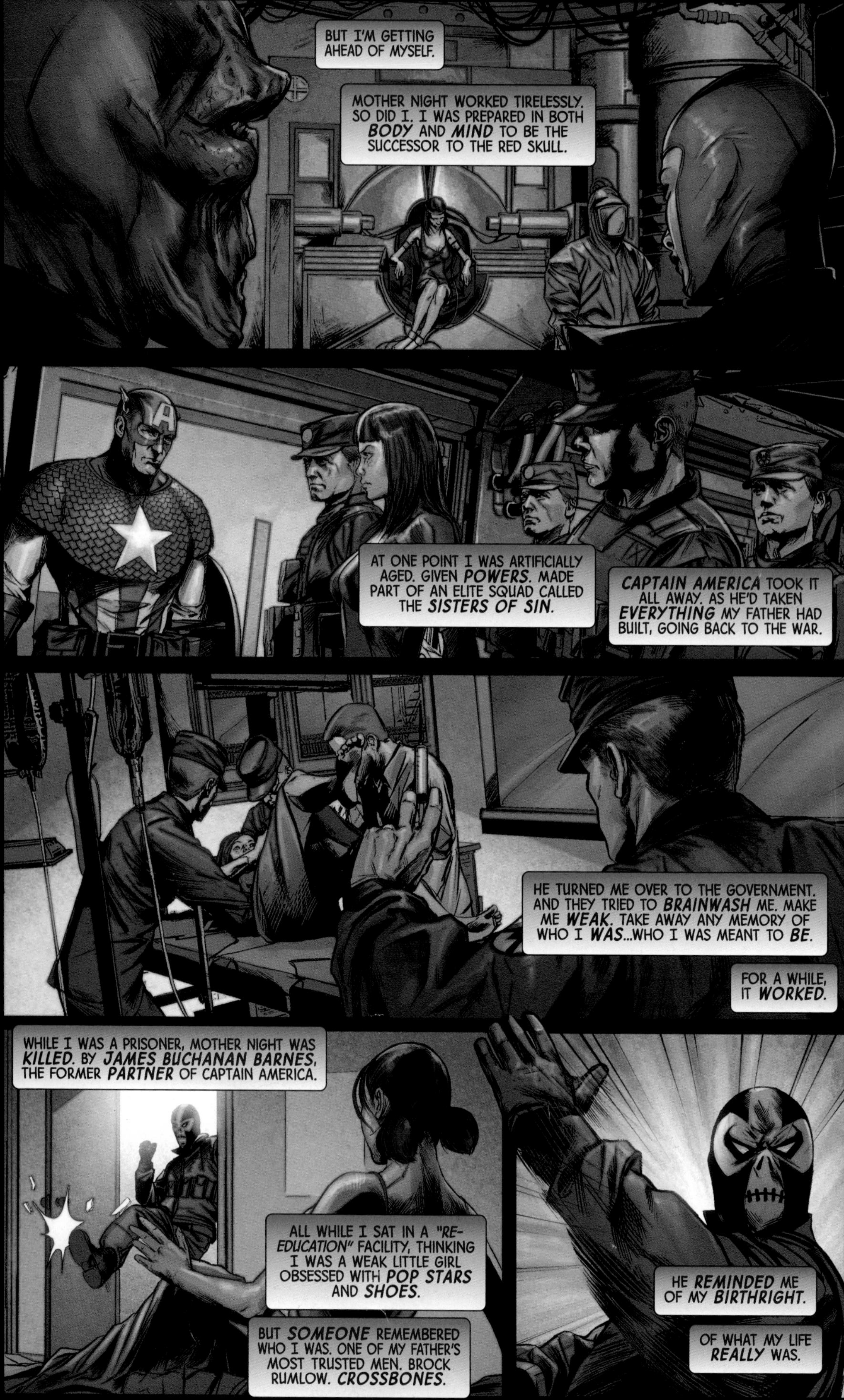
BUT I'M GETTING AHEAD OF MYSELF.
MOTHER NIGHT WORKED TIRELESSLY. SO DID I. I WAS PREPARED IN BOTH BODY AND MIND TO BE THE SUCCESSOR TO THE RED SKULL.
AT ONE POINT I WAS ARTIFICIALLY AGED. GIVEN POWERS. MADE PART OF AN ELITE SQUAD CALLED THE SISTERS OF SIN.
CAPTAIN AMERICA TOOK IT ALL AWAY. AS HE'D TAKEN EVERYTHING MY FATHER HAD BUILT, GOING BACK TO THE WAR.
HE TURNED ME OVER TO THE GOVERNMENT. AND THEY TRIED TO BRAINWASH ME. MAKE ME WEAK. TAKE AWAY ANY MEMORY OF WHO I WAS...WHO I WAS MEANT TO BE.
FOR A WHILE, IT WORKED.
WHILE I WAS A PRISONER, MOTHER NIGHT WAS KILLED. BY JAMES BUCHANAN BARNES, THE FORMER PARTNER OF CAPTAIN AMERICA.
ALL WHILE I SAT IN A "RE-EDUCATION" FACILITY, THINKING I WAS A WEAK LITTLE GIRL OBSESSED WITH POP STARS AND SHOES.
BUT SOMEONE REMEMBERED WHO I WAS. ONE OF MY FATHER'S MOST TRUSTED MEN. BROCK RUMLOW. CROSSBONES.
HE REMINDED ME OF MY BIRTHRIGHT.
OF WHAT MY LIFE REALLY WAS.

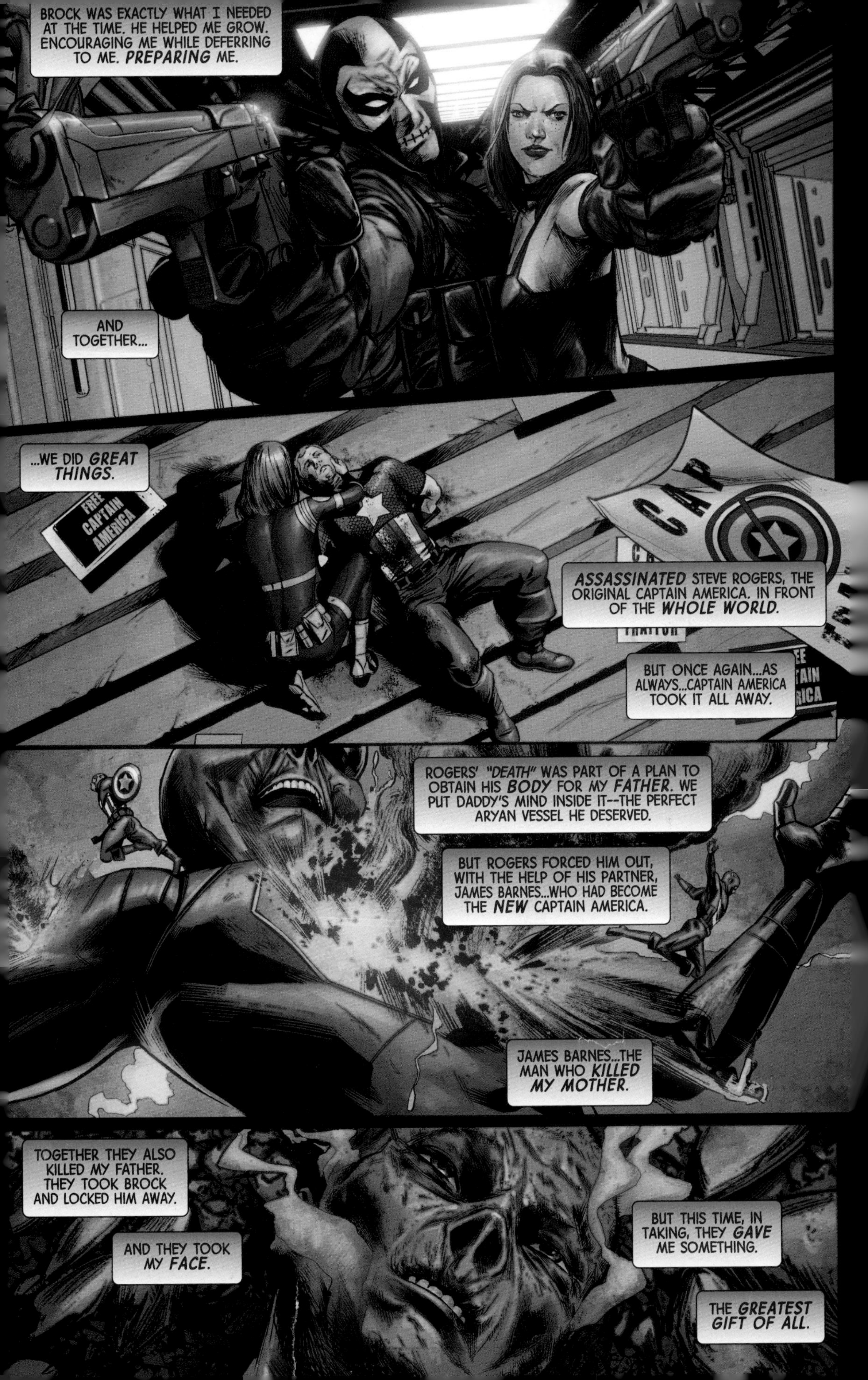
BROCK WAS EXACTLY WHAT I NEEDED AT THE TIME. HE HELPED ME GROW. ENCOURAGING ME WHILE DEFERRING TO ME. PREPARING ME.
AND TOGETHER...
...WE DID GREAT THINGS.
FREE CAPTAIN AMERICA
CAP
ASSASSINATED STEVE ROGERS, THE ORIGINAL CAPTAIN AMERICA. IN FRONT OF THE WHOLE WORLD.
BUT ONCE AGAIN...AS ALWAYS...CAPTAIN AMERICA TOOK IT ALL AWAY.
ROGERS' "DEATH" WAS PART OF A PLAN TO OBTAIN HIS BODY FOR MY FATHER. WE PUT DADDY'S MIND INSIDE IT--THE PERFECT ARYAN VESSEL HE DESERVED.
BUT ROGERS FORCED HIM OUT, WITH THE HELP OF HIS PARTNER, JAMES BARNES...WHO HAD BECOME THE NEW CAPTAIN AMERICA.
JAMES BARNES...THE MAN WHO KILLED MY MOTHER.
TOGETHER THEY ALSO KILLED MY FATHER. THEY TOOK BROCK AND LOCKED HIM AWAY.
AND THEY TOOK MY FACE.
BUT THIS TIME, IN TAKING, THEY GAVE ME SOMETHING.
THE GREATEST GIFT OF ALL.

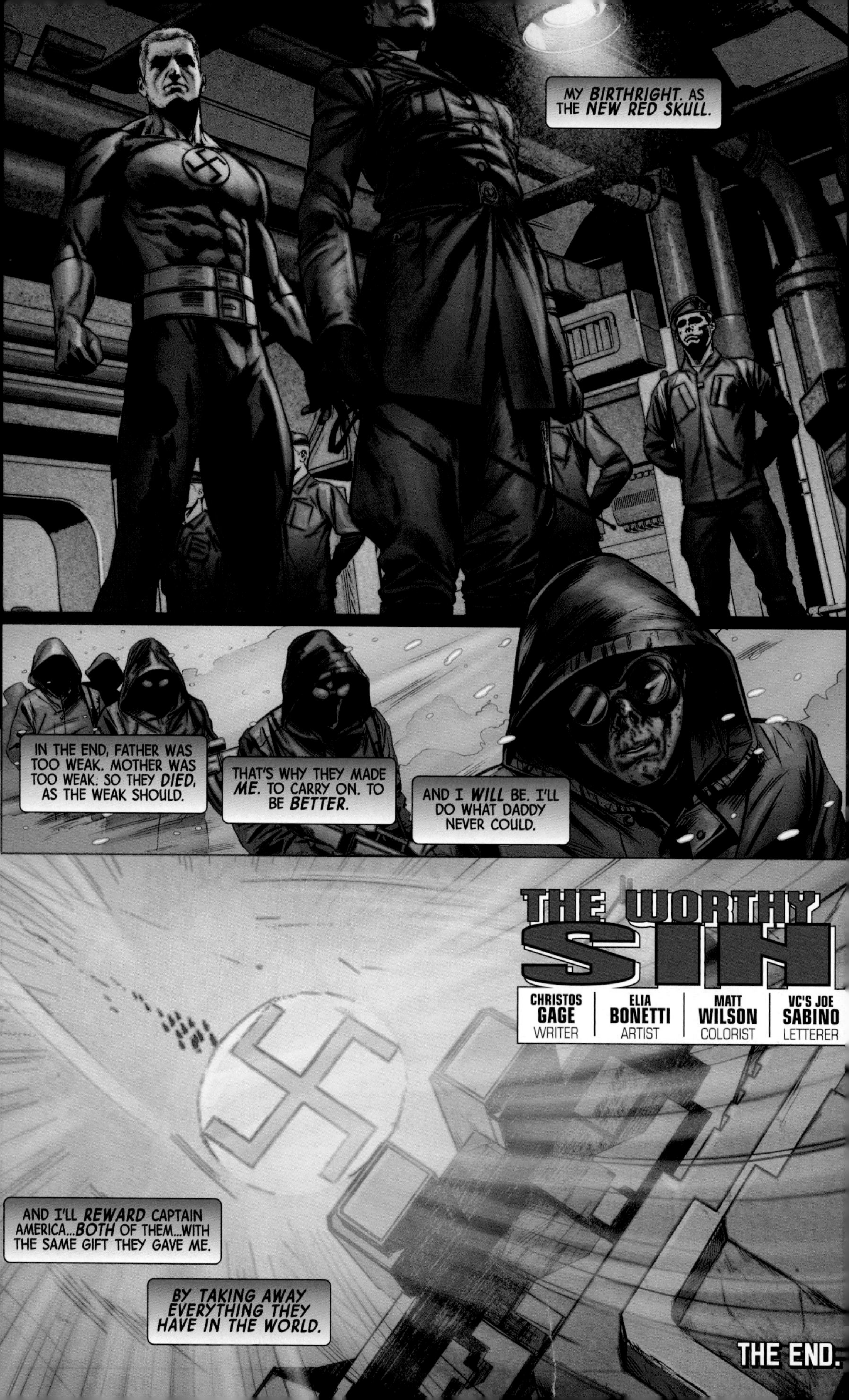
MY BIRTHRIGHT. AS THE NEW RED SKULL.
IN THE END, FATHER WAS TOO WEAK. MOTHER WAS TOO WEAK. SO THEY DIED, AS THE WEAK SHOULD.
THAT'S WHY THEY MADE ME. TO CARRY ON. TO BE BETTER.
AND I WILL BE. I'LL DO WHAT DADDY NEVER COULD.
THE WORTHY SIN
CHRISTOS GAGE WRITER
ELIA BONETTI ARTIST
MATT WILSON COLORIST
VC'S JOE SABINO LETTERER
AND I'LL REWARD CAPTAIN AMERICA...BOTH OF THEM...WITH THE SAME GIFT THEY GAVE ME.
BY TAKING AWAY EVERYTHING THEY HAVE IN THE WORLD.
THE END.

THE WORTHY

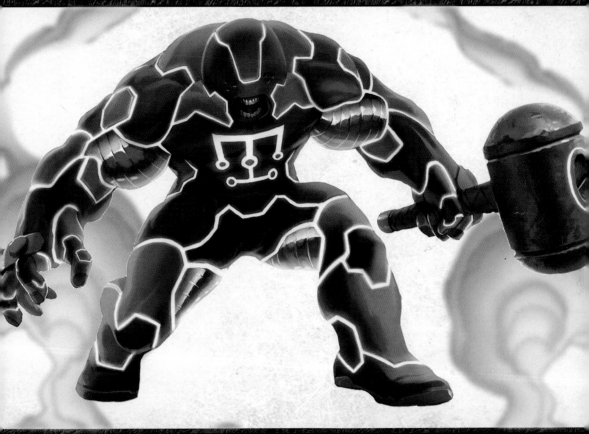

JUGGERNAUT

KUURTH:
BREAKER OF STONE

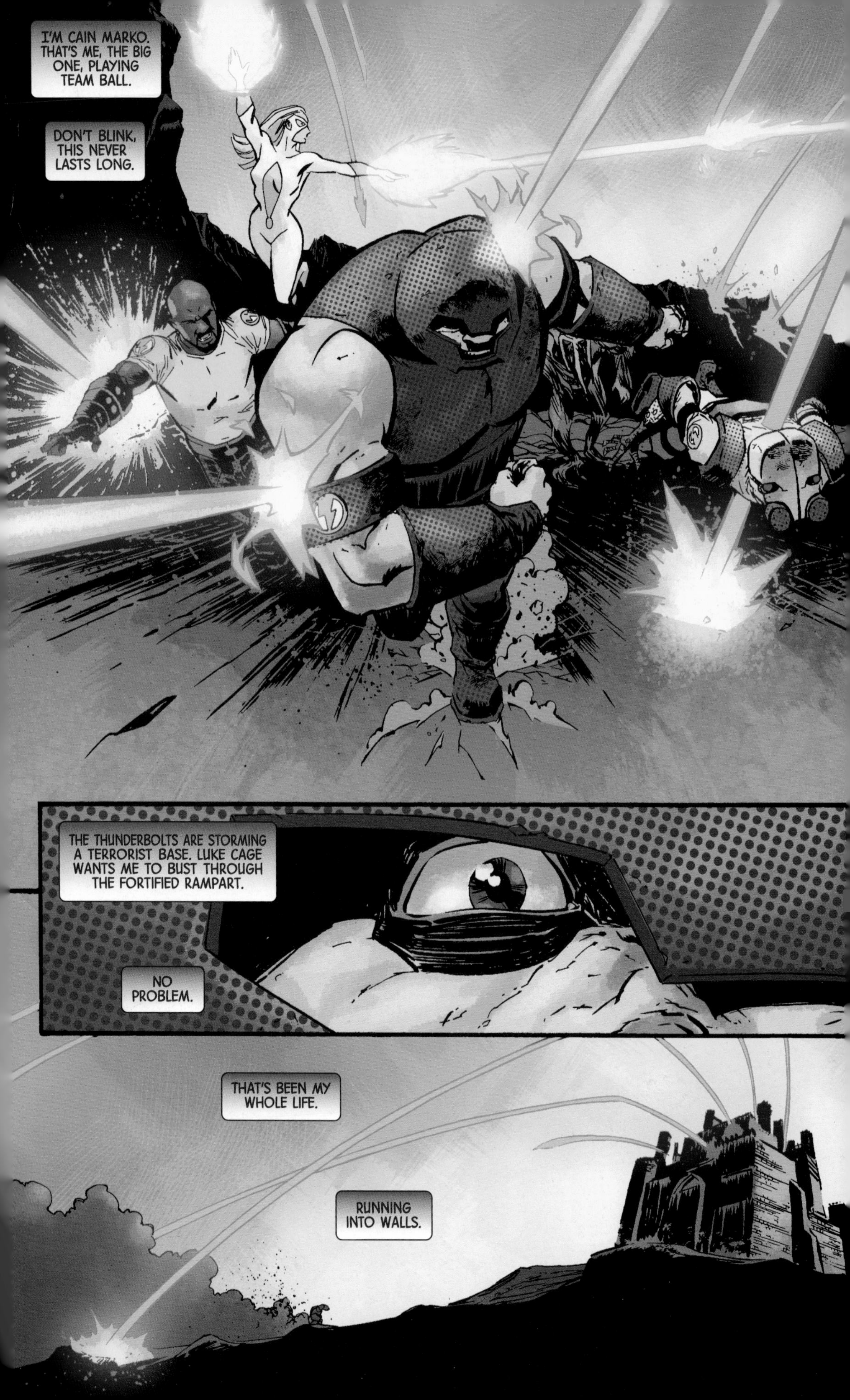
I'M CAIN MARKO. THAT'S ME, THE BIG ONE, PLAYING TEAM BALL.
DON'T BLINK, THIS NEVER LASTS LONG.
THE THUNDERBOLTS ARE STORMING A TERRORIST BASE. LUKE CAGE WANTS ME TO BUST THROUGH THE FORTIFIED RAMPART.
NO PROBLEM.
THAT'S BEEN MY WHOLE LIFE.
RUNNING INTO WALLS.

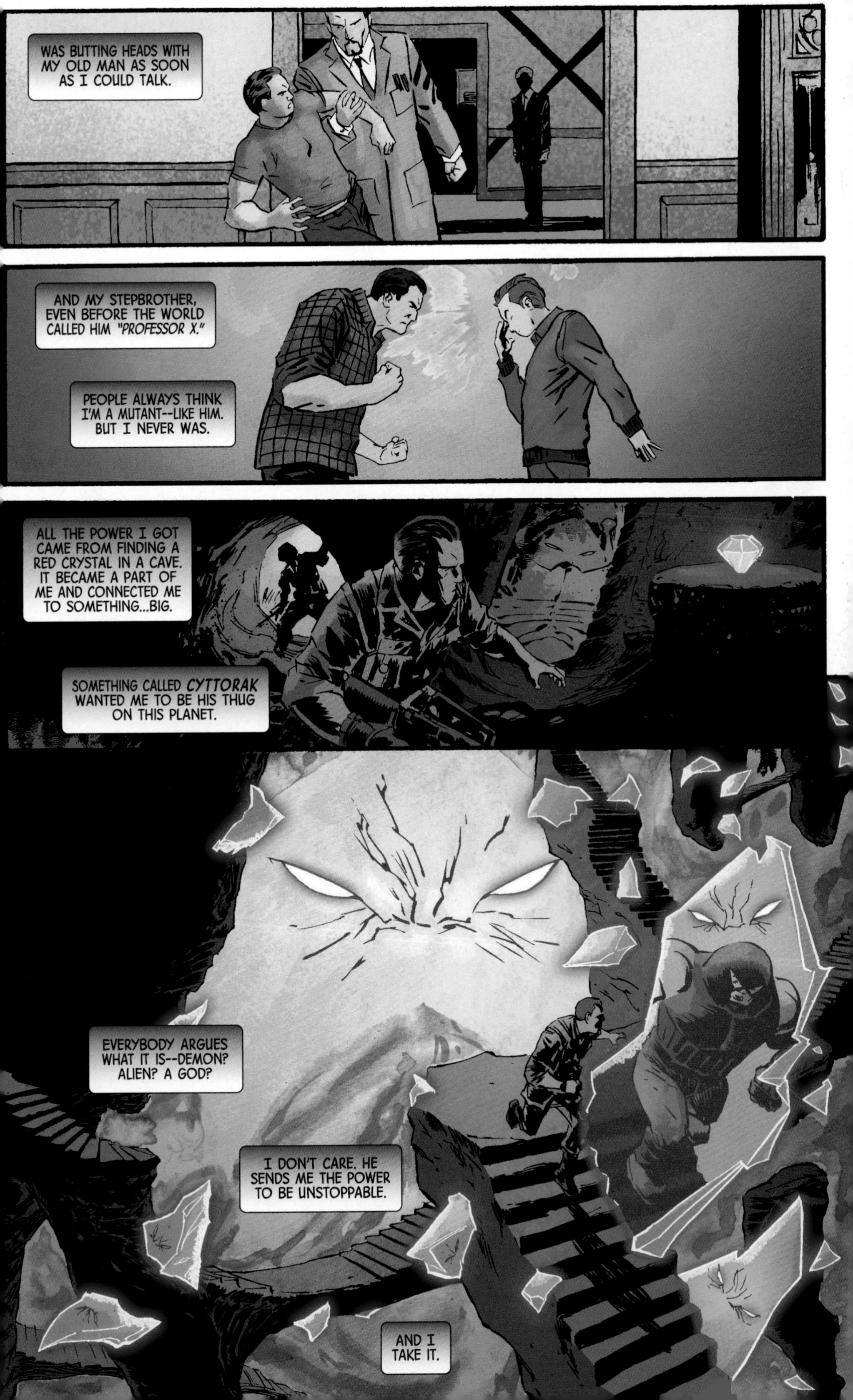
WAS BUTTING HEADS WITH MY OLD MAN AS SOON AS I COULD TALK.
AND MY STEPBROTHER, EVEN BEFORE THE WORLD CALLED HIM "PROFESSOR X."
PEOPLE ALWAYS THINK I'M A MUTANT--LIKE HIM. BUT I NEVER WAS.
ALL THE POWER I GOT CAME FROM FINDING A RED CRYSTAL IN A CAVE. IT BECAME A PART OF ME AND CONNECTED ME TO SOMETHING...BIG.
SOMETHING CALLED CYTTORAK WANTED ME TO BE HIS THUG ON THIS PLANET.
EVERYBODY ARGUES WHAT IT IS--DEMON? ALIEN? A GOD?
I DON'T CARE. HE SENDS ME THE POWER TO BE UNSTOPPABLE.
AND I TAKE IT.

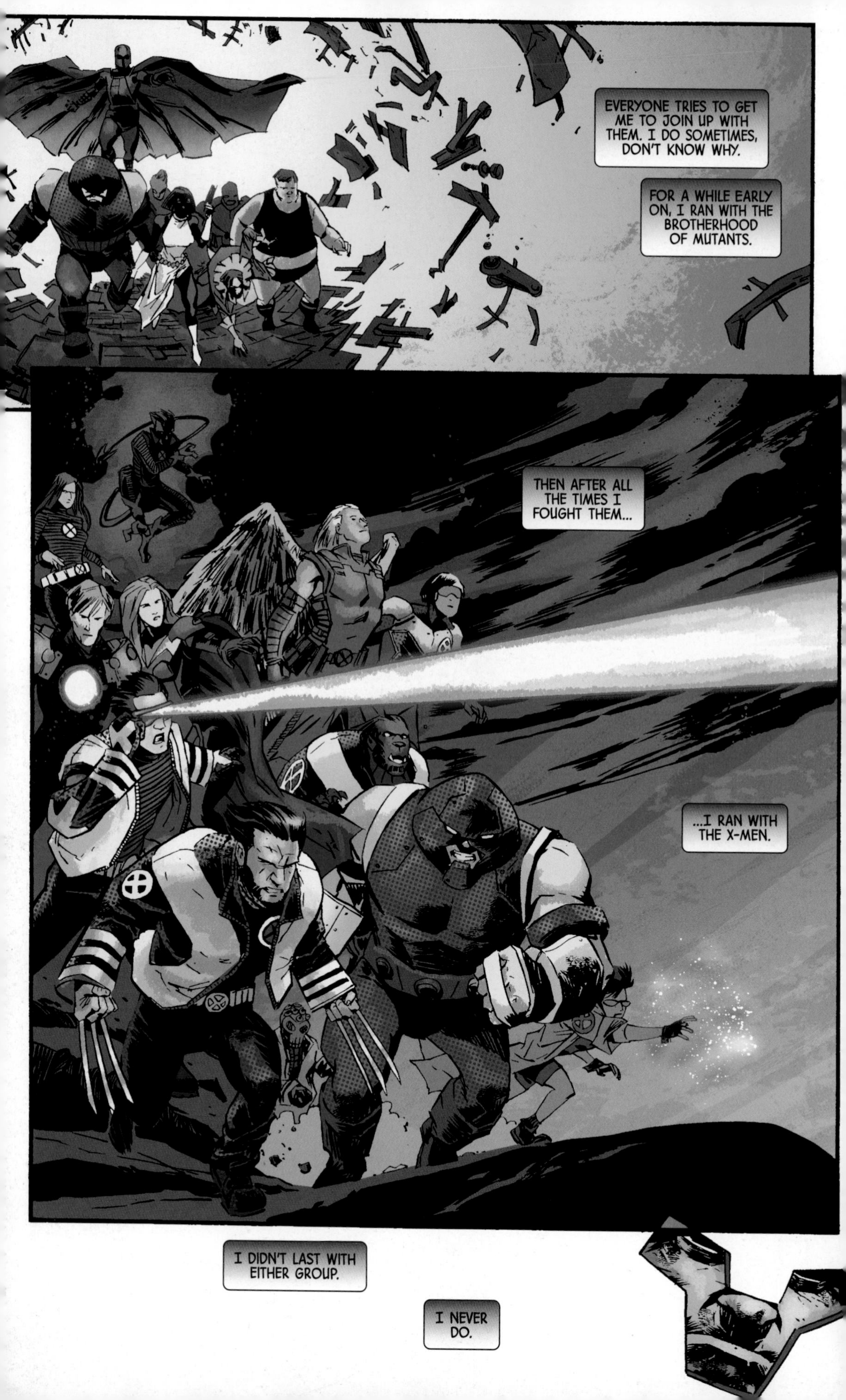
EVERYONE TRIES TO GET ME TO JOIN UP WITH THEM. I DO SOMETIMES, DON'T KNOW WHY.
FOR A WHILE EARLY ON, I RAN WITH THE BROTHERHOOD OF MUTANTS.
THEN AFTER ALL THE TIMES I FOUGHT THEM...
...I RAN WITH THE X-MEN.
I DIDN'T LAST WITH EITHER GROUP.
I NEVER DO.

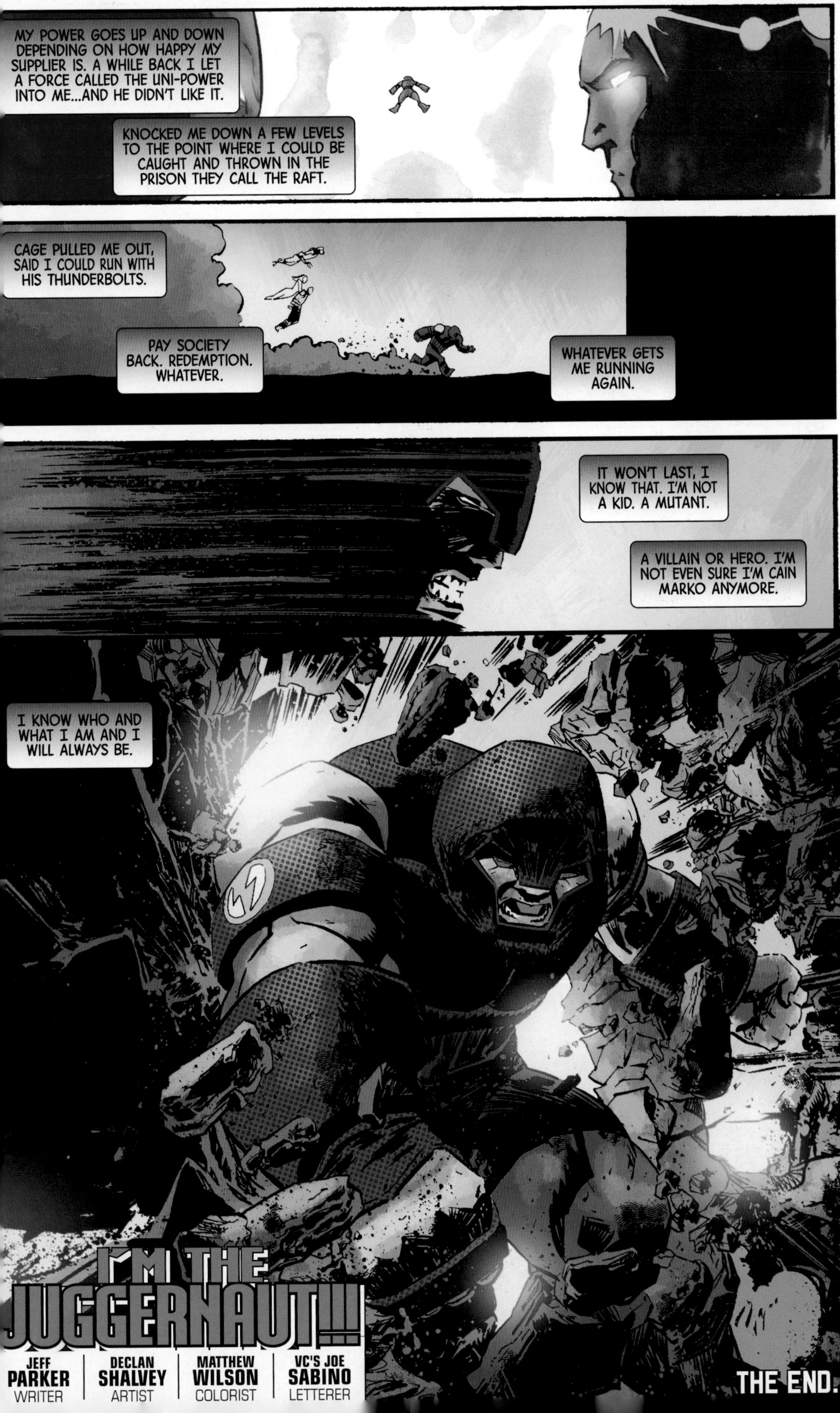

MY POWER GOES UP AND DOWN DEPENDING ON HOW HAPPY MY SUPPLIER IS. A WHILE BACK I LET A FORCE CALLED THE UNI-POWER INTO ME...AND HE DIDN'T LIKE IT.
KNOCKED ME DOWN A FEW LEVELS TO THE POINT WHERE I COULD BE CAUGHT AND THROWN IN THE PRISON THEY CALL THE RAFT.
CAGE PULLED ME OUT, SAID I COULD RUN WITH HIS THUNDERBOLTS.
PAY SOCIETY BACK. REDEMPTION. WHATEVER.
WHATEVER GETS ME RUNNING AGAIN.
IT WON'T LAST, I KNOW THAT. I'M NOT A KID. A MUTANT.
A VILLAIN OR HERO. I'M NOT EVEN SURE I'M CAIN MARKO ANYMORE.
I KNOW WHO AND WHAT I AM AND I WILL ALWAYS BE.
I'M THE JUGGERNAUT!!!
JEFF PARKER WRITER
DECLAN SHALVEY ARTIST
MATTHEW WILSON COLORIST
VC'S JOE SABINO LETTERER
THE END.

THE WORTHY

TITANIA

SKIRN:
BREAKER OF MEN

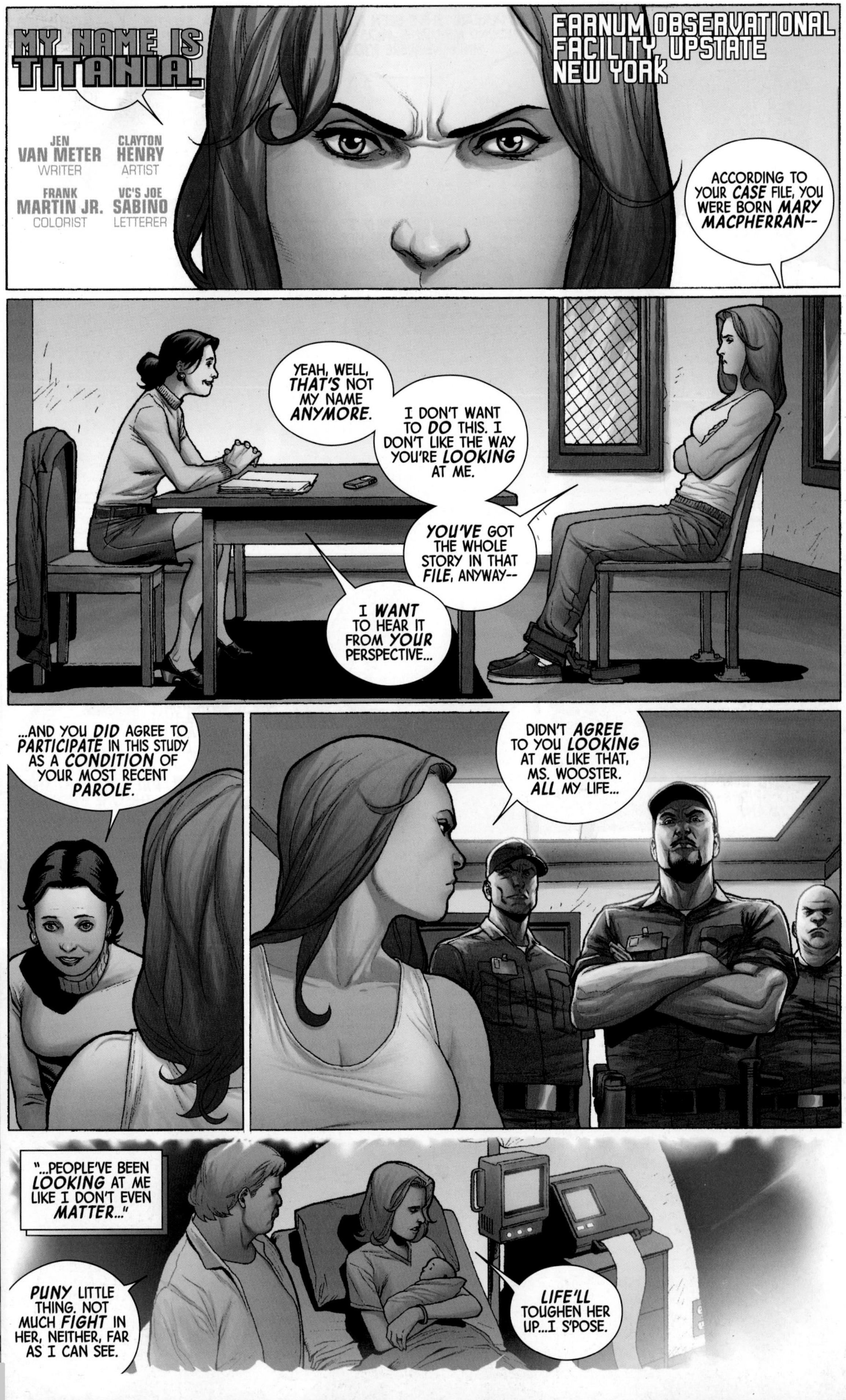
MY NAME IS TITANIA.
JEN VAN METER WRITER
CLAYTON HENRY ARTIST
FRANK MARTIN JR. COLORIST
VC'S JOE SABINO LETTERER
FARNUM OBSERVATIONAL FACILITY, UPSTATE NEW YORK
ACCORDING TO YOUR CASE FILE, YOU WERE BORN MARY MACPHERRAN--
YEAH, WELL, THAT'S NOT MY NAME ANYMORE.
I DON'T WANT TO DO THIS. I DON'T LIKE THE WAY YOU'RE LOOKING AT ME.
YOU'VE GOT THE WHOLE STORY IN THAT FILE, ANYWAY--
I WANT TO HEAR IT FROM YOUR PERSPECTIVE...
...AND YOU DID AGREE TO PARTICIPATE IN THIS STUDY AS A CONDITION OF YOUR MOST RECENT PAROLE.
DIDN'T AGREE TO YOU LOOKING AT ME LIKE THAT, MS. WOOSTER. ALL MY LIFE...
"...PEOPLE'VE BEEN LOOKING AT ME LIKE I DON'T EVEN MATTER..."
PUNY LITTLE THING. NOT MUCH FIGHT IN HER, NEITHER, FAR AS I CAN SEE.
LIFE'LL TOUGHEN HER UP...I S'POSE.

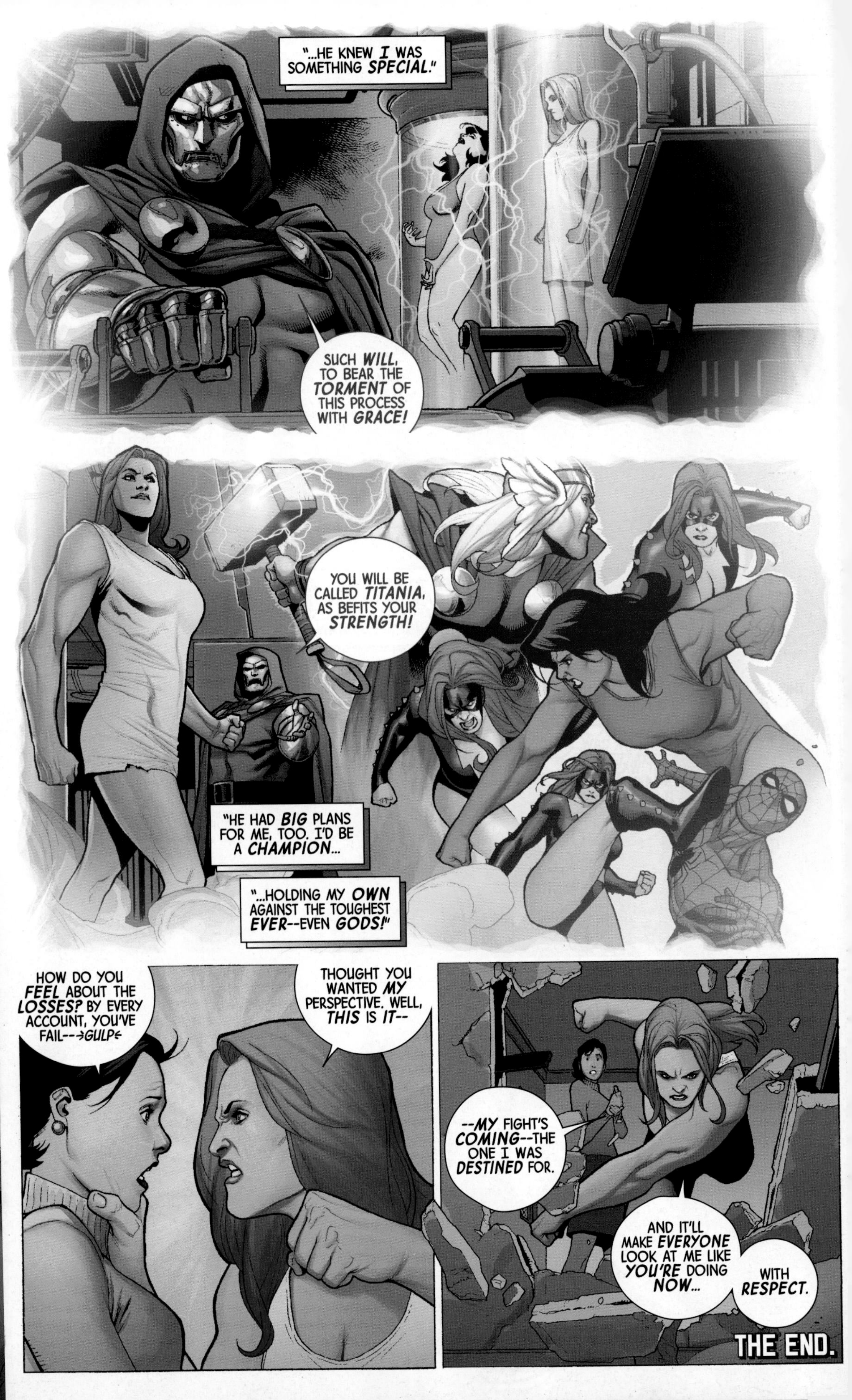
"...HE KNEW I WAS SOMETHING SPECIAL."
SUCH WILL, TO BEAR THE TORMENT OF THIS PROCESS WITH GRACE!
YOU WILL BE CALLED TITANIA, AS BEFITS YOUR STRENGTH!
"HE HAD BIG PLANS FOR ME, TOO. I'D BE A CHAMPION...
"...HOLDING MY OWN AGAINST THE TOUGHEST EVER--EVEN GODS!"
HOW DO YOU FEEL ABOUT THE LOSSES? BY EVERY ACCOUNT, YOU'VE FAIL--→GULP←
THOUGHT YOU WANTED MY PERSPECTIVE. WELL, THIS IS IT--
--MY FIGHT'S COMING--THE ONE I WAS DESTINED FOR.
AND IT'LL MAKE EVERYONE LOOK AT ME LIKE YOU'RE DOING NOW...
WITH RESPECT.
THE END.

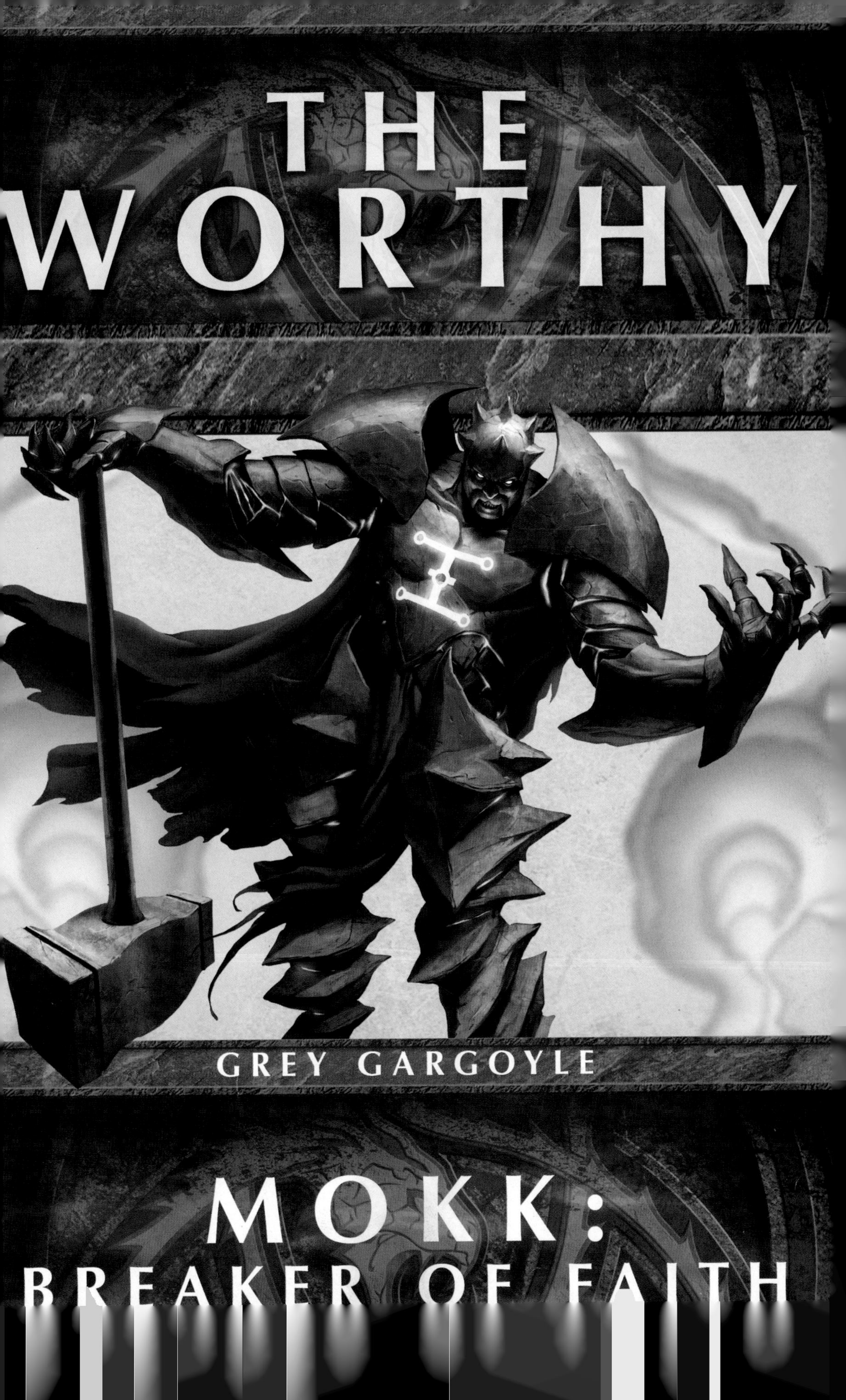
THE WORTHY
GREY GARGOYLE
MOKK: BREAKER OF FAITH

THERE ARE TIMES I BELIEVE I SHOULD NEVER HAVE LEFT FRANCE.

THAT I SHOULD HAVE BEEN CONTENT TO EXIST HERE, THRIVING IN MY OWN LITTLE CORNER OF THE WORLD...

AS IT WAS DURING THOSE INITIAL DAYS AFTER MY TRANSFORMATION.

HAD I DONE THAT... WHO KNOWS? WHERE WOULD I BE NOW?

RUNNING MY OWN CRIMINAL EMPIRE, PERHAPS? WOULD I BE PARIS' HOOD?

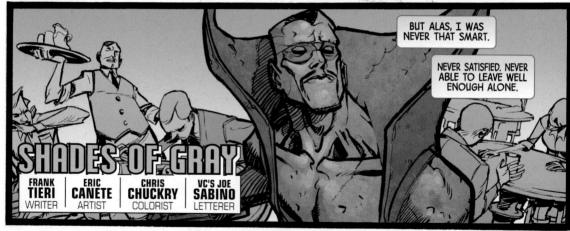

BUT ALAS, I WAS NEVER THAT SMART.

NEVER SATISFIED. NEVER ABLE TO LEAVE WELL ENOUGH ALONE.

SHADES OF GRAY

FRANK TIERI	ERIC CANETE	CHRIS CHUCKRY	VC'S JOE SABINO
WRITER	ARTIST	COLORIST	LETTERER

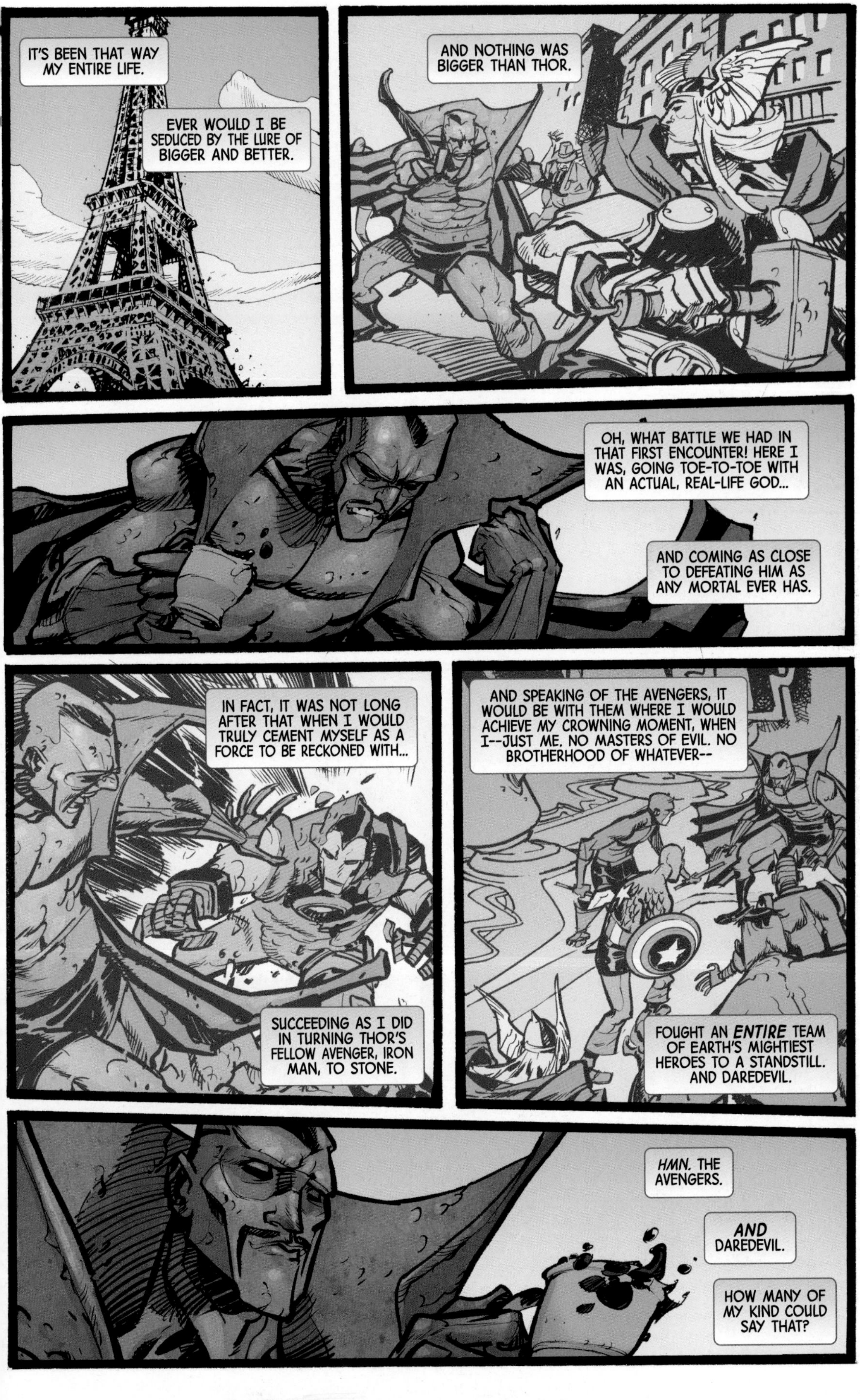
IT'S BEEN THAT WAY MY ENTIRE LIFE.
EVER WOULD I BE SEDUCED BY THE LURE OF BIGGER AND BETTER.
AND NOTHING WAS BIGGER THAN THOR.
OH, WHAT BATTLE WE HAD IN THAT FIRST ENCOUNTER! HERE I WAS, GOING TOE-TO-TOE WITH AN ACTUAL, REAL-LIFE GOD...
AND COMING AS CLOSE TO DEFEATING HIM AS ANY MORTAL EVER HAS.
IN FACT, IT WAS NOT LONG AFTER THAT WHEN I WOULD TRULY CEMENT MYSELF AS A FORCE TO BE RECKONED WITH...
SUCCEEDING AS I DID IN TURNING THOR'S FELLOW AVENGER, IRON MAN, TO STONE.
AND SPEAKING OF THE AVENGERS, IT WOULD BE WITH THEM WHERE I WOULD ACHIEVE MY CROWNING MOMENT, WHEN I--JUST ME. NO MASTERS OF EVIL. NO BROTHERHOOD OF WHATEVER--
FOUGHT AN *ENTIRE* TEAM OF EARTH'S MIGHTIEST HEROES TO A STANDSTILL. AND DAREDEVIL.
HMN. THE AVENGERS.
AND DAREDEVIL.
HOW MANY OF MY KIND COULD SAY THAT?

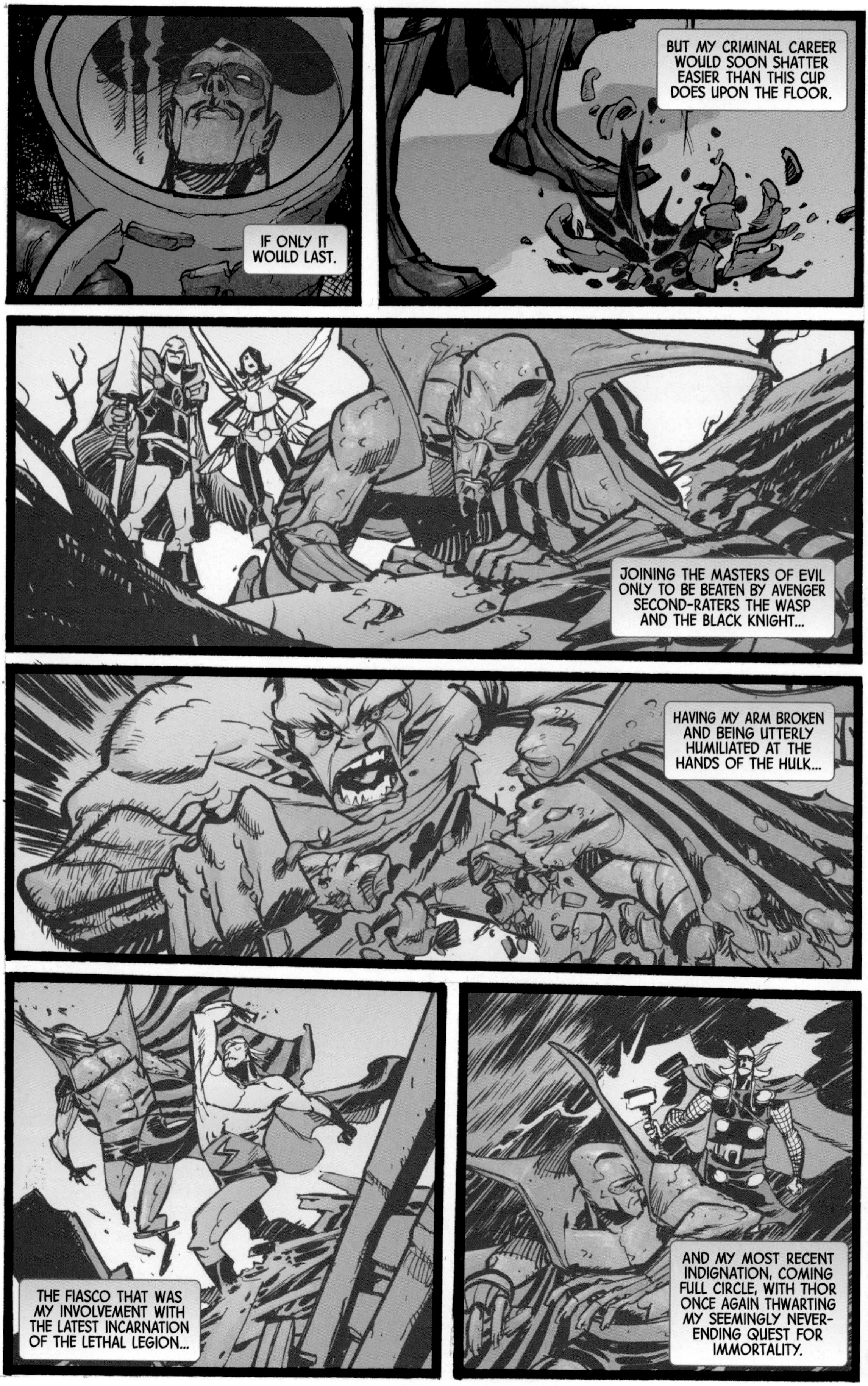
IF ONLY IT WOULD LAST.
BUT MY CRIMINAL CAREER WOULD SOON SHATTER EASIER THAN THIS CUP DOES UPON THE FLOOR.
JOINING THE MASTERS OF EVIL ONLY TO BE BEATEN BY AVENGER SECOND-RATERS THE WASP AND THE BLACK KNIGHT...
HAVING MY ARM BROKEN AND BEING UTTERLY HUMILIATED AT THE HANDS OF THE HULK...
THE FIASCO THAT WAS MY INVOLVEMENT WITH THE LATEST INCARNATION OF THE LETHAL LEGION...
AND MY MOST RECENT INDIGNATION, COMING FULL CIRCLE, WITH THOR ONCE AGAIN THWARTING MY SEEMINGLY NEVER-ENDING QUEST FOR IMMORTALITY.

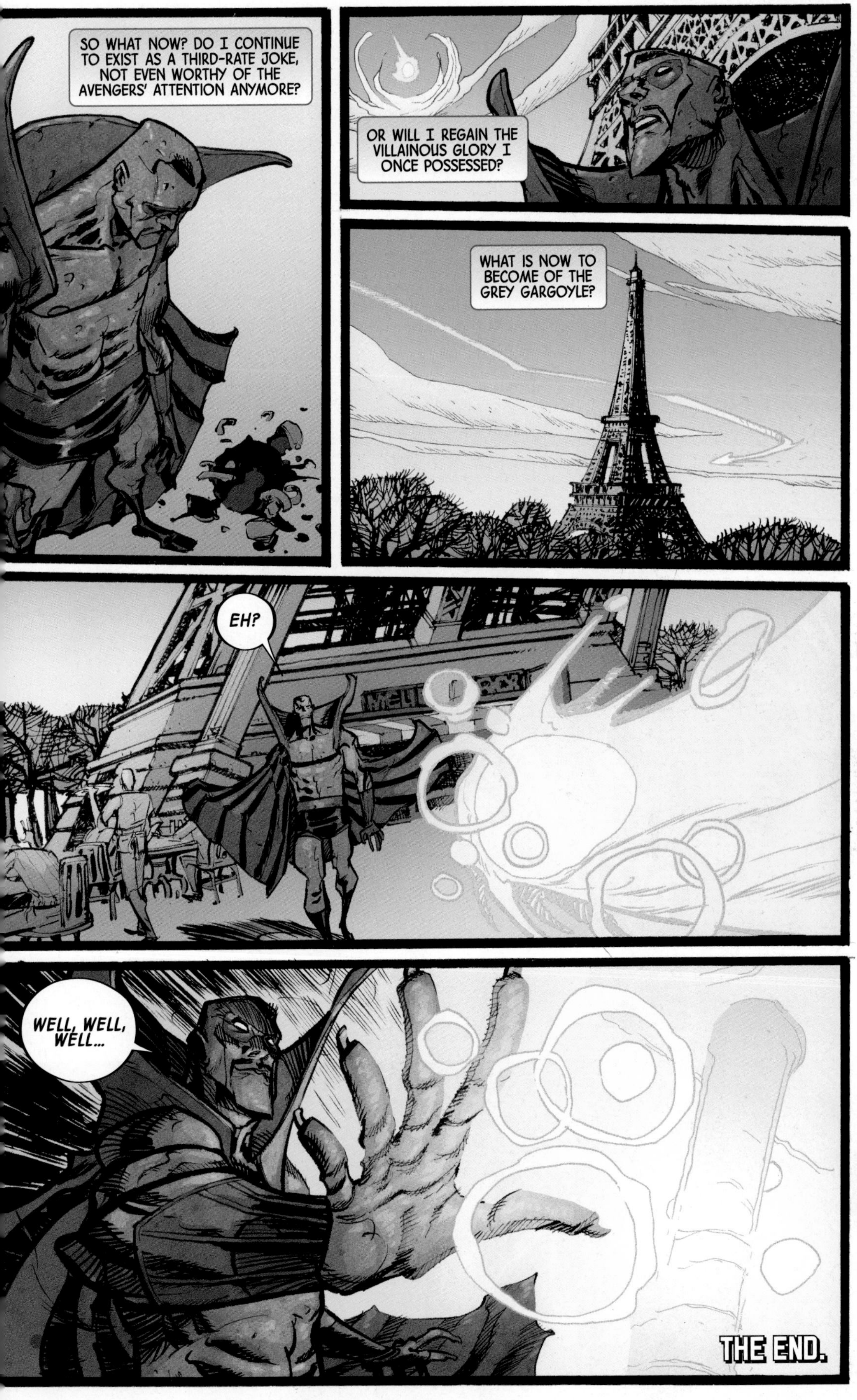
SO WHAT NOW? DO I CONTINUE TO EXIST AS A THIRD-RATE JOKE, NOT EVEN WORTHY OF THE AVENGERS' ATTENTION ANYMORE?
OR WILL I REGAIN THE VILLAINOUS GLORY I ONCE POSSESSED?
WHAT IS NOW TO BECOME OF THE GREY GARGOYLE?
EH?
WELL, WELL, WELL...
THE END.

THE WORTHY

HULK

NUL:
BREAKER OF WORLDS

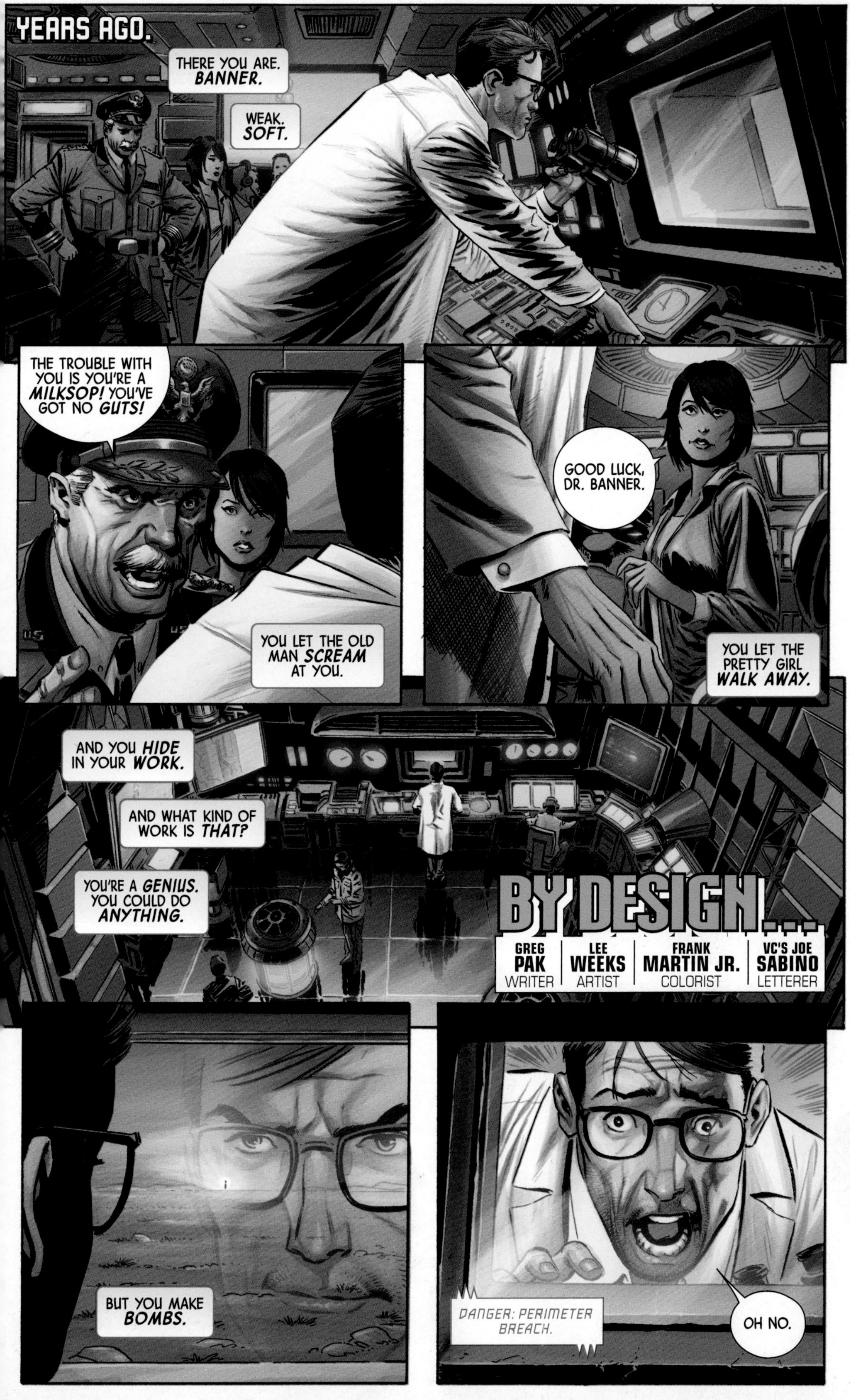
YEARS AGO.
THERE YOU ARE. BANNER.
WEAK. SOFT.
THE TROUBLE WITH YOU IS YOU'RE A MILKSOP! YOU'VE GOT NO GUTS!
YOU LET THE OLD MAN SCREAM AT YOU.
GOOD LUCK, DR. BANNER.
YOU LET THE PRETTY GIRL WALK AWAY.
AND YOU HIDE IN YOUR WORK.
AND WHAT KIND OF WORK IS THAT?
YOU'RE A GENIUS. YOU COULD DO ANYTHING.
BY DESIGN...
GREG PAK WRITER
LEE WEEKS ARTIST
FRANK MARTIN JR. COLORIST
VC'S JOE SABINO LETTERER
BUT YOU MAKE BOMBS.
DANGER: PERIMETER BREACH.
OH NO.

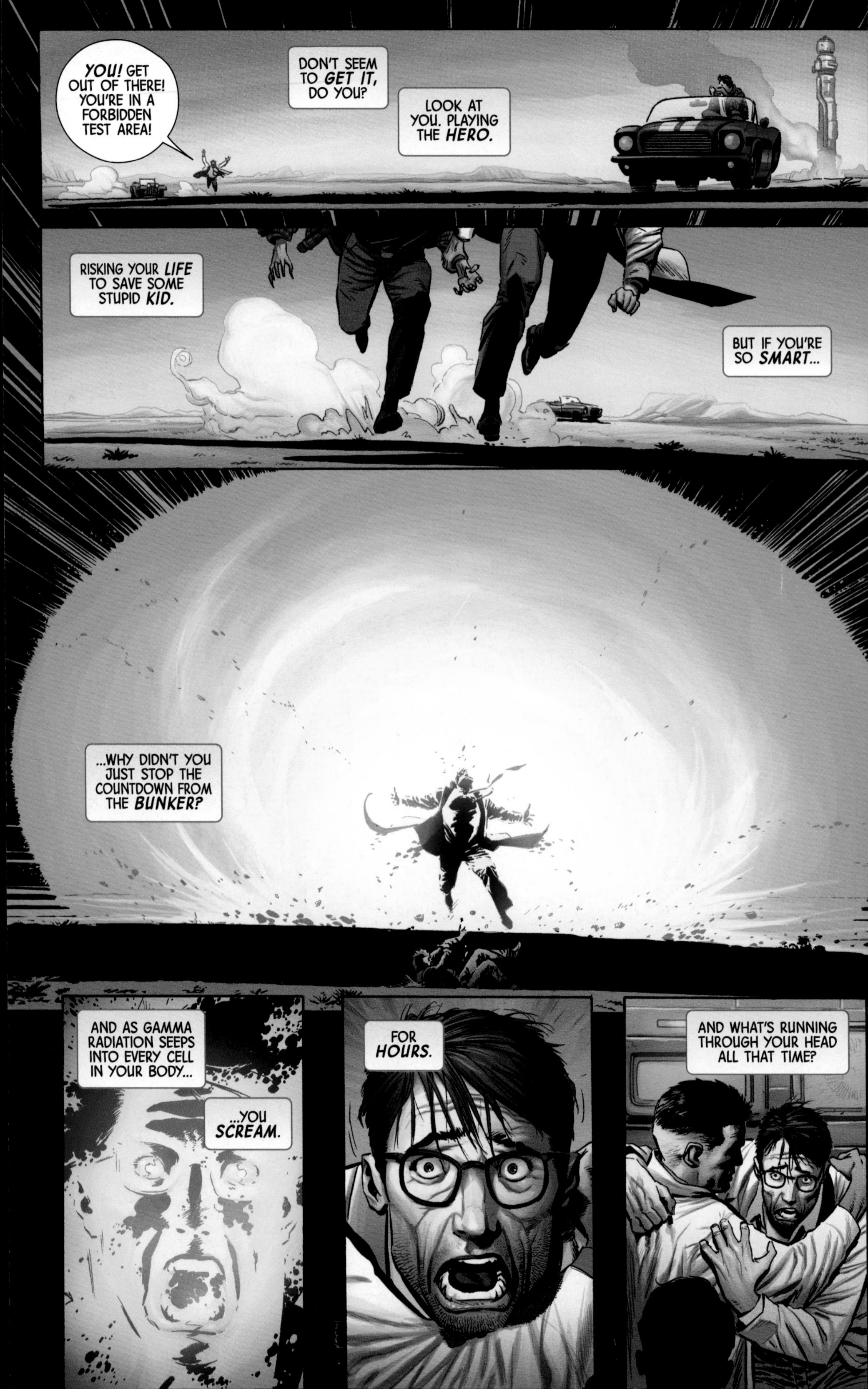
YOU! GET OUT OF THERE! YOU'RE IN A FORBIDDEN TEST AREA!
DON'T SEEM TO GET IT, DO YOU?
LOOK AT YOU. PLAYING THE HERO.
RISKING YOUR LIFE TO SAVE SOME STUPID KID.
BUT IF YOU'RE SO SMART...
...WHY DIDN'T YOU JUST STOP THE COUNTDOWN FROM THE BUNKER?
AND AS GAMMA RADIATION SEEPS INTO EVERY CELL IN YOUR BODY...
...YOU SCREAM.
FOR HOURS.
AND WHAT'S RUNNING THROUGH YOUR HEAD ALL THAT TIME?

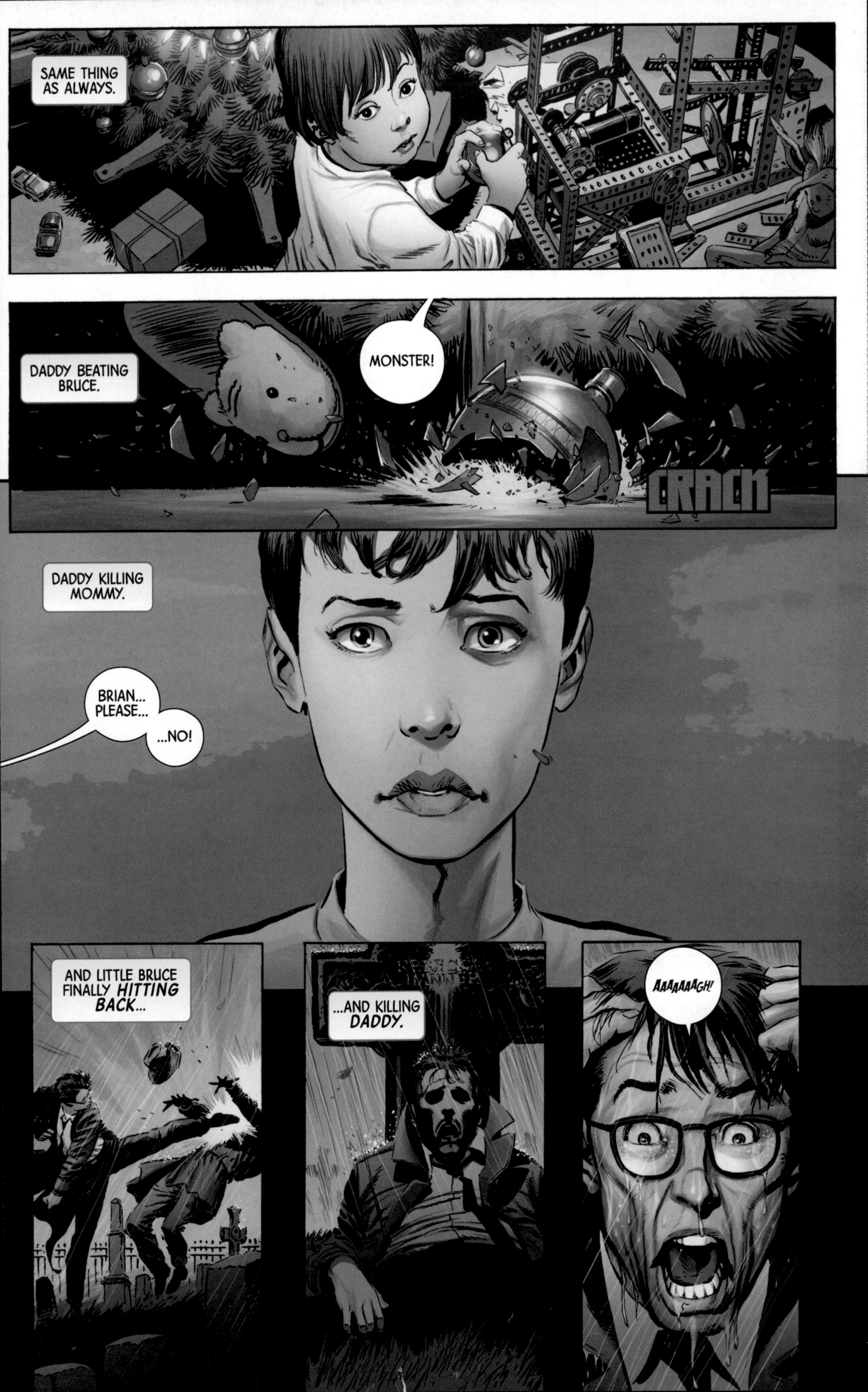
SAME THING AS ALWAYS.
DADDY BEATING BRUCE.
MONSTER!
CRACK
DADDY KILLING MOMMY.
BRIAN... PLEASE...
...NO!
AND LITTLE BRUCE FINALLY *HITTING BACK*...
...AND KILLING *DADDY*.
AAAAAAAGH!

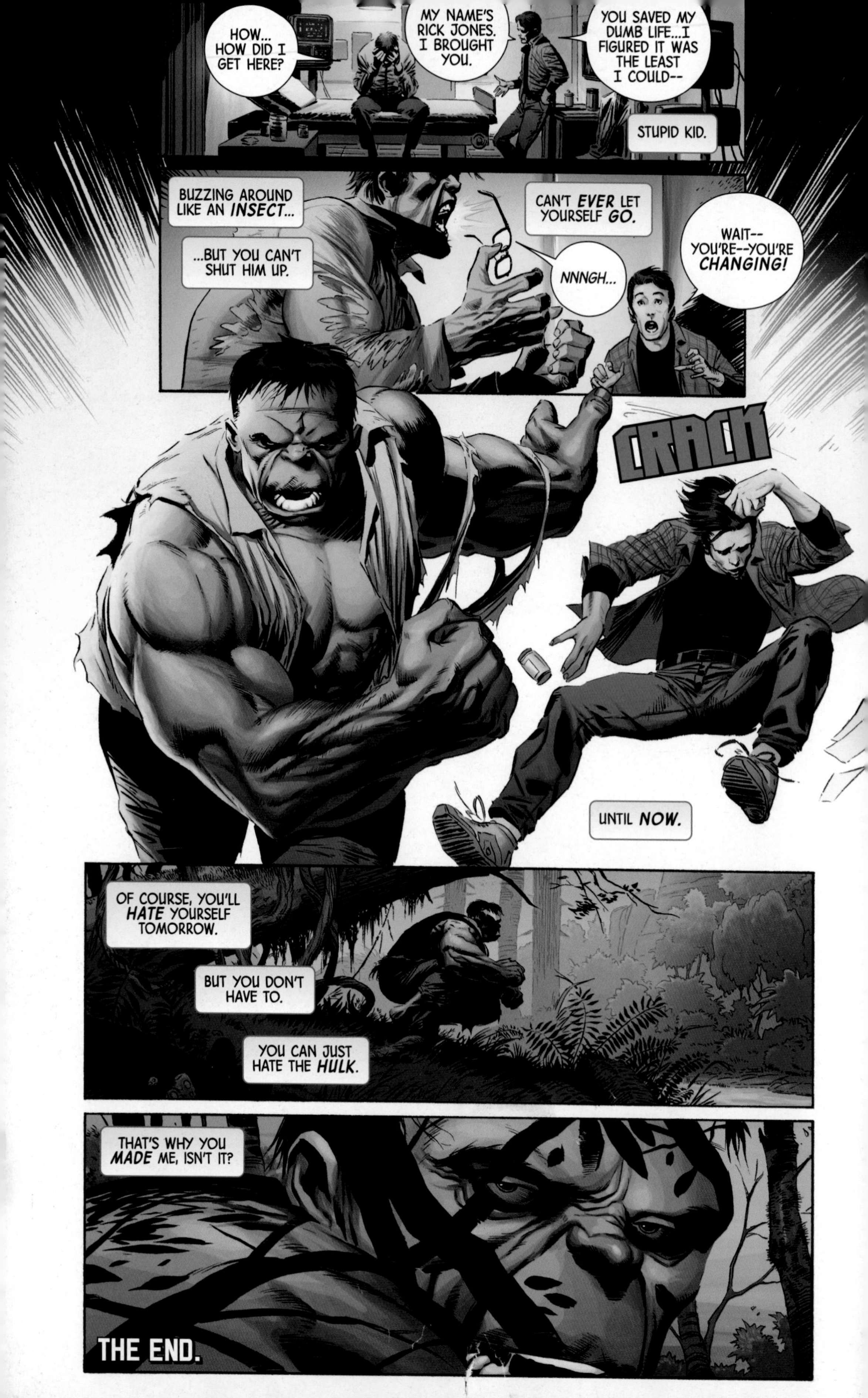
HOW... HOW DID I GET HERE?
MY NAME'S RICK JONES. I BROUGHT YOU.
YOU SAVED MY DUMB LIFE...I FIGURED IT WAS THE LEAST I COULD--
STUPID KID.
BUZZING AROUND LIKE AN *INSECT*...
...BUT YOU CAN'T SHUT HIM UP.
CAN'T *EVER* LET YOURSELF *GO.*
NNNGH...
WAIT-- YOU'RE--YOU'RE *CHANGING!*
CRACK
UNTIL *NOW.*
OF COURSE, YOU'LL *HATE* YOURSELF TOMORROW.
BUT YOU DON'T HAVE TO.
YOU CAN JUST HATE THE *HULK*.
THAT'S WHY YOU *MADE* ME, ISN'T IT?
THE END.

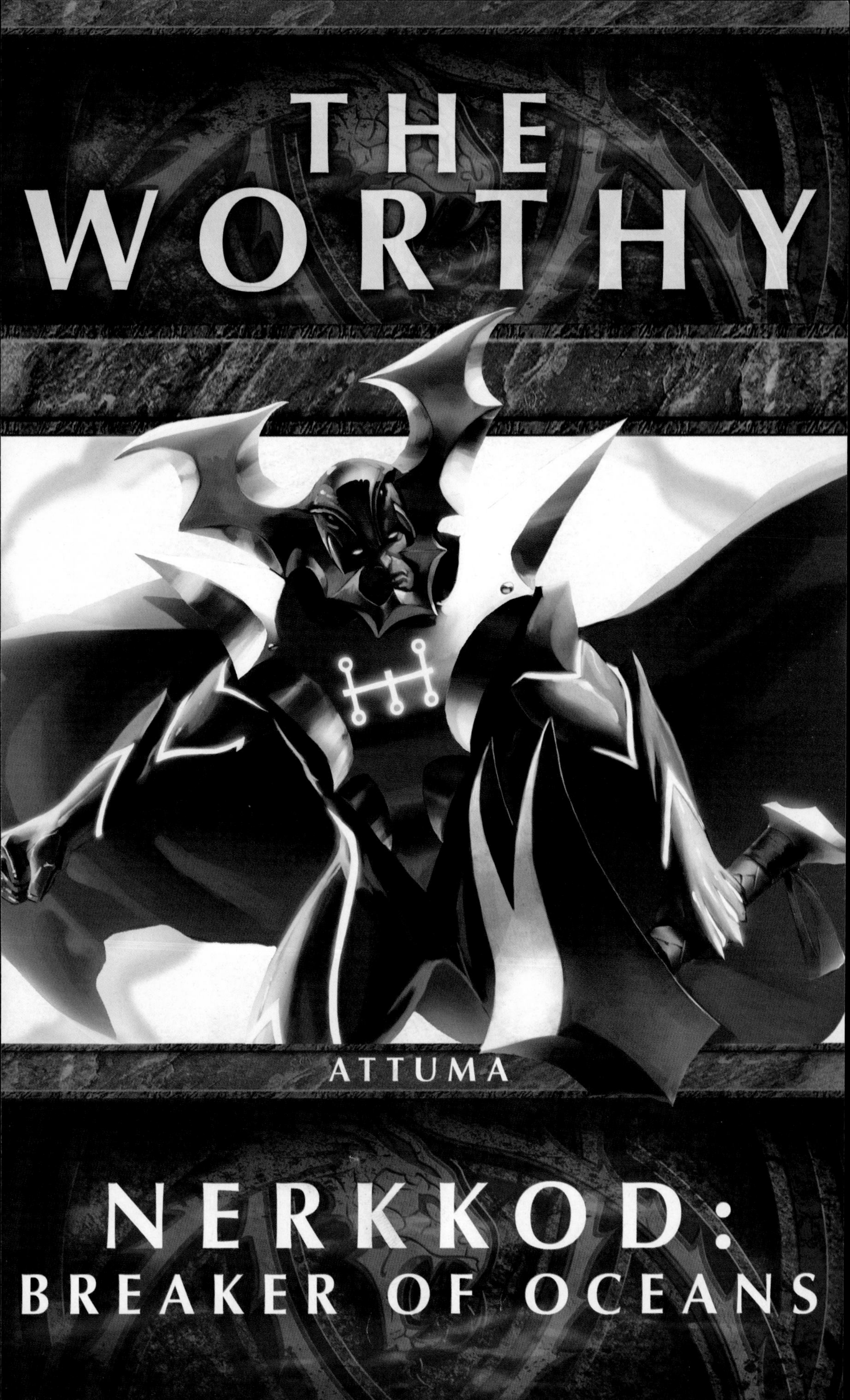
THE WORTHY
ATTUMA
NERKKOD:
BREAKER OF OCEANS

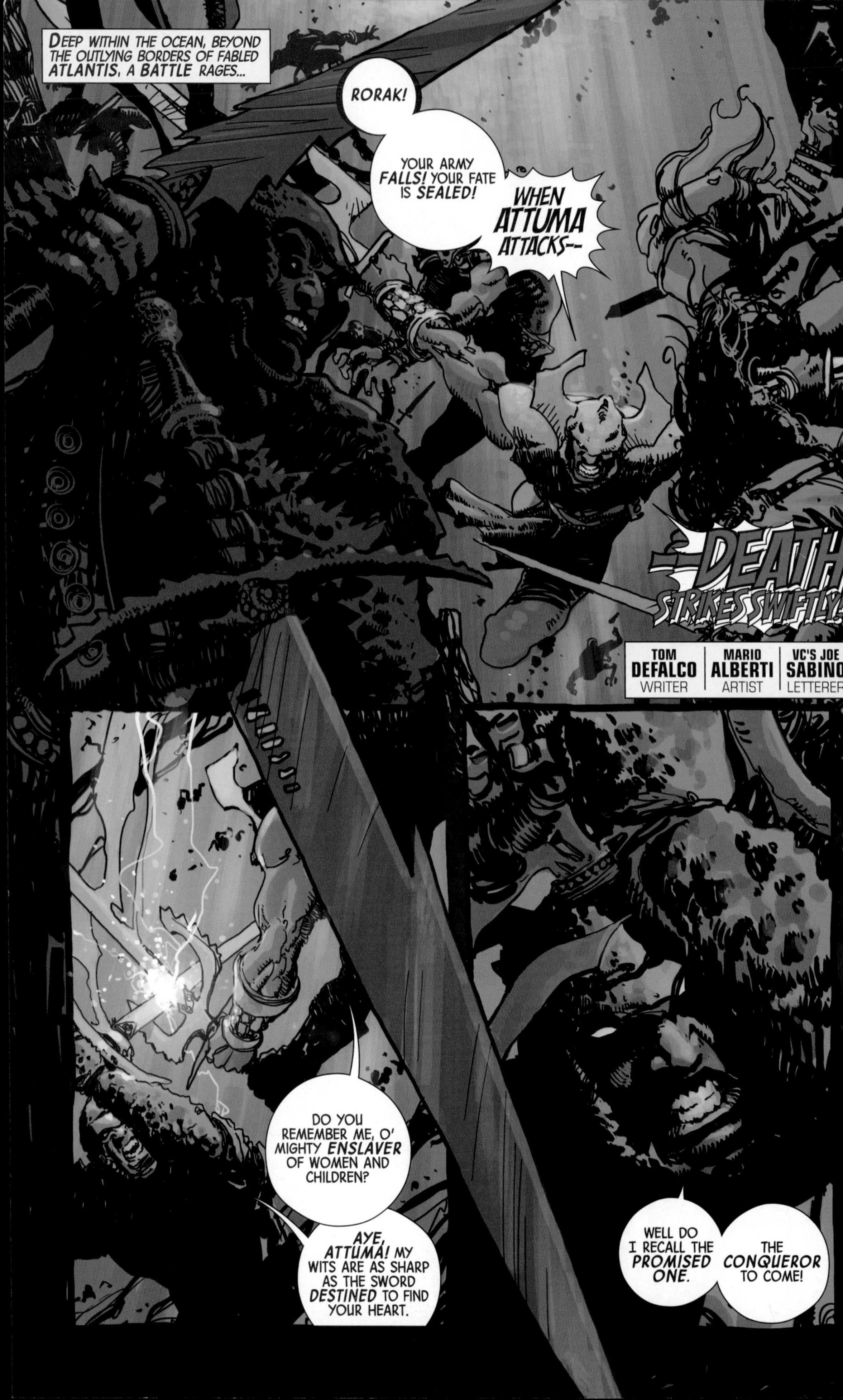
DEEP WITHIN THE OCEAN, BEYOND THE OUTLYING BORDERS OF FABLED ATLANTIS, A BATTLE RAGES...
RORAK!
YOUR ARMY FALLS! YOUR FATE IS SEALED!
WHEN ATTUMA ATTACKS--
--DEATH STRIKES SWIFTLY!
TOM DEFALCO WRITER
MARIO ALBERTI ARTIST
VC'S JOE SABINO LETTERER
DO YOU REMEMBER ME, O' MIGHTY ENSLAVER OF WOMEN AND CHILDREN?
AYE, ATTUMA! MY WITS ARE AS SHARP AS THE SWORD DESTINED TO FIND YOUR HEART.
WELL DO I RECALL THE PROMISED ONE.
THE CONQUEROR TO COME!

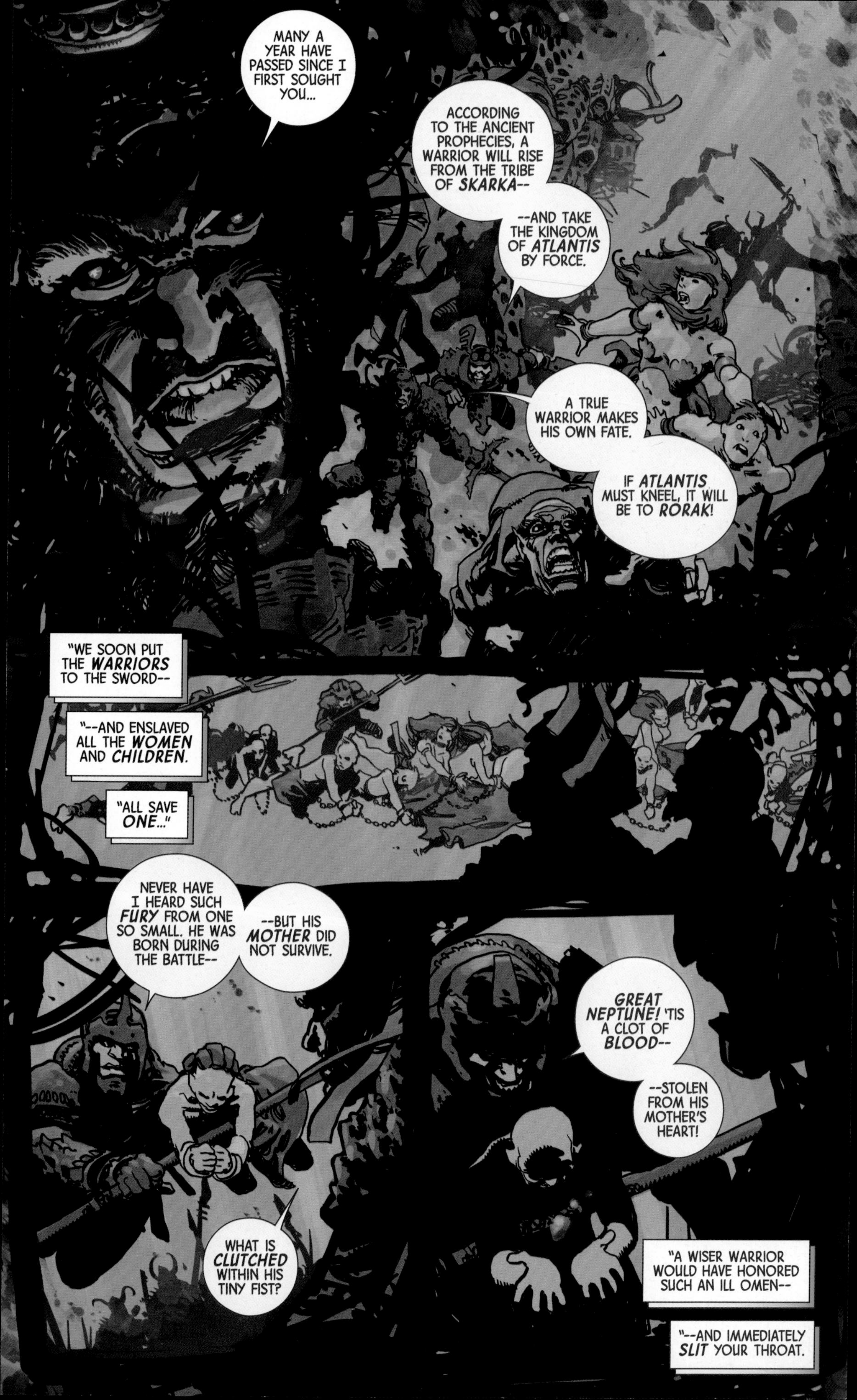
MANY A YEAR HAVE PASSED SINCE I FIRST SOUGHT YOU...
ACCORDING TO THE ANCIENT PROPHECIES, A WARRIOR WILL RISE FROM THE TRIBE OF SKARKA--
--AND TAKE THE KINGDOM OF ATLANTIS BY FORCE.
A TRUE WARRIOR MAKES HIS OWN FATE.
IF ATLANTIS MUST KNEEL, IT WILL BE TO RORAK!
"WE SOON PUT THE WARRIORS TO THE SWORD--
"--AND ENSLAVED ALL THE WOMEN AND CHILDREN.
"ALL SAVE ONE..."
NEVER HAVE I HEARD SUCH FURY FROM ONE SO SMALL. HE WAS BORN DURING THE BATTLE--
--BUT HIS MOTHER DID NOT SURVIVE.
WHAT IS CLUTCHED WITHIN HIS TINY FIST?
GREAT NEPTUNE! 'TIS A CLOT OF BLOOD--
--STOLEN FROM HIS MOTHER'S HEART!
"A WISER WARRIOR WOULD HAVE HONORED SUCH AN ILL OMEN--
"--AND IMMEDIATELY SLIT YOUR THROAT.

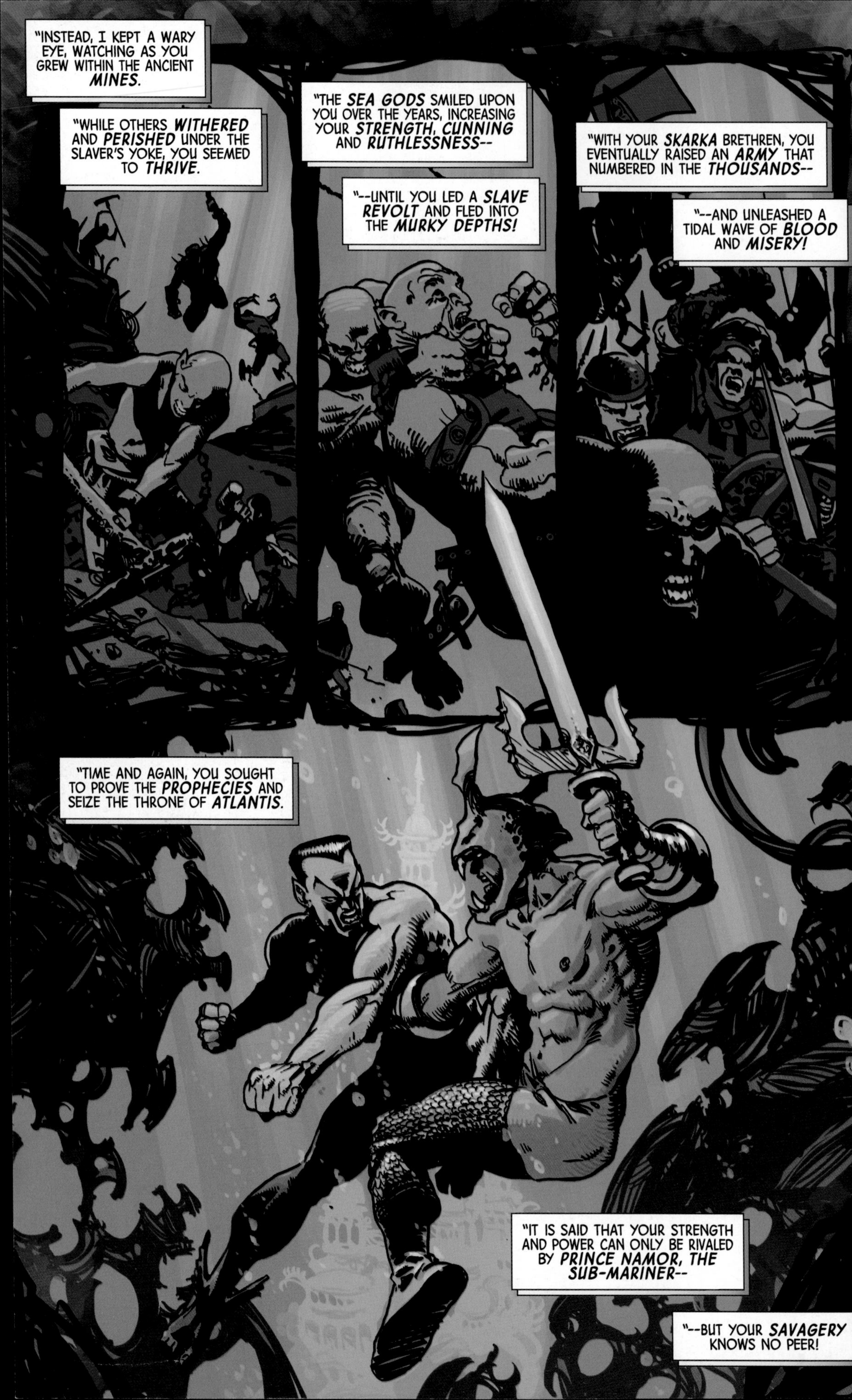
"INSTEAD, I KEPT A WARY EYE, WATCHING AS YOU GREW WITHIN THE ANCIENT MINES.
"WHILE OTHERS WITHERED AND PERISHED UNDER THE SLAVER'S YOKE, YOU SEEMED TO THRIVE.
"THE SEA GODS SMILED UPON YOU OVER THE YEARS, INCREASING YOUR STRENGTH, CUNNING AND RUTHLESSNESS--
"--UNTIL YOU LED A SLAVE REVOLT AND FLED INTO THE MURKY DEPTHS!
"WITH YOUR SKARKA BRETHREN, YOU EVENTUALLY RAISED AN ARMY THAT NUMBERED IN THE THOUSANDS--
"--AND UNLEASHED A TIDAL WAVE OF BLOOD AND MISERY!
"TIME AND AGAIN, YOU SOUGHT TO PROVE THE PROPHECIES AND SEIZE THE THRONE OF ATLANTIS.
"IT IS SAID THAT YOUR STRENGTH AND POWER CAN ONLY BE RIVALED BY PRINCE NAMOR, THE SUB-MARINER--
"--BUT YOUR SAVAGERY KNOWS NO PEER!

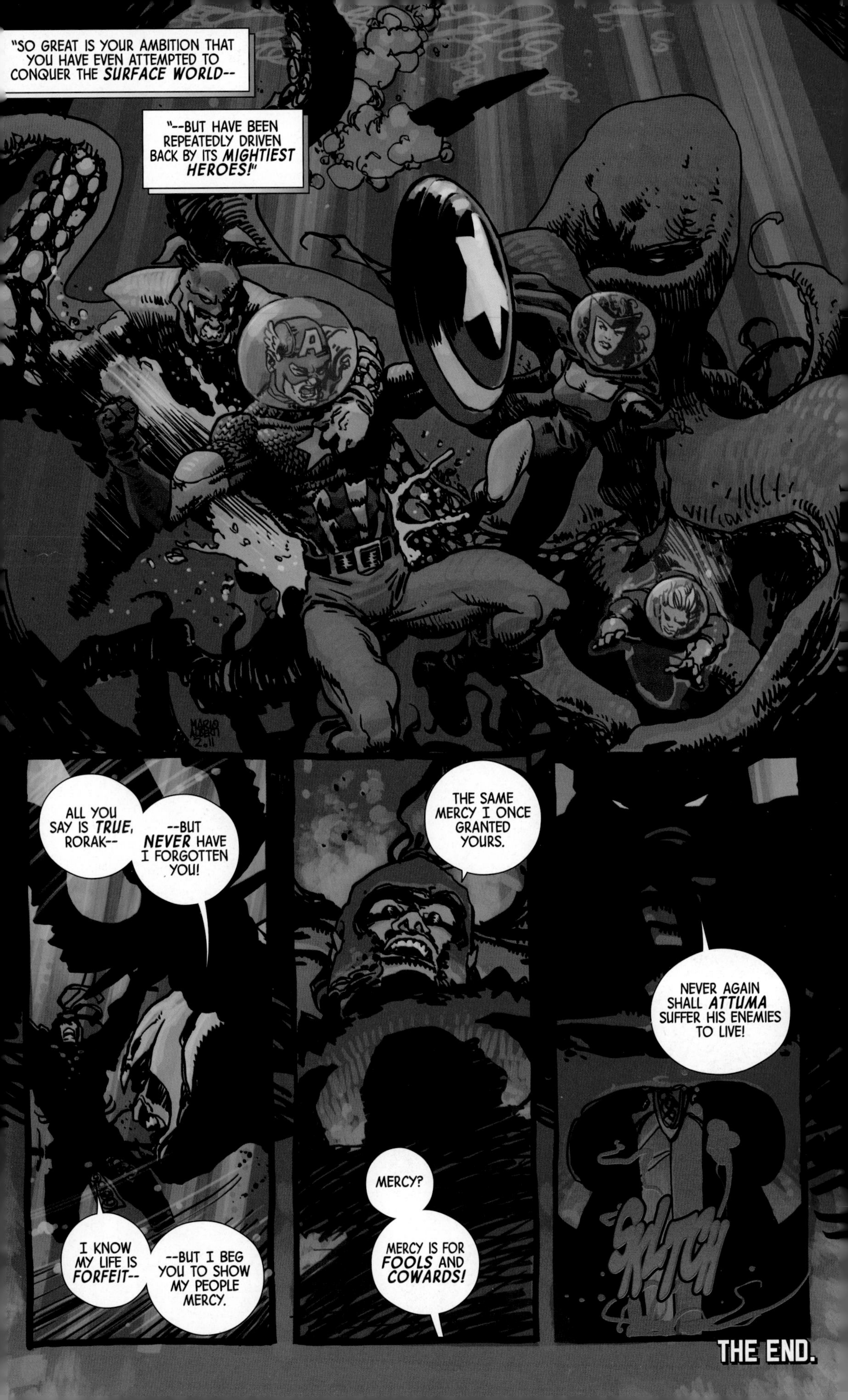
"SO GREAT IS YOUR AMBITION THAT YOU HAVE EVEN ATTEMPTED TO CONQUER THE SURFACE WORLD--
"--BUT HAVE BEEN REPEATEDLY DRIVEN BACK BY ITS MIGHTIEST HEROES!"
ALL YOU SAY IS TRUE, RORAK--
--BUT NEVER HAVE I FORGOTTEN YOU!
I KNOW MY LIFE IS FORFEIT--
--BUT I BEG YOU TO SHOW MY PEOPLE MERCY.
THE SAME MERCY I ONCE GRANTED YOURS.
MERCY?
MERCY IS FOR FOOLS AND COWARDS!
NEVER AGAIN SHALL ATTUMA SUFFER HIS ENEMIES TO LIVE!
THE END.

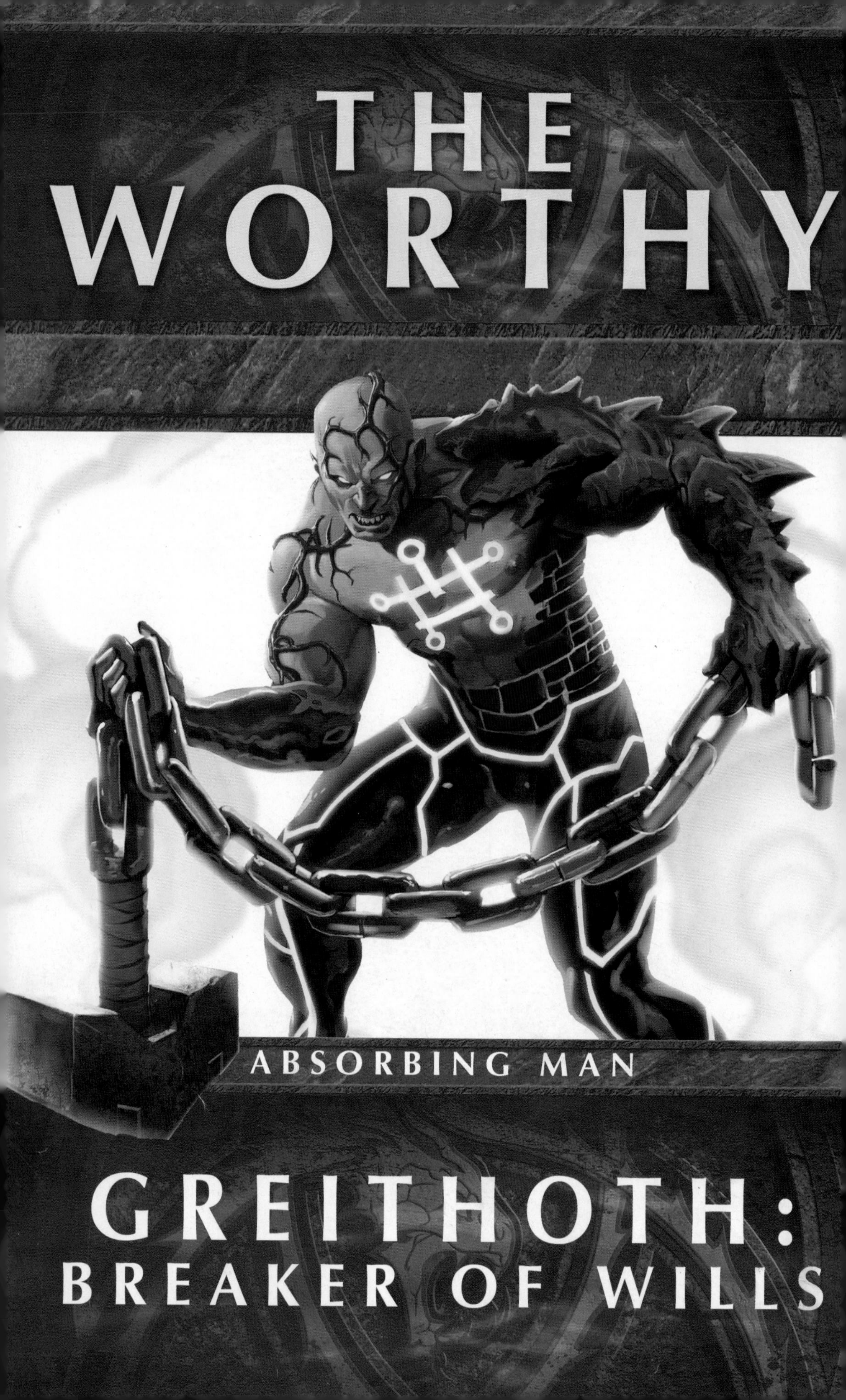
THE WORTHY
ABSORBING MAN
GREITHOTH: BREAKER OF WILLS

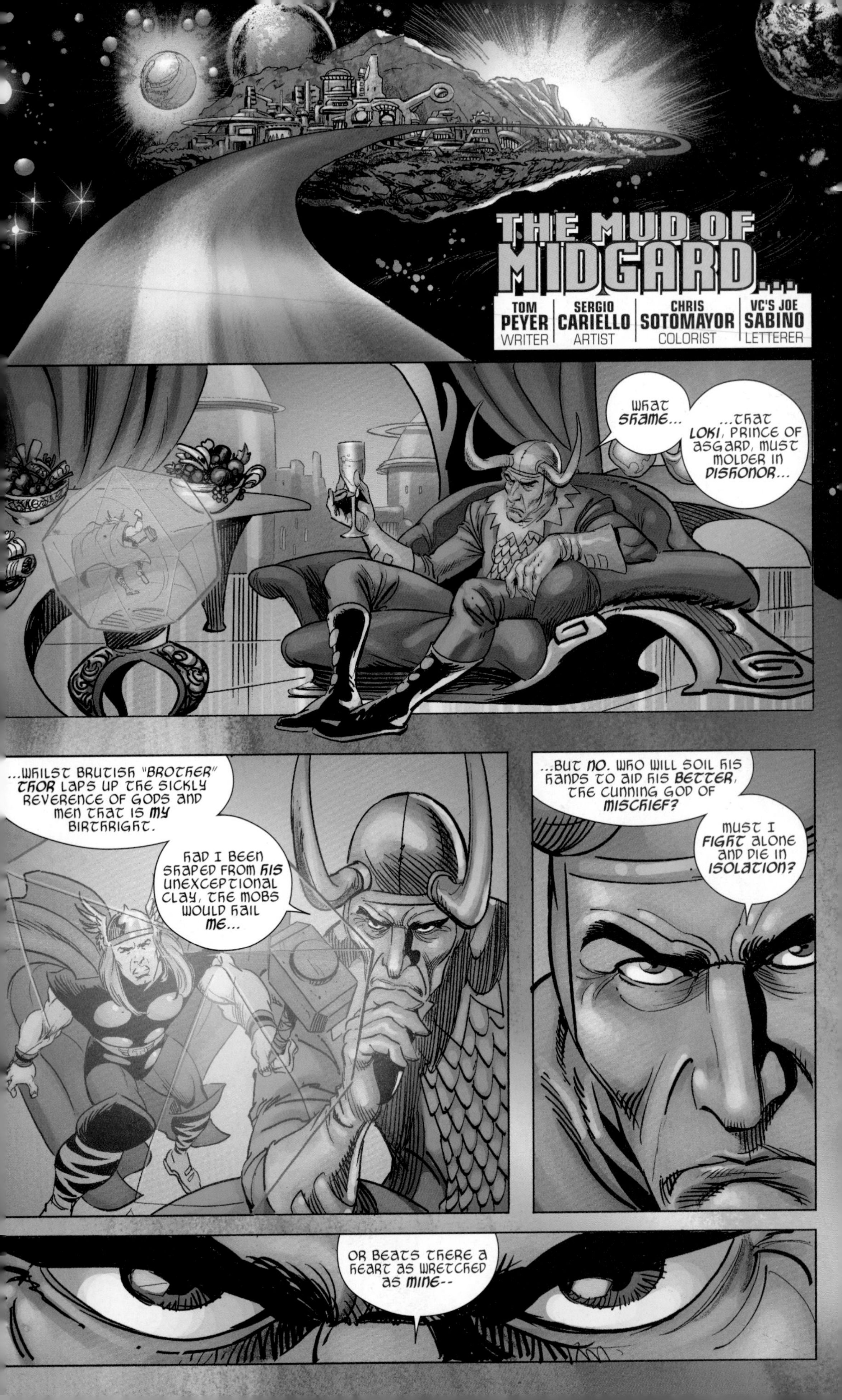
THE MUD OF MIDGARD...
TOM PEYER WRITER
SERGIO CARIELLO ARTIST
CHRIS SOTOMAYOR COLORIST
VC'S JOE SABINO LETTERER
WHAT SHAME...
...THAT LOKI, PRINCE OF ASGARD, MUST MOLDER IN DISHONOR...
...WHILST BRUTISH "BROTHER" THOR LAPS UP THE SICKLY REVERENCE OF GODS AND MEN THAT IS MY BIRTHRIGHT.
HAD I BEEN SHAPED FROM HIS UNEXCEPTIONAL CLAY, THE MOBS WOULD HAIL ME...
...BUT NO. WHO WILL SOIL HIS HANDS TO AID HIS BETTER, THE CUNNING GOD OF MISCHIEF?
MUST I FIGHT ALONE AND DIE IN ISOLATION?
OR BEATS THERE A HEART AS WRETCHED AS MINE--

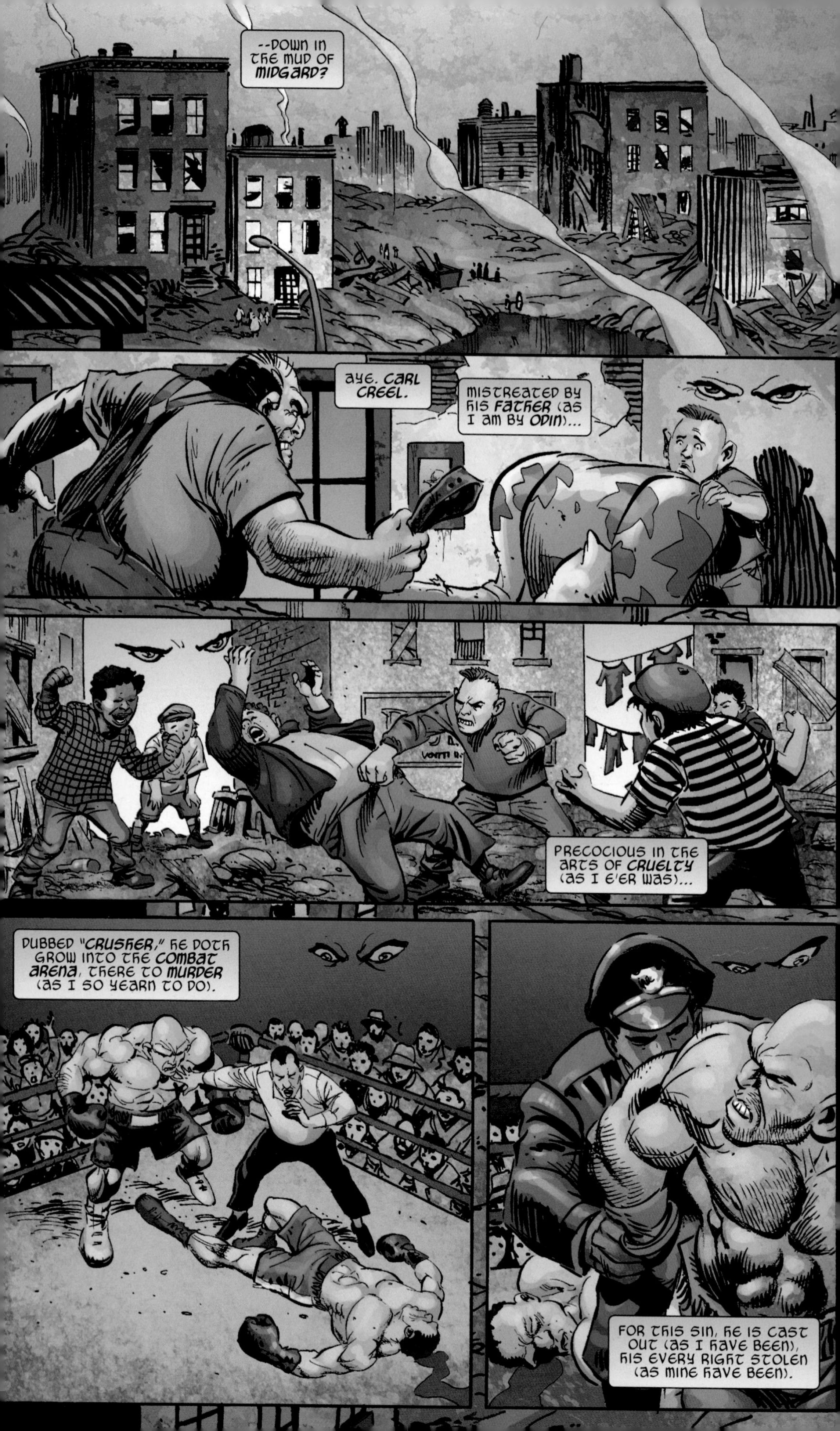
--DOWN IN THE MUD OF MIDGARD?
AYE. CARL CREEL.
MISTREATED BY HIS FATHER (AS I AM BY ODIN)...
PRECOCIOUS IN THE ARTS OF CRUELTY (AS I E'ER WAS)...
DUBBED "CRUSHER," HE DOTH GROW INTO THE COMBAT ARENA, THERE TO MURDER (AS I SO YEARN TO DO).
FOR THIS SIN, HE IS CAST OUT (AS I HAVE BEEN), HIS EVERY RIGHT STOLEN (AS MINE HAVE BEEN).

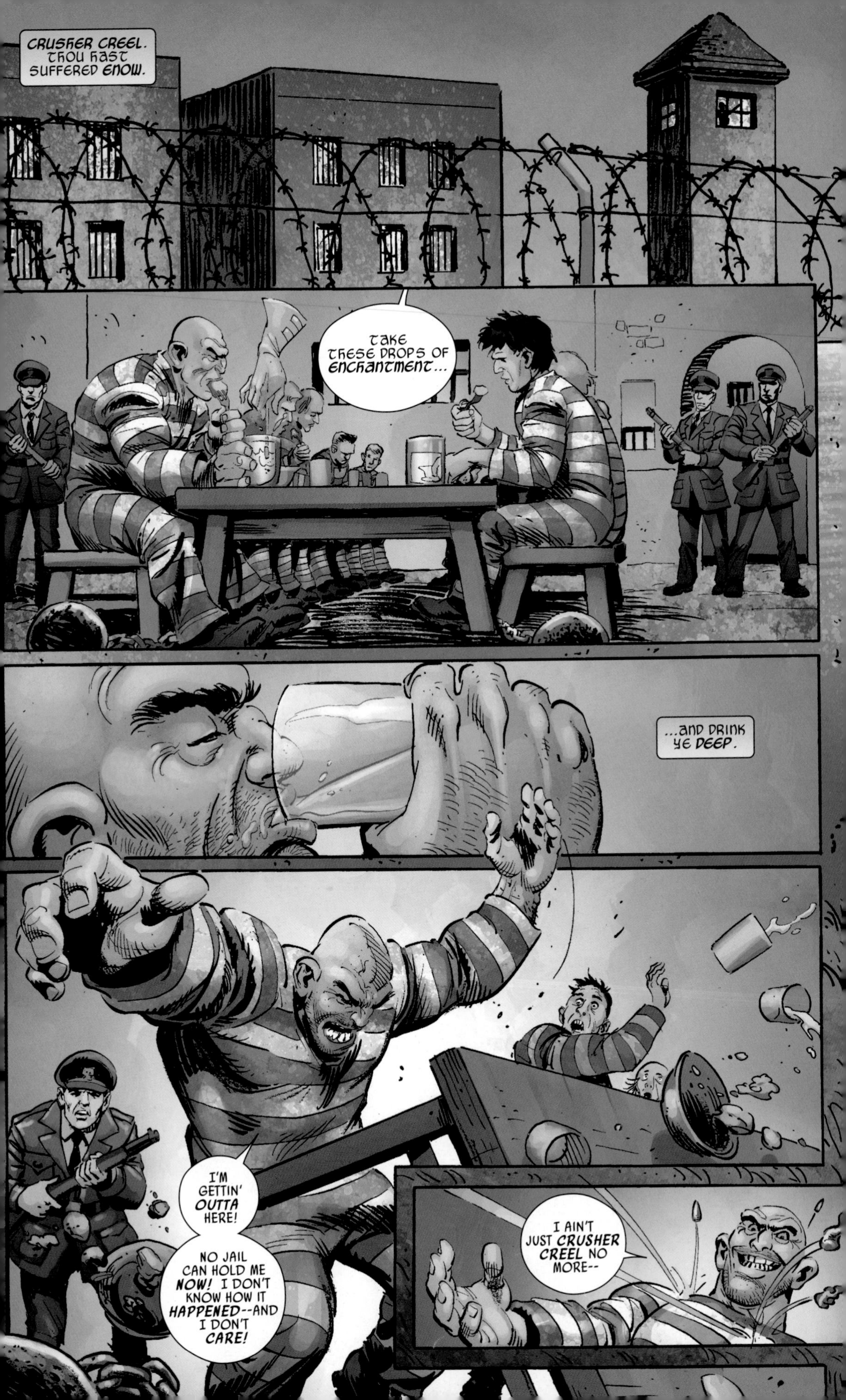
CRUSHER CREEL. THOU HAST SUFFERED ENOW.
TAKE THESE DROPS OF ENCHANTMENT...
...AND DRINK YE DEEP.
I'M GETTIN' OUTTA HERE!
NO JAIL CAN HOLD ME NOW! I DON'T KNOW HOW IT HAPPENED--AND I DON'T CARE!
I AIN'T JUST CRUSHER CREEL NO MORE--

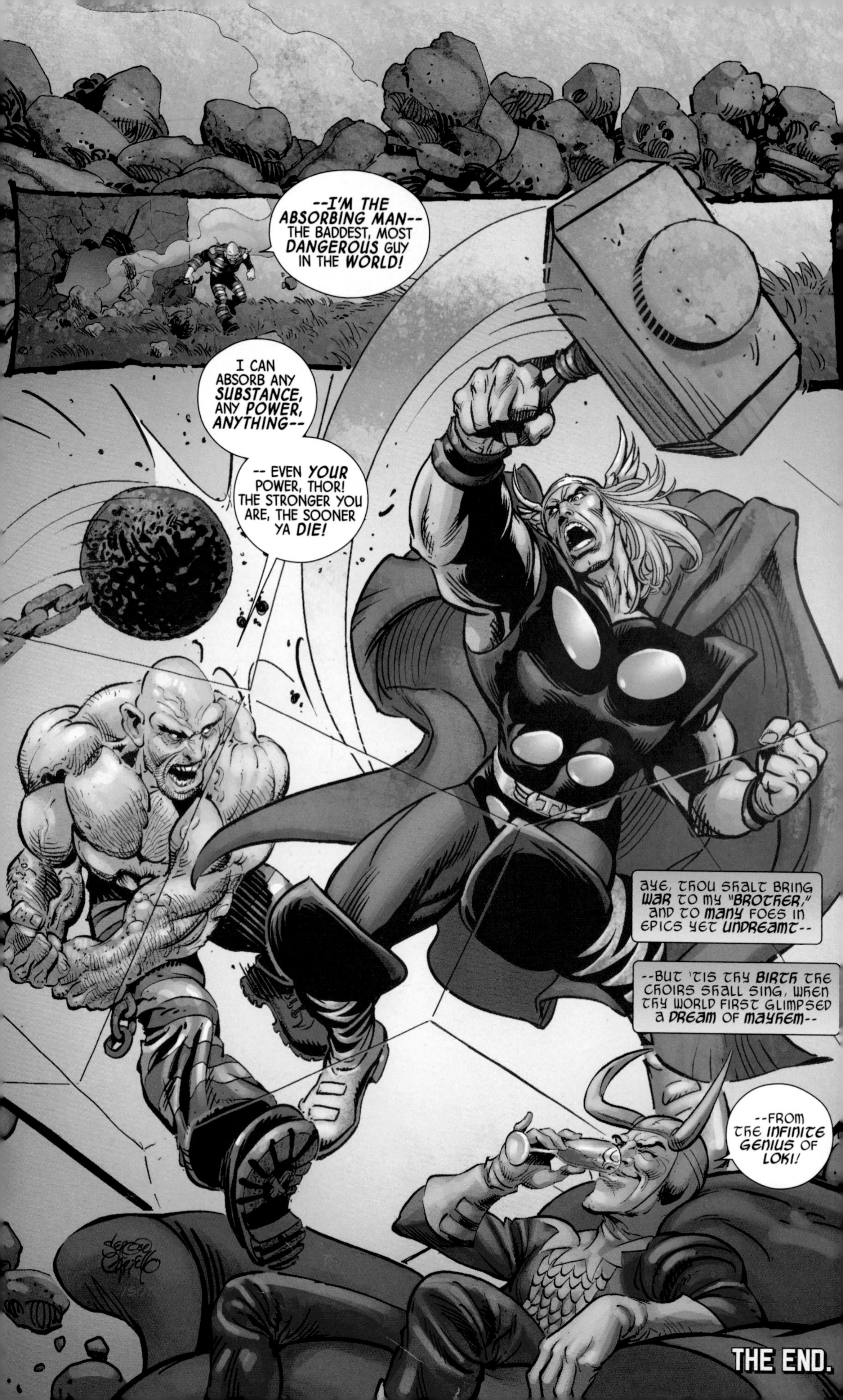
--I'M THE ABSORBING MAN-- THE BADDEST, MOST DANGEROUS GUY IN THE WORLD!
I CAN ABSORB ANY SUBSTANCE, ANY POWER, ANYTHING--
-- EVEN YOUR POWER, THOR! THE STRONGER YOU ARE, THE SOONER YA DIE!
AYE, THOU SHALT BRING WAR TO MY "BROTHER," AND TO MANY FOES IN EPICS YET UNDREAMT--
--BUT 'TIS THY BIRTH THE CHOIRS SHALL SING, WHEN THY WORLD FIRST GLIMPSED A DREAM OF MAYHEM--
--FROM THE INFINITE GENIUS OF LOKI!
THE END.

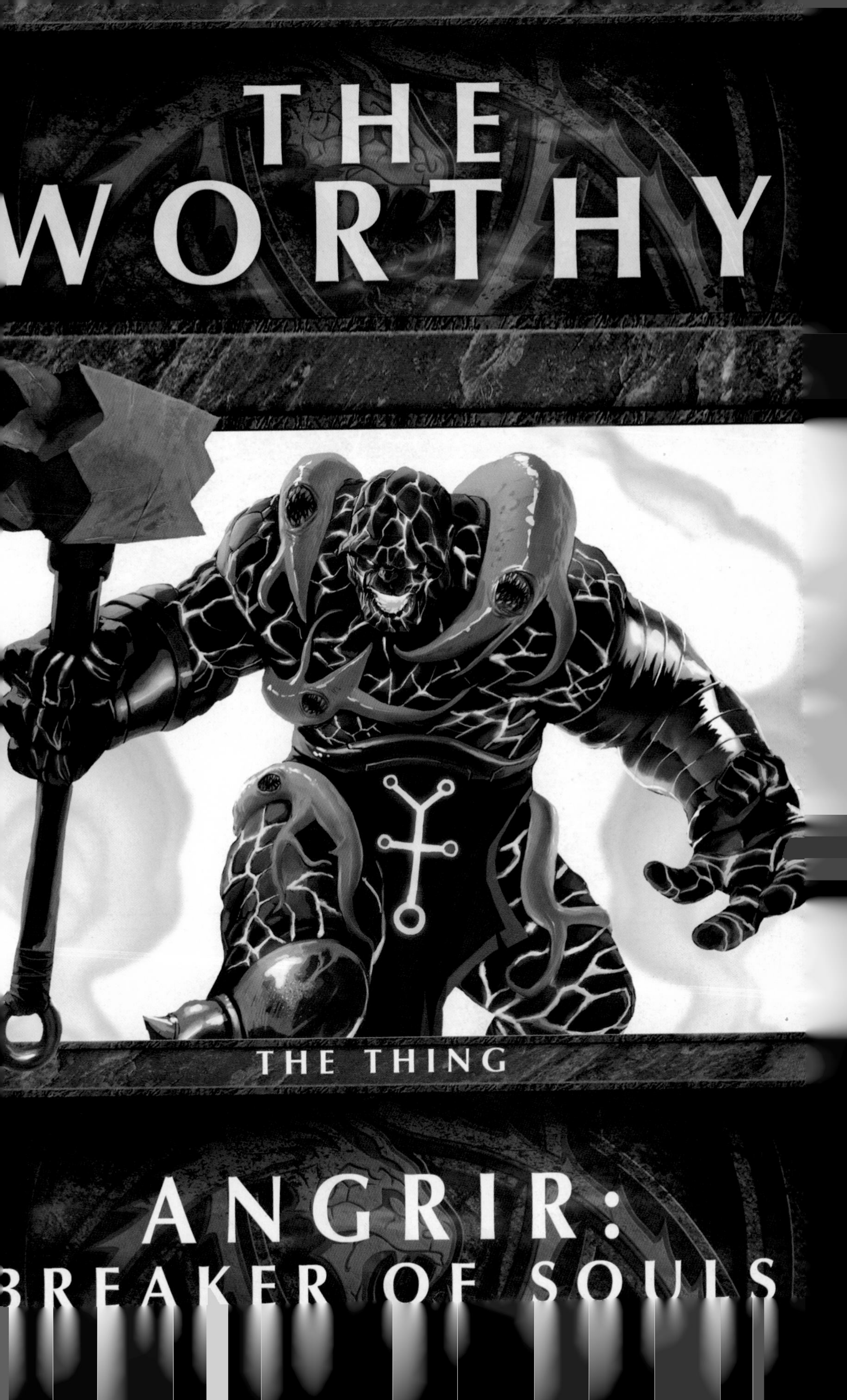
THE WORTHY
THE THING
ANGRIR:
BREAKER OF SOULS

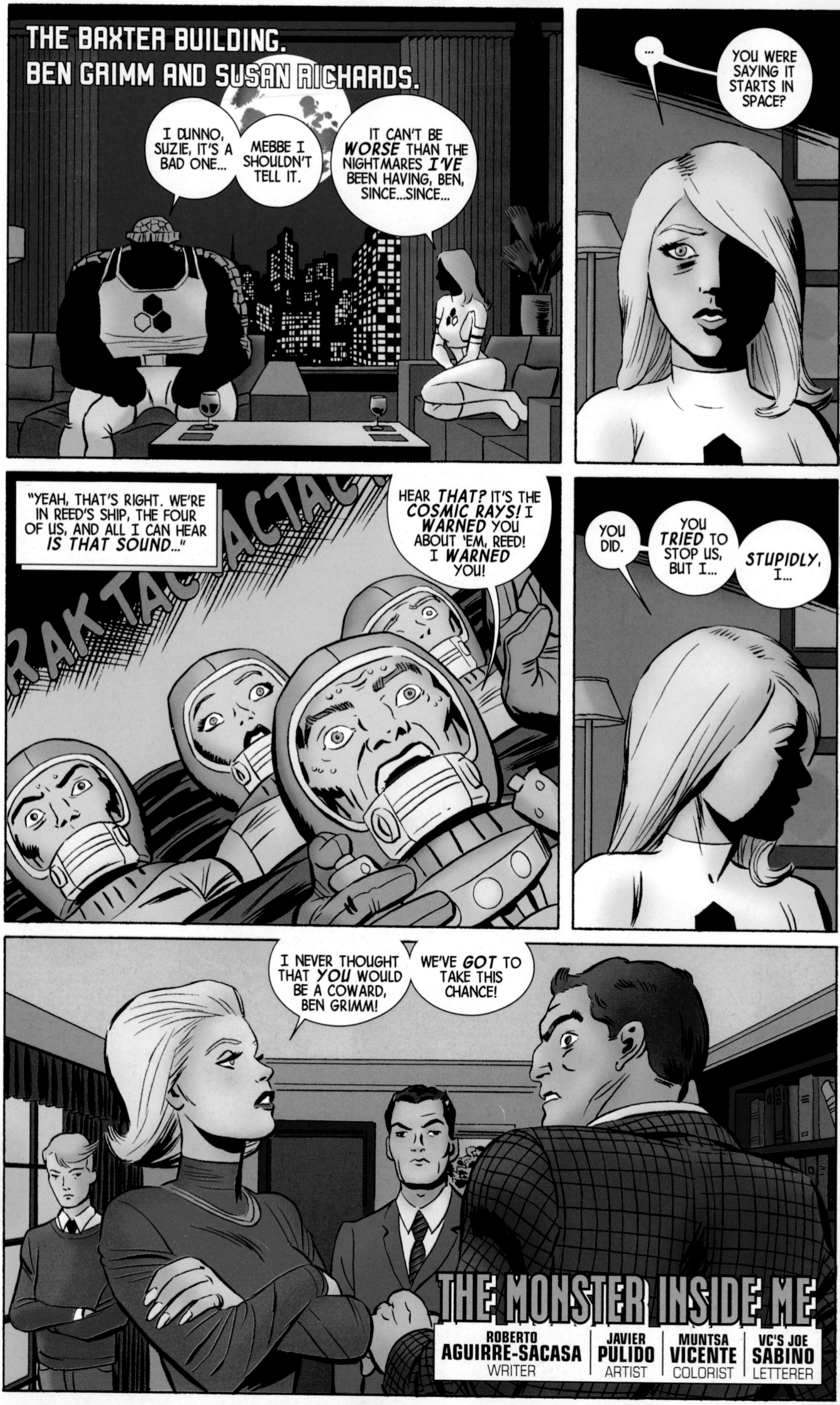
THE BAXTER BUILDING.
BEN GRIMM AND SUSAN RICHARDS.
I DUNNO, SUZIE, IT'S A BAD ONE...
MEBBE I SHOULDN'T TELL IT.
IT CAN'T BE WORSE THAN THE NIGHTMARES I'VE BEEN HAVING, BEN, SINCE...SINCE...
...
YOU WERE SAYING IT STARTS IN SPACE?
"YEAH, THAT'S RIGHT. WE'RE IN REED'S SHIP, THE FOUR OF US, AND ALL I CAN HEAR IS THAT SOUND..."
RAKTACTACTAC
HEAR THAT? IT'S THE COSMIC RAYS! I WARNED YOU ABOUT 'EM, REED! I WARNED YOU!
YOU DID.
YOU TRIED TO STOP US, BUT I...
STUPIDLY, I...
I NEVER THOUGHT THAT YOU WOULD BE A COWARD, BEN GRIMM!
WE'VE GOT TO TAKE THIS CHANCE!
THE MONSTER INSIDE ME
ROBERTO AGUIRRE-SACASA WRITER
JAVIER PULIDO ARTIST
MUNTSA VICENTE COLORIST
VC'S JOE SABINO LETTERER

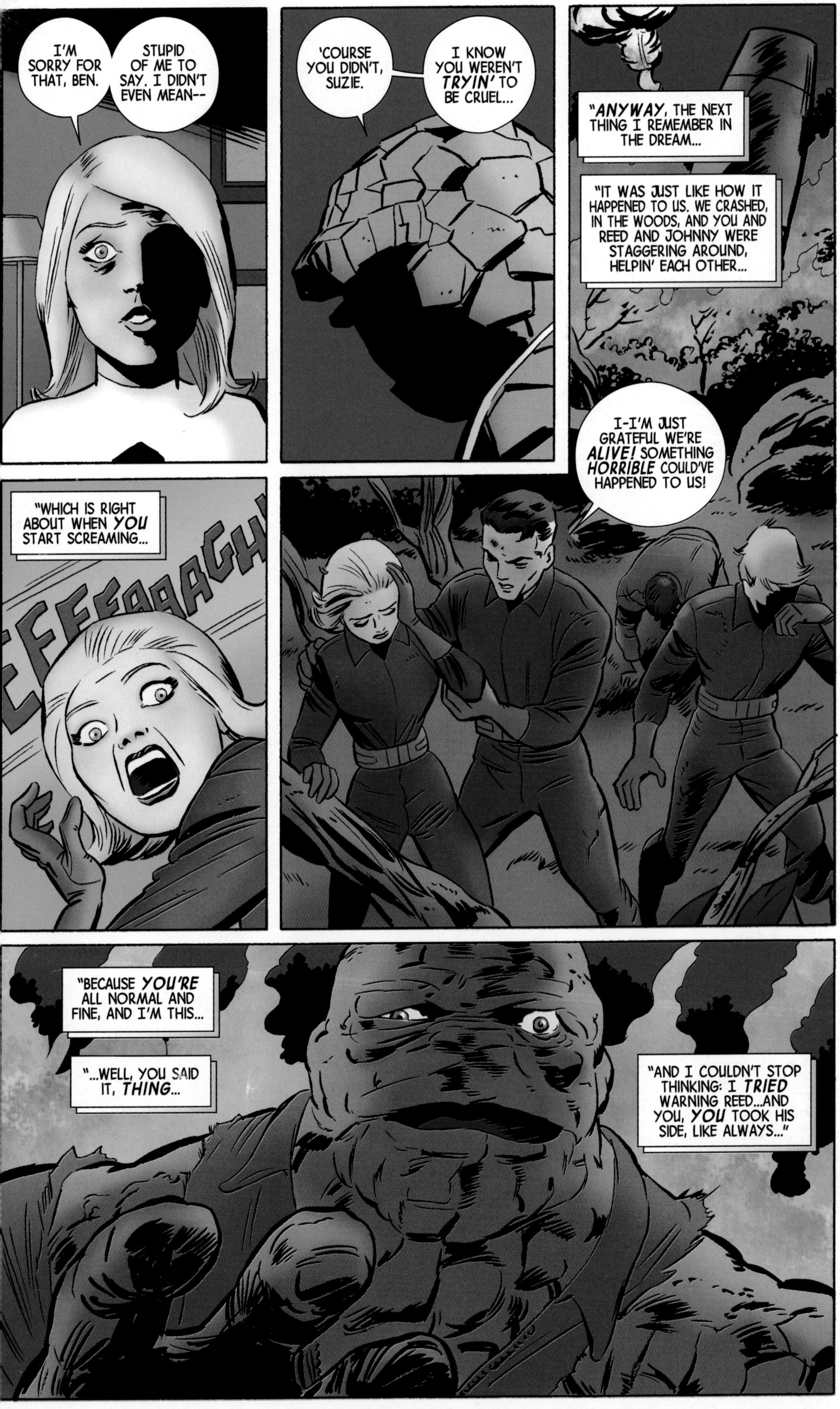
I'M SORRY FOR THAT, BEN.
STUPID OF ME TO SAY. I DIDN'T EVEN MEAN--
'COURSE YOU DIDN'T, SUZIE.
I KNOW YOU WEREN'T TRYIN' TO BE CRUEL...
"ANYWAY, THE NEXT THING I REMEMBER IN THE DREAM...
"IT WAS JUST LIKE HOW IT HAPPENED TO US. WE CRASHED, IN THE WOODS, AND YOU AND REED AND JOHNNY WERE STAGGERING AROUND, HELPIN' EACH OTHER...
I-I'M JUST GRATEFUL WE'RE ALIVE! SOMETHING HORRIBLE COULD'VE HAPPENED TO US!
"WHICH IS RIGHT ABOUT WHEN YOU START SCREAMING...
EEEEAAAAGH!
"BECAUSE YOU'RE ALL NORMAL AND FINE, AND I'M THIS...
"...WELL, YOU SAID IT, THING...
"AND I COULDN'T STOP THINKING: I TRIED WARNING REED...AND YOU, YOU TOOK HIS SIDE, LIKE ALWAYS..."

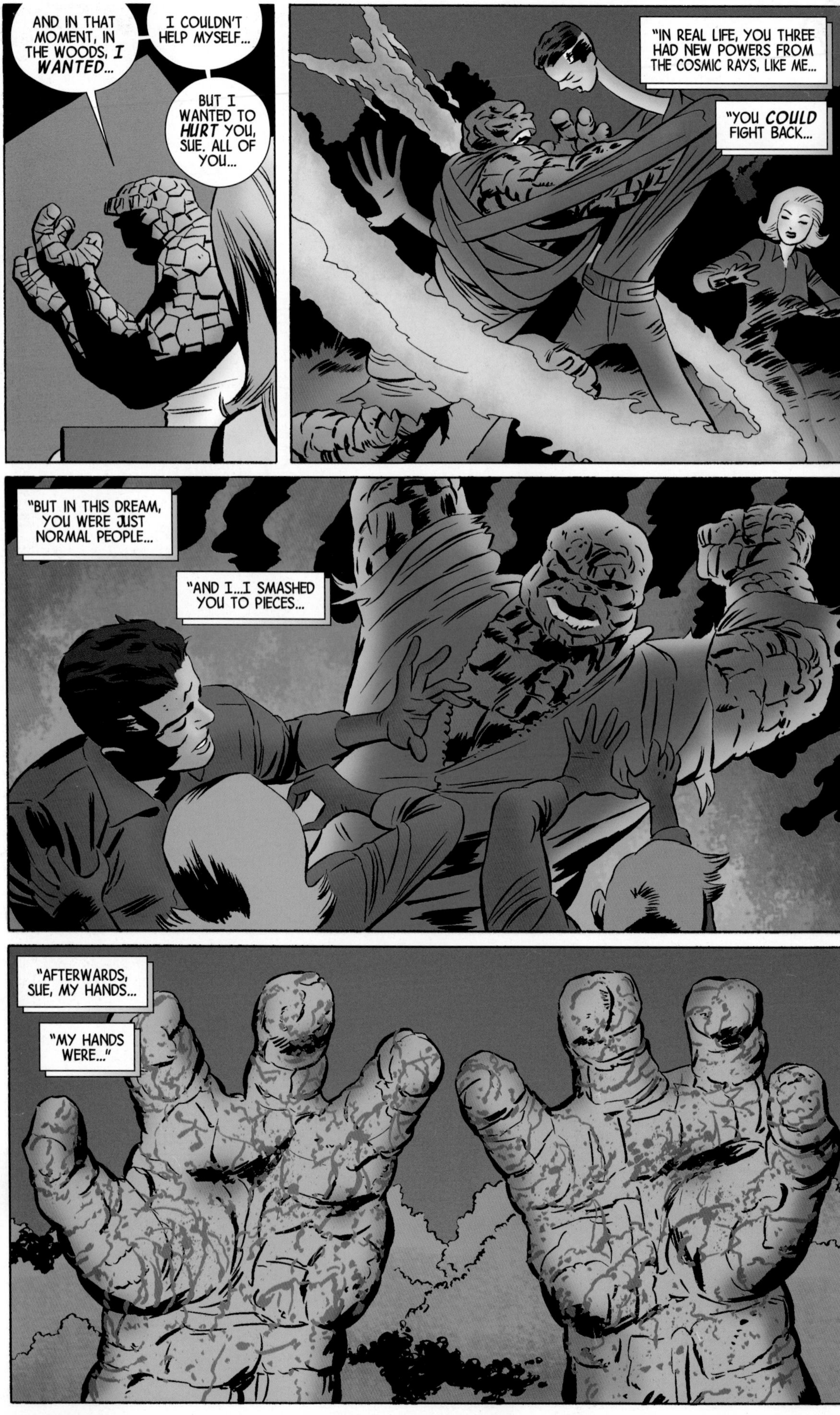
AND IN THAT MOMENT, IN THE WOODS, I WANTED...
I COULDN'T HELP MYSELF...
BUT I WANTED TO HURT YOU, SUE. ALL OF YOU...
"IN REAL LIFE, YOU THREE HAD NEW POWERS FROM THE COSMIC RAYS, LIKE ME...
"YOU COULD FIGHT BACK...
"BUT IN THIS DREAM, YOU WERE JUST NORMAL PEOPLE...
"AND I...I SMASHED YOU TO PIECES...
"AFTERWARDS, SUE, MY HANDS...
"MY HANDS WERE..."

IT'S...JUST A NIGHTMARE, BEN...WE'VE *ALL* BEEN HAVING TROUBLE SLEEPING SINCE JOHNNY DIED.

IT'S *NATURAL*.

NORMAL, IN SOME HORRIBLE KIND OF WAY...

I KNOW, SUSIE, BUT THE THING IS...

THIS NIGHTMARE?

IT'S THE FIRST TIME I'VE HAD IT IN AWHILE, BUT... I *HAVE* HAD IT BEFORE...I USED TO HAVE IT A LOT, I THINK...

BEN...

WHICH SCARES ME, SUE, 'CAUSE THAT MEANS...

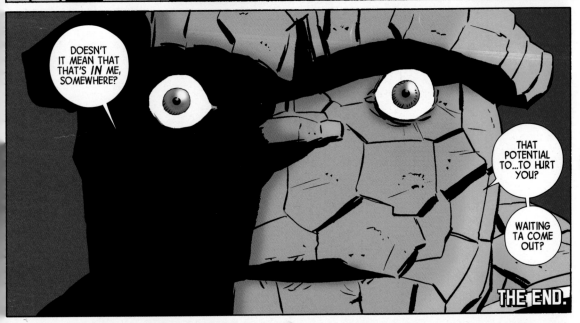

DOESN'T IT MEAN THAT THAT'S *IN* ME, SOMEWHERE?

THAT POTENTIAL TO...TO HURT YOU?

WAITING TA COME OUT?

THE END.

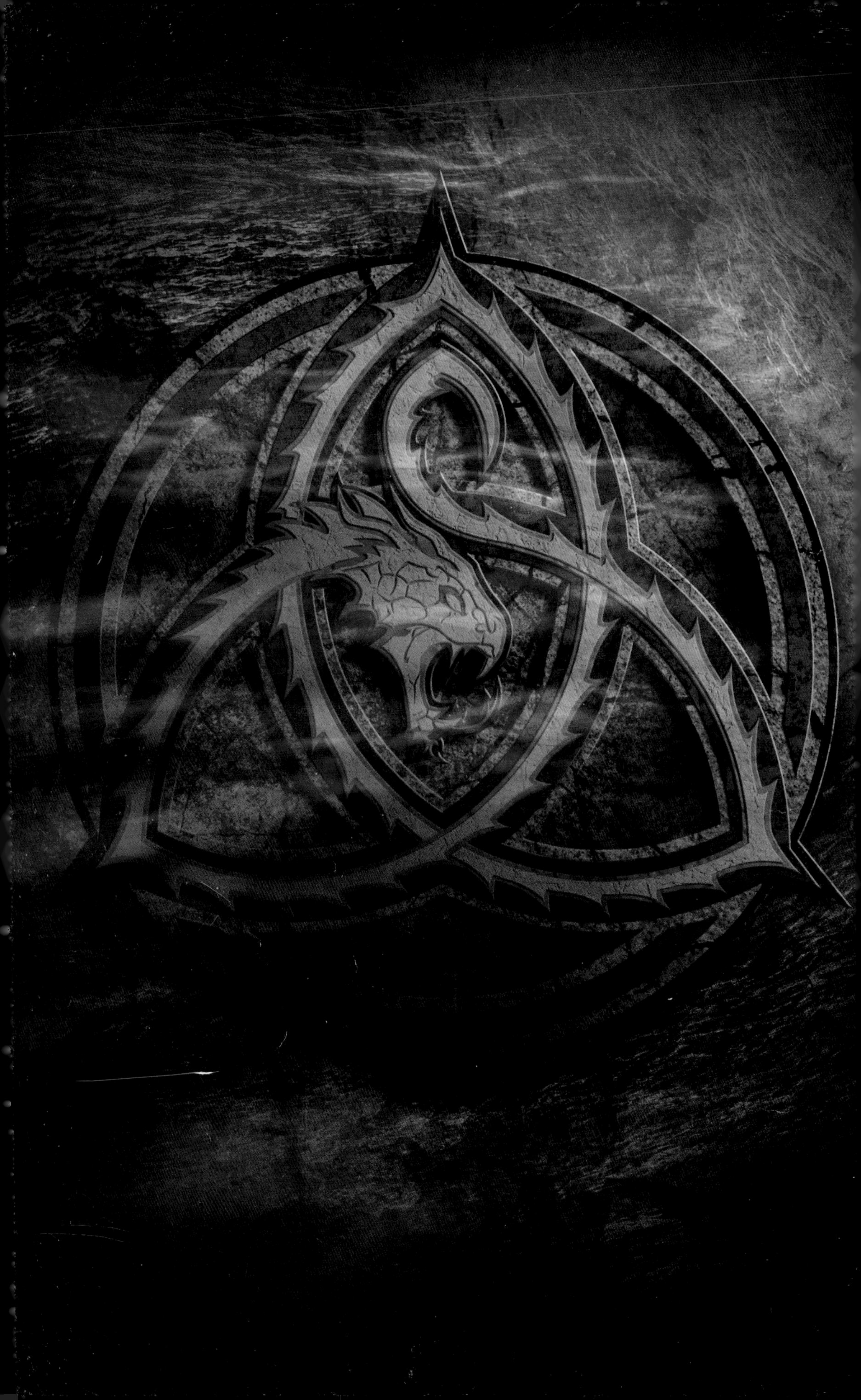